Hundred Day War

The Cultural Revolution at Tsinghua University

by William Hinton

Monthly Review Press
New York and London

Library of Congress Catalog Card Number: 72-81759
First Printing

Monthly Review Press
116 West 14th Street, New York, N.Y. 10011
33/37 Moreland Street, London, E.C. 1

Manufactured in the United States of America

Contents

Part III
The Working Class Intervenes

Introductory Note

This is not a definitive history of the Great Proletarian
Cultural Revolution at Tsinghua University. It must be considered rather a compilation of some rough notes taken from
conversations with a few participants. Others who lived through
the same events will surely find important omissions and distor-
tions. The full story can only be told when Tsinghua people
themselves get together and recreate it from the thousands of
sources that now exist but may soon be dispersed beyond recall.
Much of the story is recorded in collections of posters, leaflets,
telegrams, and letters. Much more still resides only in the heads
of people who took part. A concerted effort to collect and pre-
serve this material on the part of the cadres, teachers, and
students at Tsinghua would be invaluable. Whether it will ever
be made is another question. Already important documents have
been lost, key people have departed for distant provinces, while
those who remain and could do the job are so busy reconstructing
their institution that they tend to slight its history.

There is also a political problem, a problem of consensus.
The ideological struggle has been very sharp; furthermore, it is

still going on. Who can be trusted to sum up what happened? Who can interpret its real meaning? A dogmatic, sectarian spirit associated with the influence of Lin Piao still colors some people's thinking. What actually happened tends to get mixed up with what should have happened, and so strong is the stigma attached to those who have ended up in disgrace that the purists want to leave them out of the story altogether, apparently on the grounds that to tell about their mistaken acts and ideas is equivalent somehow to advocating the same.

For the majority who reject this kind of dogmatism there is still the problem of prematurely judging political trends that are unclear. In the summer of 1971 Kuai Ta-fu, the nationally famous Tsinghua student leader, was under investigation as a May 16 Conspirator.* Since his case had not been settled, our informants first tried to tell their story without mentioning Kuai at all. As our questions went deeper this became impossible and Kuai emerged, almost larger than life, as an anti-hero. At that very time the whole campus population was rallying to expose him and the verdict seemed inevitable. Then came the Lin Piao affair and with it the possibility that the verdict on Kuai might eventually be modified. I do not mean to suggest here that there is any serious dispute about the facts, about what happened, about what Kuai actually did, but that there is room for doubt as to what it all means politically.

As of this writing the fall of Lin Piao has not been explained, at least not to the world at large. I have, as yet, no way of telling how much of what we heard in the summer of 1971 may have been colored by apologists for Lin Piao and his line at a time when the Defense Minister and Mao's designated successor as Chairman of the Chinese Communist Party was on the verge of

---

*May 16 was the name adopted in 1967 by a group of conspirators against Mao Tse-tung's leadership who attacked from the "left" in the classical tradition of Leon Trotsky and his followers. They chose May 16 because this was the date of the first important inner-Party circular written by Mao in 1966. It spelled out the issues of the Cultural Revolution. Typically, the anti-Maoist conspirators chose to wrap themselves in a mantle of legitimacy by aligning, in name at least, with this important document.

exposure and presumably, therefore, battling for his political life on many levels.

Why then tell this story now at all?

Well, fools rush in where angels fear to tread.

I feel that the story, partial and biased as it may be, still contains important lessons. For one thing the history of the Cultural Revolution at Tsinghua helps explain what the old, revisionist education was really like and why people rose up en masse against it. For another it shows how this education, the educators themselves, and their students were transformed, or at least how this transformation began. For American readers who have been led to doubt that any real issues existed, or that anything really changed after all was said and done, this should prove useful.

Far more important is the story of how "right" and "left" political lines developed in the mass movement, and in particular how an "ultra-left" line emerged, dominated the field for a time, and then was defeated. From beginning to end the soundness and vitality of Mao Tse-tung's approach to the socialist revolution stands out. By reviewing these events one can begin to understand the crucial role which Mao played in mobilizing the mass movement when this was the key to the future and then in guiding it through one crisis after another as "right" and "left" deviations threatened to destroy it. This can be a revelation for those who think that seizing power is the ultimate act of revolution.

I feel that the question of "ultra-left" thought and action, so central to the history of Tsinghua, is especially important for young Americans to ponder. On the one hand, there are voices in the West still insisting that the ultra-left represented the real revolution in China and that in the end Mao Tse-tung, in spite of many beautiful words, crushed the flower of Chinese youth. On the other hand, many American revolutionaries are as prone as their Chinese counterparts to accept ultra-left slogans and policies. People find it hard to identify counter-revolution when it comes in "left" clothing. They think, "Anyway, left is better than right." Having learned to hate imperialism, they tend to assume that he who speaks most sharply and advocates the most extreme action hates imperialism the most; that the reddest flag is, *ipso facto,* the most revolutionary. If revolutionary politics were that simple no one would need to study Marx, Lenin, or Mao. Ultra-left politics are disastrous because they isolate the working class and make it impossible for working-class leaders to unite all forces that can be united against the main enemy. A common element disrupting unity here, as it so often has in China, is "I am the core" thinking, which maintains that I and my group are the real revolutionaries while people with other ideas, or people who have come to the same ideas at a later date, really don't deserve consideration as comrades and certainly cannot be in the vanguard.

The Tsinghua story clearly shows how damaging "I am the core" thinking can be, how it leads to arrogance, isolation, and finally to crimes against the people, all dressed in the most noble "left" rhetoric. If this can be understood, these rough notes will justify themselves.

In sharp contrast to "I am the core" thinking stands the united action of the Peking workers who ignored the most extreme provocations to bring hopelessly warring student factions together. What united the workers and eventually re-united the students was Marxism-Leninism-Mao Tse-tung Thought. Rarely has a more convincing demonstration of the power of this revolutionary theory been demonstrated than on the Tsinghua campus on July 27, 1968. If the extraordinary nature of these events and the political consciousness that made them possible can be understood in some measure from these notes, that too will justify their publication.

Part I

"Regular" Education

The class struggle is by no means over. The class struggle between the proletariat and the bourgeoisie, the class struggle between the different political forces, and the class struggle in the ideological field between the proletariat and the bourgeoisie will continue to be long and tortuous and at times will even become very acute. The proletariat seeks to transform the world according to its own world outlook, and so does the bourgeoisie. In this respect, the question of which will win out, socialism or capitalism, is still not really settled.

—Mao Tse-tung,
*On the Correct Handling of
Contradictions Among the People,*
February 27, 1957

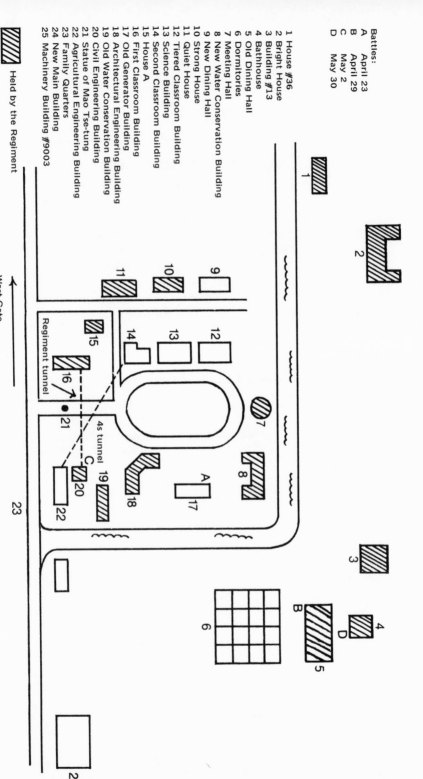

Sketch of the Tsinghua Main Campus
by Wang Yung-hsien and Tsu Hung-liang

Battles:
A April 23
B April 29
C May 2
D May 30

1 House #36
2 Bright House
3 Building #13
4 Bathhouse
5 Old Dining Hall
6 Dormitories
7 Meeting Hall
8 New Water Conservation Building
9 New Dining Hall
10 Strong House
11 Quiet House
12 Tiered Classroom Building
13 Science Building
14 Second Classroom Building
15 House A
16 First Classroom Building
17 Old Generator Building
18 Architectural Engineering Building
19 Old Water Conservation Building
20 Civil Engineering Building
21 Statue of Mao Tse-tung
22 Agricultural Engineering Building
23 Family Quarters
24 New Main Building
25 Machinery Building #9003

Regiment tunnel

4s tunnel

West Gate

Held by the Regiment

Held by the 4s

1
July on the Campus

Tsinghua University, China's most famous school of science and engineering, lies at the northern edge of the university district of Peking not far from the point where the North China Plain, stretching unbroken from the Yellow Sea, meets the Western Hills—the rock-ribbed ridges that rise abruptly into the sky in a great arc around the Chinese capital.*

This capital occupies one of the finest sites for a city anywhere in the world. Just as, on a neighborhood scale, one would build a house in a hollow encircled by hills and thus ensure both beauty and shelter, so, on a continental scale, the builders of Peking laid out their city on the vast flat in the elbow formed by the Taihang and the Yen mountains and thus combined panoramic splendor with some moderation of the cold steppe winds that blow almost all year out of Mongolia and Central Asia. Spacious as was the grand design conceived by these

---

*A satellite campus lies to the north, in Nankou, just south of the Great Wall at Nankou Pass.

ancient architects, they still left plenty of room for expansion on all four sides.

Since 1949 this rural space has been filling up with astonishing speed. Most of modern Peking's bustling, roaring, smoking new industry has been built to the east, south, and west of the city, leaving the north to the schools, new and old, and the parks, palaces, and imperial ruins that have long dominated there. Whether there have always been more trees in this suburb, whether more trees have been planted here in the last twenty years, or whether trees just naturally do better at the foot of the mountains I do not know, but certainly on coming to this area one is impressed by the great density and variety of the foliage and by the long reach of the cool shade it casts on streets, lanes, rice paddies, wheat fields, residential buildings, campus yards, and classroom buildings alike.

In the summer of 1971 Tsinghua's 200-acre campus, lying hot and humid under the July sun, seemed to us especially verdant and leafy, at least in the older, western section of the campus, and the crops — corn, beans, cucumbers, and melons — growing on much of the land between buildings spread greenness to the earth underfoot. The luxuriant growth, above and below, combined to give the whole area an unkempt look that was reinforced by slack maintenance of the lawns, the athletic fields, and numerous outlying buildings. Bushes and shrubs, planted by an earlier generation of landscapers, had not been trimmed for years. Scattered rocks and bricks still lay where they had fallen or been thrown during the hostilities of 1968. Old engineering equipment and sports paraphernalia, such as the uprooted steel frames of basketball backboards, lay in piles behind the weathered field house. Broken panes gaped from windows whose wooden frames were warped, cracked, and peeled pre-revolutionary paint. In the campus creek, black water laced with detergent foam flowed sluggishly.

All this lent to Tsinghua an air of sleepy neglect that seemed quite out of tune with the whole spirit of revolutionary Peking, and with that energetic thrust of construction, production, and innovation which the Cultural Revolution had unleashed. The explanation lay, perhaps in the fact that the campus was only slowly reviving from the long political struggle which, at its height, saw machine-guns, rifles, Molotov cocktails, and homemade cannon used by contending student factions against the classroom fortresses of each side. More than one large building had been drenched with gasoline and set afire. The whole roof of the Science Building had been burnt off and both floors of the Bathhouse had been gutted.

When we visited the Science Building it displayed a handsome new roof made of the light gray tile Peking kiln operators produce to such perfection, but nothing had been done about the charred east walls and gaping window apertures of the Bathhouse, or the firing holes hacked in the sides of the four-story dormitory buildings, or the pockmarks on these and so many other structures made by bullets, shells, and other assorted hard missles, such as the nuts and bolts that had been fired from huge slingshots made of bicycle inner tubes attached at both ends to convenient window frames. The steps of the university reception center still sagged rakishly toward a dip in the road that marked the line of an underground tunnel through which one besieged group of students, belonging to a faction called the 4s, had tried to escape. The remains of trenches and other earthworks could still be seen on the hill across from the First Classroom Building where "Bear," a member of the Chingkangshan Regiment, had appeared defiant and shirtless on the day the Peking workers arrived on the campus to stop the fighting. Bear hurled a hammer, a shovel, and finally a hand grenade at the workers on the road below, but they surrounded the building anyway.

Some of the neglect may also be attributed to the fact that the new education, now in the experimental stage, is not campus oriented but has its face turned outward toward the whole city, toward that impressive industrial region that is growing up both in front of and behind the once silent mountains. Students now spend as much time in the factories and on the construction sites of greater Peking as they do in classrooms and laboratories, and professors devote as much energy to developing liaison with the scores of factories and enterprises with which the university is allied as they do to lecturing and advising students. No longer will thousands of privileged young men and women withdraw into the leafy wonderland of Tsinghua to crack books until they are too old to laugh. No longer will they stuff their heads with mathematical formulas relating to the outmoded industrial practices of prewar Europe and America, sweat through "surprise attack" exams, and then emerge after years of isolation from production and political engagement unable to tell high-carbon steel from ordinary steel or a "proletarian revolutionary" from a "revisionist."

> In primary school dead serious about reading books.
> In middle school read dead books seriously.
> In the university seriously read books to death!

In verses like these the new student generation derides the educational spirit of pre-Cultural Revolution times and their derision carries with it, it would seem, a certain strand of disdain for a physical plant so carefully laid out and so meticulously tended by the American founders of the institution more than half a century ago. The foreigners wanted to isolate their "independent academic kingdom" from the life around it, the better to cultivate a colonial mentality among the Christian intellectuals they gathered there. The Kuomintang continued this tradition, but its administrators were too corrupt to spend money on repairs. The Communist administrators who later took control of the campus surely never felt at ease with the extravagant American style of its buildings and grounds, its lawns and pools (all built with the Chinese people's money), and so never really maintained them either. (No one ever cultivates lawns in North China in any case.) Whatever the truth may be, obviously the physical renovation of the Tsinghua campus has not stood high on the list of today's priorities. Factories, communes, workers' housing, flood control, pumping stations, coal mines, trolley buses, water mains, and a new Peking subway have all taken precedence. Today's university, after all, is not so much a *center of learning* as a *liaison center for learning* from the university of life. There will be time to fix it up when life itself has been transformed more to the taste of the burgeoning working class that now calls Peking its own.

If the Tsinghua campus seemed somewhat unkempt, it also seemed very quiet, semideserted so to speak. This was because in 1971 only a first-year class was in attendance—a class of 2,800 workers, peasants, and soldiers, almost half of whom were already out on field assignments. New classes would be added, one each year until the student body again reaches and then surpasses its traditional enrollment of 12,000. In the meantime the few students actually going to classes and living in the dorms rattled around like peas in a dry pod. When they came, a hundred or so at a time, to swim in the warm, masonry-lined lake, reclaimed years ago from a neighborhood swamp, their chatter and singing livened that area of reeds and weeds as if a flock of happy birds had suddenly descended; but when they dispersed to study and work they vanished from sight among the trees. Of course, if one toured the classrooms and work- shops, one did come now and then upon a group of a dozen or more young people intently listening to a lecture, operating some complicated machine tools, or soldering the leads of newly made transistors. But even in such important production units as the Chemistry Plant in the northeast corner of the grounds or the Truck Manufacturing Shop on the central oval, very few students or staff could be seen.

In 1971 Tsinghua was an institution in upheaval and transi- tion and the how's and why's of this momentous change were what we had come to inquire into. For this, the relaxed, quiet atmosphere was ideal. The people we wanted to meet—students, faculty, administrators, and Workers Propaganda Team mem- bers—all seemed to have plenty of time. We could talk for one day, three days, or six days if we so desired. We ended up re- turning for nineteen days in a row and still gained only an introduction to the complex history of the Cultural Revolution at Tsinghua.

We arrived by car from the city every morning promptly at nine (no matter what time we left our lodgings our solemn driver Wang always managed to enter the imposing West Gate at the same hour) and were met by our hosts for the day in front of whatever building they had chosen for our talks. The first day this was the big reception center on the main campus oval, where a huge room on the second floor had been equipped with sofas and easy chairs covered with lace-trimmed white cloth and set out in such an extended rectangle that conversations there were more like an international peace conference than an informal exchange of questions and answers. Fortunately, on the second day we abandoned this grand setting for a little upstairs room in an old dormitory building just north of the Quiet House, now famous as faction leader Kuai Ta-fu's headquarters during Tsinghua's Hundred Day War of 1968. After a week or so the talks were moved once again, this time to a creaking, single-storied brick mansion that had formerly been the home of Tsinghua's presidents and was sometimes called Ma Yi-ch'i's House after the last Kuomintanger to run the school. Ma Yi-ch'i is now on Taiwan. Since the builders of this foreign-style house had not taken proper precautions against dampness from the earth beneath, the floor joists had begun to rot away. The wide wood floors, so unusual in China, sagged precariously and in some places had even broken through. With the window frames also rotting and the bushes outside growing ever higher to block out light, and with the neglected lawn producing a fine crop of weeds, this once grand dwelling, now renamed House A, was slowly turning into something out of Edgar Allen Poe. A fine setting, it seemed, for the nocturnal comings and goings of Liu Shao-ch'i's wife, Wang Kuang-mei, who had lived here in 1966 under the pseudonym Hou P'u, or Little Hou, so that the students would not easily discover that she, of all people, was in charge of the work team that was running their lives.

When we adjourned our talks at noon each day we strolled over to a low, rambling dining hall not far to the north. It was there that Wang Kuang-mei, her work team under orders to withdraw, had once nervously served potatoes to angry rebel students and been denounced for "transparent tricks." This and other tales we heard with fascination while eating, and then either took a fitful nap in the old dormitory next to the Quiet House, went swimming in the university pool, or played several fast games of badminton on a blacktop court behind House A.

Many different cadre from Tsinghua's new Revolutionary Committee, Party Committee,* and Mao Tse-tung Thought Workers Propaganda Team helped arrange our talks and took turns being in the chair, so to speak. But the man who introduced the history of Tsinghua to us on the first morning later showed up most consistently, made most of the arrangements, and provided most of the ad hoc explanations which helped clarify things said by others. He was Liu Ming-yi, a worker from the Capital Steel Works. No one could mistake him for a campus intellectual, he was too solid and too tough. His arms were at least four inches through at the biceps and his chest filled his cotton jacket to the bursting point. His facial expression bespoke his origin as plainly as his build. His open, enthusiastic countenance was completely in tune with his habit of straight thinking and straight talking. All of this, it seemed, could have come from only one place—the shop floor. From the shop floor, too, he had acquired a naive but heartfelt male chauvinism which got him into a lot of trouble with the students and staff of the University—and with us as well.

Mao Tse-tung had said that the working class must take charge of the superstructure and transform it. Steelworker Liu was engaged in exactly this task and it was a remarkable thing to see, because he seemed to know what he wanted to do and how to go about doing it. His function at our talks was to set the political framework and then lead the discussion on from one problem to another in such a way that the past, the present, and the future all became clear. He showed absolutely no signs

---

*Revolutionary committees were the new organs of power set up everywhere in China after the overthrow of the old Party and state apparatus. They were made up of representatives of mass organizations, revolutionary old cadres, and People's Liberation Army delegates.

A Party Committee is the leading body of the Communist Party at all organizational levels, local, county, provincial, and municipal. Party committees were almost universally broken up and dissolved in 1966 and 1967 by attacks from below, but they were reconstituted in in 1968, 1969, and 1970 once the revolutionary committees had been set up.

of being ill-at-ease in an unfamiliar situation. On the contrary, he seemed to enjoy every minute of his life and work.

Our most interesting informants besides Liu were five staff members, Jen Yen-sheng, Tsu Hung-liang, Wang Yung-hsien, Kao Hung-chin, and Wu Wei-yu. They had been students or young assistant instructors when the Cultural Revolution began and had taken an active part in the militant rebel movement from beginning to end. Though they had been on opposite sides during the violent factional struggle of 1968, they sat with us day after day through good-humored explanations and never once quarreled over what had happened, over what the position of the various sides had been, or over where each had been right or wrong. This was a remarkable demonstration of the fine political work done by the Workers Propaganda Team, because not so long before these young men had been convinced that those on the opposite side were counter-revolutionary wreckers, and had maintained that questions of class power such as they then faced could only be settled by force of arms. Hence they had been trying to kill one another.

How had they fallen into such sharp opposition? How had they been brought together? How had they reached such unanimity that they could laugh about the earnest nonsense they had believed about each other not so many months before? The answers were a part of the story we had come to unravel. We had, of course, to start at the beginning. In order to get a full picture we talked not only to the rebel students, but to several professors who were in part responsible for the old Tsinghua carrying on as it did, to higher Communist Party cadres who had backed the professors and then been overthrown, to members of the Workers Propaganda Team that had arrived in July 1968 and still remains to direct the affairs of the whole University, and to new students only a few months out of the fields and the factories who are the pioneers of a new education.

Tsinghua occupies ground right alongside the main campus of Peking University, where the Cultural Revolution first took form as a mass movement. A cadre of Peking University's

Philosophy Department, Nieh Yuan-tzu, wrote the big character poster* that sparked the rebellion on May 25, 1966. All this poster demanded, in fact, was that the president of Peking University, Lu P'ing, remove restrictions on debate about the play *Hai Jui Dismissed from Office,* which he was treating as an academic controversy over historical fact rather than a political conflict over the correctness or incorrectness of Mao Tse-tung's line for socialist construction. The poster unleashed a popular hurricane because it mounted a direct attack on a "party person in power" and called him a revisionist whose "controls and plots" should be smashed. Before Nieh Yuan-tzu's poster went up most students had gone along with whatever their University Party Committee decreed, on the theory that it was automatically carrying out Mao's line. After her wide-open and scathing criticism, some of the braver and more militant students began making their own judgments concerning leading cadres, regardless of their rank or status.

At Tsinghua, where the early debates of the Cultural Revolution had been smothered even more effectively than at Peita,† the rebel students had an even bigger target than Lu P'ing. This was Chiang Nan-hsiang, who was not only the president of Tsinghua and head of its Party Committee, but was concurrently the Minister of Higher Education in the central government and a member of the Central Committee of the Communist Party of China. As soon as Nieh Yuan-tzu's poster appeared, Tsinghua students crowded the Peita campus next door to study it. When it was broadcast to the nation on June 1—an indication that it had support from Mao Tse-tung—a group of Tsinghua students, among them Kuai Ta-fu, launched an open offensive against their own Communist leadership with a poster which asked: "Is our Party Committee named *Ma* or

---

*A big-character poster is a public statement written with fairly large ideographs on a large sheet of paper and posted up on a wall or reed mat where everyone can read it. It is supposed to be brief and pithy, but many big-character posters are more like rambling wall newspapers than concentrated expressions of opinion.

†Peita is the abbreviated Chinese way of saying Peking University and is frequently used because it is more convenient.

Hsiu [Marx or Revision]?" During the next ten days the admin-istration lost control of the situation. Rebel students, staff, and teachers, buying paper and paint with their own money, covered the campus with a whole series of posters exposing Chiang Nan-hsiang and his educational line over the years.

2
Stuffed Ducks and
Surprise Attacks

What was it about Tsinghua that the rebels repudiated? Primarily the whole idea of "expertise in command," the pres-sure on the students to strive for fame and prosperity as bril-liant scientists and engineers without whose "genius" China could not advance. As the system had developed through the 1950s and 1960s, the sole measure of merit had become grades. Education, it was held, had no class character; everyone was equal before grades. Therefore striving for high grades became the main concern of everyone in the university, and the period of study (including preparatory school) had been extended to absurd lengths: from four to six years, then from six to nine years, and finally from nine to eleven years in order for the students to have time to master all the knowledge in the foreign books that dealt with their special field. In the drive for book knowledge both faculty and students eschewed practice, and the longer they sat in the libraries and classrooms the less con-tact they had with the outside world, including current prac-tice in their branch of knowledge. An accepted slogan was: "Once you master physics and chemistry you can walk under heaven" (i.e., win privilege in life). Hence, "Grades are life and death" and "Good grades ensure a good life."

All this was absolutely contrary to Mao Tse-tung's theory of education. Mao considered the goal of study not to be grades, or a prosperous life for the experts, or even the cultivation of "red engineers," but to enable "everyone who receives an education to become a worker with socialist consciousness and culture." The period of study, said Mao, should be shortened, not lengthened, and students, far from being locked year after year in their classrooms, should take a regular part in production and in class struggle.

Mao's model was Resistance University, set up in Yenan in 1936 to train cadres for carrying on the Anti-Japanese War in all fields. It was led by Lin Piao. Here, in informal classes, students and teachers alike put the development of revolutionary consciousness as their primary goal, took as long as necessary to argue things out, and worked regularly to grow food and build housing for themselves and to supply materiel to support the front.

The whole Tsinghua tradition was a far cry from that of wartime Yenan. The University had been founded in 1911 by Americans using Boxer Indemnity money. By investing in higher education in China they hoped to develop an intellectual elite in tune with American aspirations and interests, an elite that would, according to Han Suyin, "continue of its own volition the process of turning China into a client state." "This type of operation," the president of the University of Illinois wrote to Teddy Roosevelt in 1910, "is more useful than an army."

Indeed it was. For thirty-eight years, first under American and then under Kuomintang control, Tsinghua turned out a small stream of highly trained technicians, many of whom were ready to serve the Kuomintang clique and its imperial masters in whatever capacity proved most lucrative. Contrary to expectations, Tsinghua also graduated some dedicated revolutionaries, but this was a countercurrent, stimulated by the national liberation struggle in China, that the University administration tried hard to block and wipe out.

Many Tsinghua graduates went on to study abroad, particularly in the United States. This, after all, was one of the reasons the school had been established in the first place. When they returned to China a crucial number of these people were reassigned as faculty and staff at their old alma mater. Thus there grew up over the years a core of people in power at Tsinghua who were linked by the common bonds of elite origin, college study together, graduate experience abroad, and teaching at their home school. Outsiders really had no right to speak. No matter what happened, a tight little clique of "academic authorities" ruled the roost and perpetuated the system of which they considered themselves to be the finest products.

After Peking was liberated in 1949, Tsinghua was hard to transform. It was not that the Communist Party made little effort to do so. On the contrary, right after liberation a huge movement to repudiate "worship-America thought" and wipe out colonial mentality swept the campus. Students and faculty alike went out into the countryside as part of land reform teams, and many young men and women joined the Chinese volunteers fighting in Korea. Political study was put on the agenda and manual labor became a regular part of the daily life of most students and staff. At the same time, the University was shaken by rapid expansion. In the thiry-eight years from 1911 to 1948 only 2,700 students graduated; while in the seventeen years from 1948 to 1966, 27,000 students graduated—a ten-fold annual increase. The successive political movements and the expansion certainly diluted the control exercised by the old graduates who had dominated the campus for so long.

Nevertheless, Tsinghua was never fully transformed into a socialist institution carrying out Mao Tse-tung's educational line. This was in part because the Communists directly involved —such as Chiang Nan-hsiang, Minister of Higher Education, and Lu Ting-yi, head of the Propaganda Department of the Chinese Communist Party and the man responsible for educational policy—were skeptical about the socialist transformation that Mao advocated. Resistance University and its informal "development of consciousness" was all right for the guerrilla atmosphere of wartime Yenan, they reasoned, but now the Communist Party was out to transform China into a modern country and education had to be "regular." "Regular" of course meant Western traditional—set courses, "earned credit," grades in command, formal examinations—all propelling the students toward brilliant careers after graduation. And who could ensure that this "regular" education developed properly? Who else but those Western-trained "academic authorities" and the younger generation of "assistants" and "associates" they had personally developed in their own image.

The turn to the Soviet Union for inspiration, a dominant trend in China in the fifties, only reinforced this. In the Soviet Union higher education was as "regular" as anyone could desire, since Soviet educators had studied well the university systems of Western Europe and America. In fact, they had gone further in cutting the links between theory and practice than was general even in the West, and when their system was transplanted to China it helped create an academic atmosphere that was more a caricature than a copy of bourgeois education.

Professor T'ung Shih-pai of the Automation Department, a second-generation Tsinghua graduate (his father had gone from Tsinghua to the University of Pennsylvania to study architecture) recalled for us some of the highlights of his academic career.

" 'Better to have a profession than 10,000 acres of land,' was the motto my grandfather adopted. As a Ching Dynasty official and then a school principal he sent his three sons abroad to study. All my father's friends were Tsinghua graduates who went on to study in America. With such a background I had to be somebody special. During the war, while other students found their way to Yenan or joined the national army to fight Japan, I prepared to be a bourgeois gentleman at Hangchow Christian College where I was taught to turn the other cheek. At least I refused to work for the Japanese when I graduated and I took a minor job with the Yellow River Conservation Project in Sian. But the administration was corrupt and the pay so low I couldn't buy enough to eat, so I went to Kunming to Southwest Union University (the wartime combination of Tsinghua, Peking, and Nankai universities) and studied radio engineering. After the war I came to Tsinghua as a teaching assistant but avoided politics by immersing myself in music. All day long I practiced my violin in the music hall. I thought the violin sounded better than the political slogans of the embattled student movement. Finally my father arranged for me to go to the University of Illinois. From 1948 until June 1955 I studied and taught in the United States. I was prepared to return home in 1951 but the Department of Justice forbade us to leave. It was three years later that I finally defied the U.S. government and left anyway. Once home I chose to return to Tsinghua. That was natural considering my grandfather, my father, and my own past.

"At first I was worried that my knowledge might not be useful to the new society, but when I looked at what they were teaching my fears were laid to rest. At that time they were using Russian teaching material. It was no different from my own. I could still walk under heaven.

"Liu Shao-ch'i advocated learning everything from the Soviet Union, so at the start there was no attack on my methods, no struggle against me. Whatever I had learned from my teachers, I taught. 'So-and-so discovered this, what's-his-name discovered that. So study hard, my students, and become inventors.' When I described a process I used a lot of formulas to show how smart I was. When students came to me for advice I said, 'Better pack the knowledge into your head. As my grandfather used to say, a profession is worth 10,000 acres of land. So study! Learn the material by heart! Wherever you go you'll be all right!'

"In teaching work I favored the smart students. I pulled a long face at the slower ones. My first ideological education came with the antirightist movement of 1957. It was a major blow to me. Politically, people forgave me—after all, I was raw out of America. But toward my working style and my teaching methods they were very critical. They said I taught in an authoritarian way and always had the last word on everything. The last word, of course, was the way people did things abroad. If the Americans had a color code for electrical resistors—red, yellow, blue—China had to have the same. I forget the details, but in 1957 the posters went up all over attacking my worship-America thought.'

"I decided that it wouldn't do to go on like that. I couldn't just advocate American techniques. When a problem came up I would first check and see if the Soviets had a solution, and if it was the same then I would talk of that!

"In 1962 Liu Shao-ch'i came to Tsinghua and called us professors the stable elements, the 108 generals of Tsinghua.* He asked us to write the textbooks that would be used all over the country. I became the editor-in-chief of the electronics material, and right up until the Cultural Revolution the teaching material I edited had a great influence all over the country. I saw nothing wrong with it, nothing wrong at all. I thought that natural science has no class character. Capitalists use electronics, socialists use electronics. So I just dusted off my old material and spread out my wares.

"But in fact I never considered whether what I wrote was useful for the education of workers, peasants, and soldiers. I wrote not to serve the people but to display my talents and demonstrate my learning. I used all those formulas and those foreign quotes to inspire admiration, to show how able I was.

"Simple problems that could be explained with a few well-chosen sentences, I made complex. An able worker who had made a number of inventions lost confidence in himself after he heard me explain Ohm's Law. He felt he could never understand electricity.

"After my book came out, many students were intrigued by my theoretical approach and wanted to do advanced work under me. One wrote: 'After reading your book I am determined to put all the knowledge of electricity into one formula.' Obviously my influence on the young people was leading them to elevate theory to the skies and make it mysterious.

"My book took up electrical problems in the order that this science developed in capitalist countries; the first volume dealt with rectification—the conversion of alternating to direct current; the second dealt with amplification and oscillation, which related to the development of the telephone and radio; and the third dealt with radar, the vacuum tube, semi-conductors, and so on.

"I wrote this way and taught this way right up until 1966. The vacuum tube was the apex of the whole edifice long after

---

*The 108 generals were the heroes of the classical novel *Water Margin*.

its importance had waned and after even housewives' co-ops were making transistors in the back streets of Peking. There were two reasons for this. I thought I had to begin from the beginning and go through all the steps. Result: I never got around to teaching about transistors. Furthermore, I was a little shaky on the newest developments and if I didn't know about them others were not to plunge in ahead of me!

"Look at it realistically. My textbook has been a hindrance to the development of electronics in this country. I was out of touch with the state of the art, with the actual practice going on around me; I immersed my students in things I had mastered twenty years before in the United States."

Had this Professor T'ung been a "bourgeois academic authority"? He personally is convinced he had. And at Tsinghua he had a lot of company. We talked with his nephew T'ung Lin-hsiu, who had come back from the Soviet Union with a degree in architecture; with Ch'ien Wei-ch'ang, professor of mechanics, whose career paralleled Norman Bethune's in reverse (while the Canadian doctor came to China to confront the Japanese on the Taihang battlefront, Ch'ien went to the University of Toronto, Bethune's old school, to carve out a brilliant career in mechanical theory that led him to a post in rocket propulsion at Berkeley, California); with Shih Kuo-heng, a sociologist who had studied at Harvard; and with several others either trained abroad or trained at home by returned students. All had essentially the same story to tell: they had been careerists who taught careerism, overseas students who had worshipped foreign technique, theorists divorced from practice—and particularly from the rapidly developing and expanding practice of production and science in China. In so far as they had led education, they had led it down a well-trodden bourgeois path and only really confronted the political implications of this when the Cultural Revolution forced them to.

Most interesting for us was the experience of T'ung Lin-hsiu, who had been a student in the Soviet Union. He grew up and went to middle school under the Kuomintang, but because he was twelve years younger than his cousin Shih-pai and went to Tsinghua after the liberation of China in 1949, he did not consider himself an old-style intellectual like his cousin, but one of the first generation of new revolutionary intellectuals raised by the Communist Party. He became a Communist in 1952 and went off to the Soviet Union to study to become a "red engineer" without really understanding that he had put his vocation before politics. "I felt that 'red' engineers are better than 'white' engineers, but it was the 'engineer' part that was still most important."

In the Soviet Union he found the whole university very career oriented, and the study of architecture as divorced from practice as it had been in China under the old Western system. If one chose for a thesis a practical problem facing China's construction, there was no way for the Soviet teachers to handle it—so T'ung went to the library, read other men's theses, and wrote something very abstract which won him immediate recognition as an architect of promise.

On leaving the Soviet university he was given three gifts which summed up the Russian approach to academic life. The first was a leather briefcase to keep his Ph.D. thesis in, the second was a wooden box with a handpainted picture of the Kremlin on it to keep his awards and medals in, and the third was a leather wallet, also embossed with a picture of the Kremlin, the purpose of which could hardly be in doubt.

T'ung did not think through the meaning of these gifts, but when the Cultural Revolution raised the issue of the two roads, he realized that the gifts in no way conflicted with his own inner goals: they summed up the essence of bourgeois careerism.

T'ung returned from the Soviet Union at the time of the Great Leap Forward and was quite critical of the mass movement for production that was involving the students and staff of the university at that time. He was criticized as a right opportunist but received no education concerning two-line struggle.*

---

*"Two-line struggle" or "struggle between two lines" refers to struggles in society over basic issues of policy and program which reflect basic differences between the main classes contending for power. In a period of socialist revolution the contending classes are the working class and the capitalist class or bourgeoisie, and the struggle between them is reflected in every sphere. Behind the phrase

As a result he became despondent and turned his attention even more exclusively toward his vocation. Since he had made political mistakes he decided to be a "vocational Communist" and leave politics to others. Obviously, with an outlook like this, he could hardly play a positive role in transforming Tsinghua into a socialist university. In spite of his Communist Party membership, he, like his cousin, became a "bourgeois academic authority."

But what of the administrators of Tsinghua, those experienced Communists who are ostensibly in charge of higher education and had undertaken the task of transforming it along socialist lines? Were they really powerless to deal with the T'ungs and the Ch'iens in the long struggle over educational line that took place during the fifties and sixties?

We talked for a long time with Liu Ping, vice-secretary of the Tsinghua University Party Committee from 1956 to 1966 and again from 1970 until now. He is a mild-mannered, soft-spoken man of medium height and middle age who joined the Chinese Revolution back in 1938 after running away from a Honan middle school and the landlord home into which his father had been adopted when Liu's starving peasant grandparents could no longer feed their son.

In 1956 Liu Ping must have seemed exactly the right man for the Tsinghua campus. He had actually been trained at Resistance University in Yenan when it was directed by Lin Piao and personally supervised by Mao. Afterward he had become a cadre of the New Democratic Youth League at the county level and later a Central Committee member representing the Communist Youth League when it was formed in 1949.† He had rich experi-

---

lies the understanding that there is never an objectively best way to do things, but that members of different classes do things differently because they have different class goals.

†The New Democratic Youth League was the youth organization led by the Communist Party in the period of the new democratic revolution that ended with nationwide victory in 1949. The socialist revolution began in 1949 and the New Democratic Youth League was reorganized as the Communist Youth League.

ence in rural work in popular education, and in mass mobilization. At Tsinghua he moved into a strategic position. Chiang
Nan-hsiang, even though he was nominally president of the
University and secretary of its Party Committee, spent little
time on the campus. Liu Ping, as vice-secretary, was actually
in charge of day-to-day work and was in a position to refashion
the whole Tsinghua system if he really made that his goal.

In fact Liu Ping did nothing of the sort.

"When I got here," Liu Ping said, "Liu Shao-ch'i and Lu
Ting-yi were saying: 'What we had before were training classes.
Now we need regular universities.' I fell for it.

"Chiang Nan-hsiang said: 'That old Resistance University
method won't work. This is something new and different. Here
we must produce scientists. A little Marxist-Leninist theory, a
little study of society, a little military training won't solve the
problem.'

"When we were at Resistance University Mao Tse-tung
told us that the center of our work should be changing the
thinking of our students. We should strive for three things:
(1) a staunch political orientation, (2) flexible strategy and
tactics, and (3) a good working style.

"But when I came here everyone said the task was just
the opposite. We weren't here to change people's thinking but
to teach knowledge, science. Here we put technique above all,
expertise above all, and organized mountain-climbing teams to
scale the peaks of science.

"So I thought, 'Maybe this polytechnical school is different
from Resistance University, where the main subjects were
politics and social theory.' So I too put technique in command.

"As to teaching methods, Mao Tse-tung advocated the
method of enlightenment as opposed to the stuffed-duck method. But we had regulations here that tied the students hand
and foot. In Yenan the classes had been lively, we had had
debates, discussions. I thought, 'Maybe that is suitable for a
training class, but here where there is so much science to learn,
perhaps we must cram the facts in. So I fell for the stuffed-
duck method.

"Chairman Mao said all along: 'Cut the school years

shorter.' At Resistance University the time was short—at first three months, later a year, then the graduates went out to work. Of course, technical courses needed more time than the social sciences, but they didn't need all the time we argued for. Lu Ting-yi suggested ten years, but we ended up with two years in senior middle school, six years in college, and three years in graduate courses, making it eleven altogether. That was doing Lu Ting-yi one better. That is how we creatively carried out Lu Ting-yi's instructions and applied them to Tsinghua! The argument was that too little time would keep the standards of the graduates down, so we added rather than subtracted.

"I thought, 'I have no experience. I know nothing of technical things. Probably more time really is needed.' So I worked together with the others to carry out this eleven-year system. But the majority were not satisfied with it. They came in as young people and they went out with gray beards!"

The staff and the older professors at Tsinghua never tired of telling Liu Ping that he was in no position to lead them. In 1957 this became a campus-wide issue. As Liu Ping put it:

"In 1957 the Rightists* jumped out and said, 'You are only a clod, a country bumpkin. You don't have any technical knowledge at all.' Under this kind of pressure I was convinced that I was indeed a country bumpkin, that I knew nothing of education, and since I didn't know I had better listen to others, and especially to Chiang Nan-hsiang. Thus I got pushed around. I had no idea that this was class struggle."

"But why did the Rightists make you their target?" I asked.

"They attacked me because I was vice-secretary of the Communist Party Committee even though I had no academic standing. Chiang Nan-hsiang was a graduate of Tsinghua. He graduated before the Anti-Japanese War. Now the slogan was, '*wei hang* can't lead *nei hang*' [Those outside the trade can't lead those inside]. Chiang Nan-hsiang was obviously an in-

---

*In 1957 people who opposed socialist construction and preferred to build a bourgeois society were labeled "Rightists." Among them were intellectuals, students, former Kuomintang officials, and former independent businessmen, as well as Communists sympathetic to them.

sider while I was an outsider. I hadn't graduated from college.
I hadn't even graduated from middle school, and I was a country bumpkin to boot. I was doubly an outsider—an old Communist transferred from mass work. How could a middle school
student lead professors? They made that clear at the very
beginning of my work here. The day after I arrived I gave
a lecture on Communist leadership, but before I got through
a whole pile of notes came up from the audience. The gist was,
'Stop all that nonsense. We've heard it all before.'

"Then when the Rightists went on the offensive in 1957
they attacked me personally and said, 'Bumpkin, get out!' In
the countryside the peasants never drove me away. When I
worked in a factory and led the fight against economism the
workers welcomed me. I was always treated as a comrade. But
here they wanted to drive me away! I was surprised at their
attitude. I should have drawn some conclusions, but I didn't.
Along came victory in the movement. We pulled out two to
three hundred Rightist students and a similar number among
the faculty.* So I thought all the Rightists had been pulled
out and the class struggle had been resolved. I accepted the
theory of the dying out of class struggle.

"Once we had defeated the Rightists, Mao Tse-tung set
out the thesis that our education should serve proletarian politics and be combined with productive labor. He also raised
the ideas of communes in the countryside and of the Great
Leap Forward. I was very happy. I saw all these new developments. I saw our students going to Honan to make iron and
steel. I saw the mass movements and I was happy. Mass movements were something that I was familiar with. I played a central role. I became the director of steelmaking at Tsinghua. It
was not the same as messing around in laboratories.

"Then, in 1960, we had drought and flood, the Soviet Union pulled out, tore up their agreements. Suddenly Liu Shao-
ch'i stepped forward and said that our students were doing
too much labor, that the quality of education had been lowered,

---

*"Pull out" means to remove from office or activity and to expose
politically.

and that it wouldn't do to go on like that. So we got the students back from the countryside, withdrew them from the 'three revolutionary movements,'* and set up all sorts of regulations about passing courses: what sort of grade allows you to go on and what sort of grade means you must drop out.

"Although I personally liked to see the students going out to work, when the capitalist-roaders said this was a mess, I thought they were probably correct. It fit my world outlook at the time. And all this came from inside the Communist Party. The capitalist-roaders were inside. I never thought that this was class struggle reflected inside our Party, so I didn't resist it. I bought it. I didn't recognize that the principal contradiction was between the socialist and the capitalist roads and that this was especially true after private ownership had been abolished, forcing the struggle to go deeper.

"As the revolution objectively deepened and moved from the base to the superstructure, I moved from the countryside to the city, into the heart of the superstructure, a great university. But subjectively I didn't recognize what had happened. As far as I was concerned there was a big gap between the subjective and the objective and this created the basis for making the mistakes I made."

3
A Revisionist in Spite of Himself

Liu Ping's story was a long one but he had it well in mind. He knew what he wanted to say, so it was hardly necessary to ask any questions. It took him one whole afternoon to review the old Tsinghua system and his own surrender to "regular education." It was so hot that I had to keep several layers

---

*The three revolutionary movements are (1) class struggle, which includes almost all significant political struggle; (2) the struggle for production, which includes all productive effort in industry and agriculture; and (3) scientific experiment, which, by revealing new objective laws, revolutionizes production and social practice.

of heavy paper under my hand to prevent sweat from soaking into my notebook. The heat did not let up all night. The next morning Liu Ping, not the least bit jaded by the unrelenting high temperature and matching humidity, took up what he considered to be the most crucial question of all—Communist Party leadership. This was of course linked to the question of who, which class forces, led the Party.

"As to the question of the Communist Party as the vanguard, Mao Tse-tung teaches that the Party must lead regardless of the situation, no matter what the place. The Party must always be in command. But Chiang Nan-hsiang said that in the University the Party must be a professors' party, a lecturers' party. Once it becomes a party of the professors and lecturers, then it can run the University. What he meant was that when professors are recruited into the Communist Party, then the Communist Party will rule the school because the professors always rule the school.

"So we actively recruited professors into the Communist Party. The slogan was "To recruit Mei Lan-fang [a famous Peking opera star] is better than recruiting 100 banner carriers.' With this type of thinking we tried to develop the professors politically and bring them into the Party. Hu Chien, a second vice-secretary of the Party Committee and an old comrade of mine, analyzed which individuals looked like the most promising material. Then the central headquarters sent members to talk with them and look them over. We divided the professors and teachers into three groups—left, middle, and right. The standard we used for left (good) was whether or not they supported the Communist Party leadership at Tsinghua. Whoever had some kind words to say about the Communist leaders of the University we labeled 'left.' Actually these 'lefts' supported our revisionist line, so what kind of 'lefts' were they?

"When we had decided on a few 'lefts,' we informed Chiang Nan-hsiang. After consultation we sent some members down to help individual prospects. What kind of help did they give? They had everyone study Liu Shao-ch'i's book, *On the Self-Cultivation of Communists.*

"The Communist Party branches in the departments, when

told by the central headquarters to consider somebody for membership, took this as an order. So they did their best to win these prospects to the Party. Most people, when asked if they wanted to join, said, 'Of course. Why not?'

"So the individual agreed. But what of his history? Our position was that all intellectuals had a complicated political history so we needn't look into it too deeply. This was Chiang Nan-hsiang's position. We just judged by whether they behaved well and by that we meant whether they supported our revisionist line.

"Of course, the Communist Party is a party led by Mao Tse-tung. We had to go through the steps laid out in the Party Constitution. But we did it quite formally and used as standards our revisionist standards, our loyalist standards. When recruiting workers and peasants we had used different standards. Why adopt something new for intellectuals? Because we thought we had no expertise. How could we lead a modern university? We must make our party a party of professors. Without professors we can't lead."

"But," I asked, "wasn't support for the Party, how well any given peasant supported the Communist Party leadership, in fact the same standard that you used for recruiting in the villages?"

"Yes," answered Liu Ping, "but in the villages there was open class struggle going on. You could judge by how a peasant behaved in this struggle and pick out the activists."

"But, as you explained it today, there was class struggle here on the campus then. Couldn't you judge in the same way here?"

"I didn't really study Mao Tse-tung. I thought I understood the struggle but I didn't really. I failed to use the viewpoint of class struggle to look at what was going on," replied Liu Ping. He continued:

"Once the professors joined the Party, we brought them quickly into the branches, department- and university-level Party Committees. But once they got in they spread their own thinking about education throughout the Party. Hence the professors' ideas became the decisions of the Communist Party, the policy of the Communist Party. This gradually changed the nature of the Communist Party as a proletarian vanguard. But I never saw this as a two-line struggle!"

"Do you mean to say that intellectuals should not be recruited into the Party?" I asked.

"Of course not," said Liu Ping, somewhat startled. "It was not wrong to recruit intellectuals. But the question was, were they up to the standards of proletarian vanguard fighters? We need intellectuals. They are an important force. The problem was that many of the professors had problems in their ideology and in their history and we took them in anyway. For instance, we accepted a professor who had been a district leader of the Kuomintang; now we have expelled people like that. We also accepted good people, patriotic people, who wanted socialism but were really not vanguard material. In the course of the Cultural Revolution these people have developed and they are still in the Communist Party. Then there are those who really were reactionary bourgeois academic authorities in their respective fields even though politically they were not reactionary, people such as Liang Szu-ch'eng, a civil engineer and architect. Now they have learned many new lessons and really want to change. In the Cultural Revolution Liang's reactionary academic theories were repudiated, but we wanted very much to save and develop this person. He had not been involved in reactionary politics. After repudiation by the masses he criticized himself and even though he was sick he studied Mao Tse-tung Thought intently.* He wanted to remain in the Communist Party. This man has been patriotic, he has sup-

---

*Mao Tse-tung Thought refers to the whole body of Mao Tse-tung's writings, which are considered by Mao's followers to be a development of Marxism-Leninism in the middle decades of the twentieth century. The Red Book contains some highlights of Mao Tse-tung Thought. Mao's *Selected Works* contain much more. A collected works has not yet been edited or published. To say "Mao Tse-tung Thought" instead of "Maoism" is an expression of modesty because it quite clearly places Mao on a level below Marx and Lenin as a developer of basic theory. This was, at least, the original intent of the formulation. It has no mystical connotations.

ported the Party and socialism. So he remains with us. He is over seventy years old and sick now. I went to see him to discuss the matter of his Party membership. When he spoke of it and of Mao Tse-tung he was moved to tears. We have to take all these aspects into account and unite with him."

Since Liu Ping had been at Resistance University in Yenan under Lin Piao, I wondered how he had so easily abandoned the concepts of mutual aid and mutual study that were so vital to revolutionary education there.

"Well," he replied thoughtfully, repeating much that he had said before, "the first day I came here they all told me Resistance University was no good. Here we had regular education. I was a clod, a country bumpkin. What I thought was: These people are experts, I had better listen to what they have to say. Not only was I enmeshed in their system, but all my direct superiors from Lu Ting-yi on down were supporting the 'regular' idea. If you had left me on my own I would have modeled the education here along Yenan lines because that's the education I knew. But what I studied at the Higher Party School was a complete duplication of Russian experience, which came from people who were on the Central Committee. As for me, I couldn't tell one line from another."

"But didn't you come in from the countryside to overthrow the old system?"

"Yes, of course," said Liu. "I came to overthrow the old system, but I was gradually absorbed into it. The most difficult thing is that the revisionists wave a red flag and pose as revolutionaries. The leaders never said this was a bourgeois school. They said this was a great socialist university. But actually it had the same old content, and I fell for it!

"Chiang Nan-hsiang said, 'If you don't have some professional competence how can you stand on your feet around here?' He wanted me and Hu Chien to become professors in the Political Science Department. I had only been through two years of middle school and Hu Chien had only been through primary school. How could we become professors?

"But if the title of professor was too grand for us, we still felt that we needed some professional status, some acquired skill, so we decided to study Russian. At this time we were learning everything from the Russians. So Hu Chien and I decided we would amass some capital, some academic standing, if we mastered the Russian language. It was not wrong to study a foreign language, the more you know the better, but our thinking was, 'Old cadres who can speak a foreign language! We won't be looked down on then!'

"Hu Chien studied a year and quit. I studied a week and quit. We weren't using proletarian thinking. We didn't use our experience at Yenan to transform Tsinghua. Instead we got transformed by this old bourgeois university!

"When I came here," said Liu Ping, summing up, "I followed others in political line, educational line, Party construction, and professional viewpoint. Thus I made serious *line mistakes*. But I didn't realize it. I wasn't one bit aware of it. I made serious mistakes but I thought only that I had worked hard for the Communist Party and the Revolution!"

Just as surely as Professor T'ung Shih-pai had been a bourgeois reactionary authority, so the cadre Liu Ping had been a "capitalist-roader," a "party person in authority taking the capitalist road." Nevertheless, before June 20, 1966, such an idea had never entered his head. On that day he returned to the Tsinghua campus for the first time in several months. He had been away leading the work teams of a whole province as they carried through the Socialist Education Movement in the countryside.* On his way back he had stopped over in Peking to attend a week-long meeting of higher cadres involved in rural work.

"I thought I was on the 'left.' Hadn't I led 4,000 students in the transformation of a whole province? Back home on the campus the students had started putting dunce caps on the heads of administrators, but here I was at the Peking Hotel studying. Of course, we had heard about the goings on on

---

*The Socialist Education Movement was launched throughout China's countryside in the early 1960s in order to consolidate and develop collective agriculture after a period of retreat toward individualism led by Liu Shao-ch'i.

the campuses but I had had no details about Tsinghua. And anyway, I thought, "I am on the left. No one will struggle against me!'"

Liu Ping was in for a traumatic shock. When his chauffeured car drove into Tsinghua's West Gate on the bright morning of June 20, it was stopped by a crowd of angry students. They pulled him rudely from his comfortable seat, set a tall conical dunce cap on his head, and dragged him before a mass meeting so that he could be repudiated.

But I am getting ahead of my story.

The educational system perpetuated by "bourgeois academic authorities" like T'ung Shih-pai and Ch'ien Wei-ch'ang, and reinforced by such "capitalist-roaders" as Liu Ping and Chiang Nan-hsiang, was particularly hard on students of worker and peasant origin who had had no opportunity to go to the more prestigious middle schools in China's coastal cities. Worker and peasant students were very much in the position of Black and Third World students from the rural South and the ghettoes of America who find themselves ill-prepared to compete academically with the sons and daughters of suburban professionals and the business elite, when and if they ever reach the "college of their choice."

Poor peasant students at Tsinghua told us about a class in the Agricultural Engineering Department that entered the University in 1960. They were all of worker or poor peasant background and they resented the treatment they got—the unwillingness of professors to explain their blackboard formulas, the reluctance of advanced students to help the less advanced, the sudden-death examinations that eliminated wholesale all those who were poorly prepared. The Party secretary of this class was an experienced older cadre. He led his classmates in criticizing the whole system and pointed out that it added up to a wrong line in higher education. This upset the school authorities. Their first act was to remove this man as Party secretary. But the class stuck together and continued to fight, so in the name of catering to its academic difficulties the whole group was prematurely graduated. This removed them from Chiang Nan-hsiang's hair, so to speak. It was said that they gave the University a stomach-ache. Take a laxative and purge the stomach! Instead of being allowed to complete their course, which was to end in 1964, they were suddenly sent out to work in 1963.

Another blatant case involved a woman tractor driver from the Northeast who was a model worker and also famous as a parachutist. When she came to Tsinghua she had been in good health and was politically advanced. But the professors looked down on her as a girl with "a big stomach but a small brain." They called her dumb to her face and constantly undermined her morale. Her health deteriorated week by week and finally, after two years, she had to have part of one lung cut out because of tuberculosis. The regulation was that certain exams had to be taken, but when the time came this sick woman was still in the hospital. Instead of making special arrangements for her, the authorities said that if she didn't take the exams she would be expelled from the University. Her classmates went to the hospital at night to help her study and she came to the exam straight from her sick bed. Half way through the ordeal she fainted. Of course she didn't pass and she had to leave school. Because she had not fulfilled the task given her by the Party she applied many times to return, but the authorities repeatedly rejected her on the grounds that they had to maintain the high academic standards of their institution. They told her she just did not qualify. The prestige of Tsinghua was at stake. She begged to be allowed to sit in on courses without credit, but this they would not allow either, so she was driven from the campus altogether.

In sharp contrast to the short shrift shown to this labor model were the great lengths to which the University administration went to welcome a rather brilliant student from Shanghai who was steeped in bourgeois ideology. The admissions personnel knew all about this youth's politics and family background and some wanted to turn him down. Others argued that since he had an above-90 average he must be seriously considered. Finally the Party Committee itself took up the question and Vice-Secretary Hu Chien made a special trip to Shanghai to interview the prospect. He came back insisting

that the young man must enter Tsinghua because he was so
brilliant. When this fellow finally came to the campus he so
angered the other students with his reactionary ideas that they
wanted to repudiate him publicly. They called him "Little Tito."
But the Party Committee protected him.

"Their slogan was, 'Before grades all are equal,'" said my
student informants. "Their idea of a politically reliable person
was a person with an average of 80 or above. The Party Committee had no other standard. This created many problems
concerning who should be admitted and how they should be
handled afterward."

"It was all very clear at home," said Wu Wei-yu, a former
Hupei peasant and the first in his family ever to receive a
higher education. "At home after land reform the poor peasants
and hired laborers had prestige and the landlords had none.
But here at the university the professors were still riding high
all over the stage while we poor peasants were suppressed."

Wu had never left his home in Huangmei county until
he came to Tsinghua in 1965. He still looked more like a peasant than a college graduate. Unshaven stubble on his heart-
shaped face made his dark complexion seem ever darker. Long
hair hung down over a pair of very bright eyes that set off a
nose rather Western in its prominence. His manner was energetic, combative, well suited to his stocky, labor-tempered
body.

"Tsinghua," he went on, "was really an independent kingdom made up of graduates of Tsinghua, and even the higher
cadres from outside had it tough. An outsider sees problems
very soon and begins to raise questions. But then he gets isolated and that's the end of that."

Part II

It Is Right to Rebel

It is necessary to trust the masses, rely on them and respect their initiative. It is necessary to boldly arouse the masses and to let the masses rise up in revolution, educate themselves, run their own affairs, and liberate themselves.

—Mao Tse-tung, as quoted in
Peking Review, August 20, 1966

4
Liu's Work Team

"Right at that time the pressure was great. We were in our dormitory arguing intensely when we heard someone shout, 'The Work Team is here!' Looking out the window we saw two trucks full of people pull up and stop. We ran down all four flights of stairs rejoicing and shouting at the top of our voices, "Mao Tse-tung has sent people to help us!' We really welcomed them. We wept for joy. We scurried around to find rooms for them and carried in their bedrolls. And we asked them a thousand questions, hoping to clear up all our problems. They admitted right away that the Party Committee had problems. We were delighted. We thought so too."

The speaker was Tsu Hung-liang, a former student militant now on the Party Committee staff. He was describing the events of June 10, 1966, when students welcomed the work team sent by Liu Shao-ch'i because the University authorities had counterattacked so fiercely. During the ten days of unregulated upheaval that preceded this turning point, the young rebels at Tsinghua had centered their attack not on the older conserva-

43

tive professors who, after all, were only carrying on as they had been trained to, but on the "party people in authority"—like President Chiang Nan-hsiang, Party Vice-Secretary Liu Ping, and Party Vice-Secretary Hu Chien—who held real power in their hands and were ultimately responsible for the state of the education the students were receiving.

Members of the Party Committee did not, of course, sit idle under this unprecedented attack. As posters exposing them appeared they mobilized their supporters among the students and staff for rebuttal. A veritable avalanche of replies professing loyalty and denouncing "counter-revolutionary" wreckers greeted each critical thrust. The political directors of the various departments called in and warned the offending rebels, as the Rightists had been warned in 1957. Since the rebels were attacking a Party Committee, they were asked what side they stood on, the side of revolution or of counter-revolution? Party members who had joined the rebels were hauled before their departmental committees and threatened with expulsion. "Where is your Party spirit? Where is your class stand?" The assumption behind these arguments and threats was that the Communist Party was a monolith equally revolutionary at all levels and that an attack on any Party Committee or Party leader represented an attack on Mao Tse-tung. Since this assumption had been widely accepted for many years, the arguments were convincing to many. Even if they didn't understand the issues, most people at least had faith in the Party, and it therefore made sense to rally behind its local representatives. Others, not nearly so sanguine about the revolutionary nature of the University leaders, were still intimidated by their threats and so fell in line.

But the bolder rebels remained uncowed. They continued to press the attack, and day by day won more adherents, in part because their arguments were convincing and in part because the student masses resented the arrogance and the repressive tactics of the school authorities.

Then on June 10, as activity on the campus mounted to a fever pitch, the cadres of a work team began to arrive from the city. The rebels, thinking that the work team had come to support them, were overjoyed, as Tsu so vividly described.

By June 13 the full team was on hand—500 cadres sent by the Peking Party Committee with the concurrence of the Central Committee (where Liu Shao-ch'i was temporarily in command since Mao Tse-tung had left for a trip to the south). Ostensibly the team had come to help the students in their rebellion against the "capitalist-roaders," but team leaders later admitted that Liu had been alarmed by the rebellion, which was spreading like wildfire through the campuses of the whole country, and had urged the team members to rush to Tsinghua "like firemen going to a fire." Other teams with similar instructions were dispatched to key campuses in Peking and elsewhere, wherever the mass movement threatened Party Committee control.

The Tsinghua Work Team called a mass meeting on June 13 to introduce itself. Team leader Yeh Lin announced a two-pronged program. On the one hand, all department- and university-level cadres were suspended and ordered to report in groups for study. On the other hand, all students were called upon to return to their classrooms for a major campaign of self-and-mutual criticism. Lin then read out a series of regulations concerning student activity. He forbade any contact among the students of different classes, different departments, and different campuses. To insure the latter he ordered the campus gates locked: no one could go out or come in without special permission. He also forbade the posting of statements without prior approval from the Team.

Since the Work Team admitted that the school authorities had problems, militant rebels next day seized some of those staff members who had been most arrogant, put tall dunce caps on their heads, and paraded them through the campus to a mass meeting where they were to be repudiated. But the Work Team cadres, as soon as they found out what was going on, rushed to stop the proceedings. "You are like a bunch of sheep," said one. "What a low political level you have, repudiating people in this crude fashion!"

The students, having just studied Mao Tse-tung's *Report on an Investigation of the Peasant Movement in Hunan*, read out the passage about peasants putting hats on landlords' heads and Mao's comment: "This is fine!"

"But," said the Work Team leader, "such things are out of date."

"How can you say that Mao Tse-tung is out of date?" exclaimed the students. Surrounding this brash cadre, they demanded that he make a thorough self-criticism. Until he did they would not let him go.

After formal repudiation meetings were banned, the students conducted informal ones at meal times by asking leading cadres to stand on their chairs and listen to critical opinions while everybody, except those speaking, ate their rice. But this too the Work Team stopped by gathering the cadres together not only for study but for sleeping and eating. When the students went looking for their targets of the day they could not find them. No one announced where the cadres met or ate.

"We couldn't accept all this," said Tsu.

Like Wu Wei-yu, Comrade Tsu was the first member of his family ever to receive an education. His father and mother had both made shoes all their lives in a small shop in Hengyang, Hunan. The shoemaker's son was perhaps the liveliest of our informants, although all of them were full of energy, displaying high spirits and very keen memories. Tsu talked rapidly but clearly, laughed easily, and moved his head abruptly as his eyes darted from one listener to another. He was twenty-five years old but looked much younger. His hair was clipped short above a child-like face and his teeth were spaced wide apart in a big, expressive mouth. In sharp contrast to Wu, his build was slight and his complexion very light, but he had the same combative, forceful manner that marked so many student leaders. A frown creased his face as he continued.

"The working style of the Work Team members was very bad! They had all come in from the Four-Clean Movement in the countryside.* Maybe peasants listened to them when

---

*The Four-Clean Movement is another name for the Socialist Education Movement. The "four cleans" are to clean up politically, economically, organizationally, and ideologically—to substitute socialist standards for capitalist standards in both personal and community life in these four fields.

they talked so arrogantly, but we weren't peasants. We were mature students who could not be treated like clods. We saw it as a problem of method. In our dormitory we never even discussed Yeh Lin's report, but only his attitude. It angered us.

"As we looked out the window we saw posters going up on the wall of Dormitory #4. They were written by the students in the Mathematics Department. We ran down to have a look. 'We rebel!' said one. 'We have no confidence in the Work Team.' 'The number one task is to clarify who is a friend and who an enemy, but the Work Team confuses this,' said another. 'Mao Tse-tung teaches us to rely on the masses. Why suppress the masses?' asked a third.

"We thought these posters were great so we decided to write a few ourselves. We simply raised questions at random. We listed twelve problems concerning the Work Team: Why don't they trust the masses? Why do they gather the cadres together? Why do they prevent repudiation? We didn't have any organization then, we just wrote the posters and looked around for people to sign them. More than twenty people signed the first one and we pasted it on Dormitory #3. Even before we had it up someone came and took a picture of it. We didn't care. We weren't making any secret of our opinions. Just then another student came by, read our message, and signed his name. The man with the camera then took a picture of all the names.

"As we climbed our stairs a member of the Work Team came running, out of breath. 'Do you know what waving the red flag to oppose the red flag means?' he asked.

"We laughed. How ridiculous! Why should a few mild criticisms create such a reaction? What a low political level!

"By evening our group had two, not just one, Work Team members assigned to it and people we didn't know began hanging around in front of our dormitory entrance. But we didn't pay much attention; we went right on attacking the capitalist black-gangers and nothing much happened."*

---

*The use of the word "black" for "bad" is universal in China. In a country with no black minority, it has no racial connotations. Since it is deeply embedded in common speech, I translate it lit-

Then, on June 23, Kuai Ta-fu, one of the most militant of the rebels, put up a big poster asking: "What's this all about, Comrade Yeh Lin?"

This poster concerned Liu Shao-ch'i's wife, Wang Kuang-mei. It was rumored that she wanted to come to the campus to hear the complaints of the students first hand. A woman cadre had appeared at the Chemistry Department, Kuai's home base, on June 22, and many students had talked their hearts out, thinking they were talking directly to a representative of the Central Committee. They then found that they had not spoken to Wang Kuang-mei at all, but to an ordinary member of the Work Team, none of whom the students trusted. Kuai asked what was behind all this trickery.

The Work Team's response was to call a public meeting in the name of the masses, who were said to be enraged by Kuai's questions. The Work Team mobilized all its supporters to pack the hall, take the best seats, and express indignation. Those who opposed the Work Team came later and had to take whatever seats were left. As a result the majority inside the hall were reliable supporters of Yeh Lin, while the masses who opposed him gathered outside.

Thirty-year-old Wang Yung-hsien told us about this meeting. He was a middle peasant youth* from Yentai, Shantung, who had been in the Electrical Engineering Department of the University since 1961. Short, plump, with a flushed round face and a long lock of hair hanging over his forehead, he was the most mature and the most amiable of the former students we talked with. He had also held a higher position in the mass movement than the others. He had been a member of the headquarters committee of the 4s faction and commander of its whole western front.

"I went late to the meeting," said Wang. "By the time I got there the whole hall was crowded. It was so full that

---

erally with this clarification, aware that in foreign language publications the Chinese now substitute other words.

*A middle peasant is a self-supporting, land-owning peasant who neither hires others nor rents out land (like a rich peasant), nor hires out to others nor rents land to till (like a poor peasant).

many people who couldn't find a place to stand were leaving. But I was privileged. I could put on an armband which carried the designation 'picket.'* Since I was vice-leader of our department's picket squad I could go wherever I wanted. I got into the meeting and pushed my way right up front to the stage to help keep order.

"That was no small task, for this turned out to be Kuai's great debate with the Work Team leaders. So many people had come forward with critical opinions that Kuai was on the offensive and the Work Team was on the defensive. If the latter hadn't packed the hall it would have been a rout. As it was, the confrontation was much larger and more bitter than we expected. Before it was over Kuai's supporters had forced their way in and taken over one side of the hall while the Work Team and its supporters held diminishing ground on the other side. Each side applauded its own speakers, shouting and clapping, and the meeting ended in a near riot. Kuai's supporters clearly had the best arguments, and besides they were united and well disciplined."

"We were very excited," said Wu, breaking in at this point. "We shouted and clapped as loud as we could. Later, whether you clapped for Kuai or not became the dividing line between being a counter-revolutionary or a revolutionary."

"The whole meeting was run according to Peking tradition," continued Wang. "You clap for your own side and you send up notes. We clapped for Kuai and sent up notes in support, and we also sent notes to the Work Team questioning both their arguments and their political level.

"The chairman of the meeting was none other than Liu Tao, Liu Shao-ch'i's daughter. She debated with Kuai but was no match for him. She couldn't even rally her own forces and finally ended up saying, 'My mother says the Work Team must be trusted!' We responded with a sentence from a recent editorial: 'Revolutionary posters are the mirror that shows up cow-devils and snake-gods.'

---

*"Picket squads" were organized by the Work Team to go wherever there was trouble.

"Since Liu Tao couldn't control the meeting, we rebels were on top. This forced Yeh Lin and the Work Team vice leader to come out onto the stage. Right there they dropped all pretext that this was a meeting of, by, and for the masses.

" 'You have made the Work Team your target. Doesn't that mean that the Communist Party is your target?' shouted Yeh Lin.

"He then announced that Kuai Ta-fu's poster was definitely counter-revolutionary. Hence Kuai Ta-fu himself was a counter-revolutionary. This made us angry. We shouted: 'How can you decide this by looking at one poster? Where is your evidence?'

"Yeh Lin's answer was to hold his head high, raise both arms in the air, and shout, 'I represent Mao Tse-tung. I represent the Communist Party!'

"We clapped, whistled, and booed in an effort to drive him from the stage and he shouted back, 'If I don't represent the Communist Party, who does? Does Kuai Ta-fu? You must choose between us!'

"When we started to debate these questions neither Yeh Lin nor the other Work Team members had anything to back up their argument, so they tried to settle the case by putting 'big hats' on us all. They called us counter-revolutionaries who opposed the Work Team, opposed the Municipal Party Committee, and opposed the Central Committee. Thus they tried to substitute political pressure for reasoning. They had begun by debating concrete problems, but now, at bay and unable to back up their arguments, they just put 'hats' on us all and called us names.

"At this point Liu Tao intervened, saying, 'My mother says there should be no more debate.'

"We asked, 'Where in hell is your mother? She's not here.'

"Little did we know that Wang Kuang-mei was actually on the campus, hiding out in the president's old house. She was in touch by telephone and from time to time called in her instructions. We later learned that she wanted to come to the meeting in person but had been advised to stay in the background."

"After it was over we all gathered in excited knots and

agreed that the Work Team was unreasonable, that it was in fact terrible," said Tsu. "The more we talked the more we felt that they had violated Mao Tse-tung Thought. Most of us didn't sleep all night but instead wrote new big-character posters. The title of ours was: 'Is this the attitude of true Marxist-Leninists?'

"In this poster several students analyzed the big 'meeting for debate' and the Work Team's attitude toward criticism. We called on the Work Team to trust the masses* and to rely on the masses to carry the Cultural Revolution through to the end."

Counterattacks such as this led to differences inside the Work Team which its leaders did not know how to resolve. In order to hold the Work Team together, Wang Kuang-mei stepped ginerly out into the open, saying, "Liu Shao-ch'i has asked me to look into affairs here at Tsinghua." She called several hundred Work Team members together in the Chemistry Building and told them the line that must be followed, which was that the big "meeting for debate" had been a counter-revolutionary incident and that Kuai Ta-fu had been proven to be a counter-revolutionary. She then accused everyone who had joined the opposition of having conspired to pack the meeting hall in order to challenge her daughter, Liu Tao.

In fact, the majority in the hall had acted spontaneously. Only a few had made prior contacts or had gone to the meeting with a group. By the next day, partly as a result of the Work Team's repressive attitude, student sentiment was almost unanimous—eighteen of twenty in one class signed a critical poster, and this was by no means an unusual proportion. Students in another class wrote a poster saying, "Yeh Lin, what are you angry about?" By the time they completed it and took it outside they found a whole battery of other posters attacking Yeh Lin and the Work Team already in place.

"In our class," said Tsu, "we rebels had at first only numbered six. After that night's meeting the whole class joined the

---

*Revolutionary Chinese generally use the word "masses" where we would use "rank-and-file," "the people," or "population." Here the "masses" are the students, faculty, and staff of the University and their families.

rebels. We couldn't all get into one room to talk it over. People sat on the upper and the lower bunks, on the window sill, on chairs, stools, and the floor—twenty in one room. We six from the original rebel group did most of the talking and gave background information.

"We told our comrades how the team had suppressed the masses in the other departments and other units. We said, 'You can see from last night's meeting that the Work Team is no good!'

"The Work Team member assigned to our class stood quietly to one side taking notes. We didn't care, we went right on discussing. We thought the Work Team was the most serious problem. Of course, we had fallen behind in the struggle against University President Chiang Nan-hsiang, but it was more important to carry this new struggle through to the end.

"That night we wrote six more big-character posters. I myself wrote one that questioned Chiu Chih-ping, vice-leader of the Work Team.* My poster said: 'How big you talk! What do you mean, you represent Mao Tse-tung? This statement alone shows that you don't have an ounce of Mao Tse-tung Thought in you.'"

Other posters said:

"Pursue this problem to the end!"

"Are Work Team members teachers or scolders?"

5
Pull Out Kuai

In one night those who opposed the Work Team went from the defensive to the offensive and from the minority to the majority. Whereas before critical posters could only be found on dormitory walls, now these same attacks showed up at central spots on the campus and on the long reed mats erected in front of important gathering places. That morning

---

*He is now Political Director of the Fukien Military District.

the whole campus hummed as groups denounced the Work Team and debated the questions raised.

The Work Team cadres did not accept this sudden reversal. They organized whatever supporters they could to continue the debate, to repudiate hostile posters, and to write posters of their own denouncing Kuai. If at sunrise all the public proclamations on the campus had been anti-team, by noon pro-team statements had begun to appear, and by two o'clock they were plastered everywhere, often right on top of the statements they were designed to refute. Hundreds of people gathered in front of the Meeting Hall to debate the issues, while "loyalists" circulated among them, taking notes which could be used against pro-Kuai elements in the future.

Finally the Work Team cadres took the initiative in organizing formal discussions, setting as the topic for debate in the various classes, "Why do you think Kuai Ta-fu is a counter-revolutionary?"

This did not work out well. Only one person in Tsu's group said he thought Kuai deserved the epithet. All the rest said he definitely did not. Since the majority expressed themselves so unanimously, the Work Team members assigned to this class stopped promoting the idea and fell silent. His isolation did not prevent him from taking careful notes, however.

At four o'clock the Work Team called for a meeting of all students in the first category—the "staunch revolutionary left." What they had done was to divide the student body into five categories. First, the "staunch revolutionary left," made up of those who supported the Work Team; then four categories of people with problems. The first two of these included all those who lacked understanding, whose wrong opinions were due to their low political level, and hence who could be treated as still among the ranks of the people. The third and fourth of these categories included those whose opposition reflected a bourgeois class stand and hence who demonstrated a contradiction between the people and their enemies. They were, in other words, the counter-revolutionaries.

"Out of my whole group," said Wang, "only one student was qualified to attend the meeting of the 'staunch revolution-

ary left.' He was the one who thought Kuai a counter-revolutionary. With such a meeting underway we knew something
bad would happen, and sure enough, the next day the Work
Team sent for me and gave me an official Communist Party
warning. I was expelled from the picket squad, membership in
which had allowed me to come and go at will, and had to
turn in my armband. Classmates were mobilized to write posters against me, asking, 'Where is your class stand?'

"On June 28 I was required to make a self-criticism. The
Work Team leaders said my problem was very serious. But
since my brother was a revolutionary martyr, they decided not
to call me a counter-revolutionary. Four others weren't so
lucky."

Tsu described the Work Team's counteroffensive in equally
stark terms. "In the morning we put up our posters. By afternoon we found many posters on our dormitory wall attacking
us. Then we saw that the curtains were drawn over the windows
of the Meeting Hall and that guards had been posted all around,
a veritable sentry line. Only one of our classmates had been
invited to this meeting. When he came back he said, 'You are
all counter-revolutionaries.' Since we 'counter-revolutionaries'
were so numerous, they had to find students from other departments to come and debate with us. The idea was to try
and win us over, but actually they used a mental club. 'You
must thoroughly and completely confess your counter-revolutionary plots against the Communist Party and socialism,' they
said."

Thus it went with anyone who protested the line or the
actions of the Work Team. They were accused of anti-Party
activity and threatened with serious consequences. Whole
dormitories were asked to write self-criticisms, and no self-
criticism was considered to be valid unless it raised the problem to the level of principle—that is, unless it agreed that the
mistakes under discussion were both objectively and subjectively counter-revolutionary. Even this was not enough, because
each admission had to be backed up with facts, facts which
didn't exist. Thus there was really no way to write a criticism
that would satisfy the Work Team.

All those who clapped for Kuai on June 23 were called counter-revolutionary. More than 800 students found themselves in this category. Once the "counter-revolutionary cap" was placed on any student's head he lost his freedom. He was confined to quarters and was kept under guard day and night. Student guards even followed their suspects to the toilet. He was asked to write concrete self-criticisms endlessly, and at big and small meetings he became an object of mass attack. At that time there were big, small, old, and new "counter-revolutionaries" all over the place. In one class of thirty people, twelve were labelled counter-revolutionary and twelve more were called sympathizers. The remaining six were not enough to stand guard over the others. They had to call in help from other classes.

Students labelled this whole movement the "white terror." More than a few broke under the pressure and tried, with indifferent success, to write the confessions the Work Team was demanding.

Tsu described his own retreat:

"When the Work Team struggled against us I was thinking, 'My family is so poor, we have struggled all our lives, how could I oppose the Communist Party and Mao Tse-tung Thought?' They asked us to answer a whole series of questions. After they had spread all those rumors about Kuai Ta-fu I thought, 'Maybe I am objectively anti-Communist.' So I made a self-criticism saying just that. But they wouldn't accept it. They said that in Chairman Mao's *Talks at the Yenan Forum* objective and subjective are linked. One can't be objectively against the Communist Party without being involved subjectively as well."

Kuai, abandoned by one comrade after another, wrote the waverers a letter:

Liu Ts'ai Ch'ang, Wang Tieh-ch'eng, and all comrades who have supported me or sympathized with me:

Now we are facing an extremely severe test. I firmly believe that up to now most of you have been staunch revolutionaries. But under Comrade Yeh Lin's high-pressure policy some of you have wavered and some have surrendered. Some are presently confessing their "crimes." Though your lips move and your hands write, actually I believe the vast majority of you, really, deep in your hearts, don't admit to the people that you have committed any crimes. Because in fact you have not. The revolutionary spirit you had before cannot be wiped out by anyone.

If temporarily, under high pressure, you have to bend a little, I can forgive you.

But if you really go over, if your heart is dead, if you sell out your own comrades and betray your conscience, then in the future the revolution will not forgive you.

As I've already told you several times, our opponents are very soft. Under the proletarian dictatorship, they don't dare do anything to the revolutionaries. On the surface they look very strong and harsh, fierce and bullying, but actually they are paper tigers. They are frightened to death of us. The masses are temporarily deceived, but they will wake up eventually. In order to be responsible to the Central Committee of the Communist Party and to Mao Tsetung we have to develop our fearless revolutionary spirit. Fear nothing. Before liberation, under the "white terror," the heroic revolutionary martyrs carried on a life-and-death struggle, throwing away their heads and pouring out their blood; they brought our people's power of today. We successors, under the proletarian dictatorship, have we anything to be afraid of?

I sincerely wish that at this very difficult and crucial time you will stand firm. The revolutionary train, at high speed, now turns a sharp corner. Sit still, hold fast, don't fall out and break yourself in pieces.

I won't force my opinions on those who resolutely betray us, but I have to tell you that you can only sell information on us. You can by no means sell out our revolutionary souls. Remember, the revolutionary big winds and waves are going to wash out all the dross and save the precious metal.

Finally, I want to point out that even if temporarily only I am left, I will resolutely fight to the end. So long as one monster still exists on Tsinghua campus, I will resolutely sweep him out. If I don't reach this goal, I won't close my eyes when I die.

Comrades, stand up and stiffen your backs, the Central Committee of the Communist Party and Chairman Mao Tse-tung fully support us. Unite and fight bravely. Final victory is bound to be ours. Resolutely defend the Communist Party Central Committee and resolutely defend Chairman Mao Tse-tung. Resolutely defend Mao Tse-tung Thought. Resolutely defend proletarian dictatorship and socialism. Long live Chairman Mao.

Kuai Ta-fu, June 28, 1966

If many gave in and many others wavered, still a small band, with Kuai Ta-fu at its core, stood firm and exchanged blow-for-blow polemically with the Work Team. They studied Mao Tse-tung's writings diligently and pasted slogans beside their beds, such as:

If we live we'll fight for Mao Tse-tung's line.
If we die we'll die for Mao Tse-tung's line.

or

Fierce-browed I coolly defy a thousand pointing fingers.
Head bowed, like a willing ox, I serve the children.*

The rebels were convinced that as true supporters of Mao Tse-tung they would win out in the end, so they mobilized for all-out struggle against a Work Team that claimed to be Mao Tse-tung's sole representative and constantly urged everyone to have boundless faith in its decisions because it represented the Communist Party, the Central Committee, and Chairman Mao.

"We have boundless faith in Chairman Mao and Mao Tse-tung Thought," the students countered, "but as for faith in you—who are you? You are nothing!"

In the rebels' eyes the Work Team was nothing, but its leader, Yeh Lin, wielded state power at Tsinghua and used it to organize a whole series of mass meetings to expose and repudiate Kuai Ta-fu and his comrades. If Kuai Ta-fu (great

---

*This is a famous couplet written by Lu Hsun, China's most famous modern writer, to express his defiance of the reactionaries and his willingness to serve the people.

wealth) was target number one, then Kuai Er-fu (second wealth) and Kuai San-fu (third wealth) became targets number two and three. Kuai's, it seems, were to be found in every dormitory and every department. "Pull out Kuai" became the slogan of the day. It was spread far and wide by the Work Team.

In order to understand what happened later it is important to explain the extraordinary role that Kuai Ta-fu played at the time. Kuai was a wiry young man of poor-peasant origin who had long been noted for brilliance and self-confidence. He wore glasses in heavy square frames that accentuated the width of his forehead and made his sharp chin seem even more pointed than in fact it was. People remembered Kuai for his short stature, his triangular face, and his explosive oratory.

Kuai Ta-fu operated like the commanding general of an army that had absolute confidence in the rightness of its cause and absolute faith in final victory. When his support fell away around him he never wavered or retreated one inch. On the contrary, he always seemed to be on the offensive, taking up and refuting each point made by Work Team leader Yeh Lin in public speeches and a constant stream of wall posters that, even when they were almost immediately ripped off the walls, still tore the mantle of legitimacy off the Work Team and shook the whole campus and the city of Peking. Clear cut, sarcastic, like gusts of spring wind, his polemics dispersed cant and obscurantism. If the Work Team was to stand at all it had to destroy Kuai, but the more vigorously it mobilized against him the more tenaciously he mounted the counterattack. On June 29, Kuai sent an open letter to Yeh Lin in the form of a big-character poster that went up in the middle of the campus where thousands could read it. Here are some excerpts:

> Comrade Yeh Lin, how are you? Today I would like to say a few words to you.
> To tell the truth, I absolutely did not expect that "little tiny Kuai Ta-fu" would have such power to threaten, that the Work Team had no alternative but to concentrate all its energy to beat me down. Never has there been such a large-scale movement—the whole school writing big-

character posters against one person, parading, demonstrating, holding campus-wide rallies, and broadcasting over the air—all these means have been used. Such a mobilization was never mounted against Chiang Nan-hsiang! I can't help but feel a twinge of joy. Who would have expected that Kuai Ta-fu was, "like a brick in a pivy, both stinking and hard and would never give up even unto death." You probably feel a little bit nervous. But if you feel very firm inside and you still have other tricks that you haven't brought out yet, that is fine. I am waiting. Just a side point here—I will use every means that I can to counter your attack . . .

Comrade Yeh Lin, please open your eyes and take a look. Who is supporting you? Those people who are loyalists. Now they just shake their bodies like the Monkey King and change into the revolutionary left. These speculators in revolution have become your most helpful assistants. Even the former "black ganger" Yeh Lu and his crowd now all shout loudly, "Support Comrade Yeh Lin." But the real left, the left that all along was clearsighted, just because it has raised correct criticism of you, you see as a nail in the eye, a splinter in the flesh. You mount an attack, put on political pressure, force us to make self-criticisms, force us to confess so-called crimes. I feel hurt when I see this situation. I feel this may also be what you, a real revolutionary, are not willing to see. . . . Your high-pressure policy creates an atmosphere of terror. It reminds me of the high-pressure policy of the black Party Committee of the school at an earlier time. They made people afraid to speak out, then they began to be afraid that they couldn't square their reports with the top, so in a great rush they demanded that the students raise criticisms. As for the situation in our school now, Comrade Yeh Lin, I'm really worried about you. If you don't give lying reports, how can you square things with the new Municipal Committee? How can you square things with the Central Committee and Chairman Mao?. . . .

Dear Comrade Yeh Lin, time is very short, time is pressing, you had better hurry and draw up a plan and prepare for the next step. I am waiting patiently. I don't know why, my confidence grows stronger and stronger.

When I pick up Chairman Mao's works I feel that Chairman Mao is right beside me.

Wishing you good health, a revolutionary salute.

—*Kuai Ta-fu,* June 29, 1966

In this and many other posters which Kuai wrote at the time one can see small sprouts of the kind of thinking that eventually transformed him from a motive force of the revolution at Tsinghua into one of its targets. Kuai's unusual self-confidence bordered on arrogance, an arrogance which when matched against an oppressive Work Team was positive and progressive, but when matched against fellow students who did not accept his leadership turned into something ugly and dictatorial. When Kuai read Mao Tse-tung's words he felt that the Chairman was standing right beside him, but when he looked at the cadres of the Communist Party he tended to see nothing but "capitalist-roaders," and when he looked at the teachers of Tsinghua he tended to see nothing but "bourgeois academic authorities."* From this it was but a small leap to "I am the core," which made unity in the struggle against revisionism all but impossible.

In a secret message to his closest companions Kuai warned that as long as they were called "counter-revolutionaries" they should not admit the slightest weakness or the slightest error, lest it be used by the Work Team to beat them down. In the situation that then existed this was perhaps a justifiable tactic, but it laid the groundwork for a cynical disregard for truth in the factional struggles which followed, each side hiding its own mistakes and lying about its actions while grabbing at

---

*In the self-criticism Kuai made after the Work Team left, he admitted that he did not believe that 95 percent of the teachers and 95 percent of the cadres were good, as Chairman Mao had stated repeatedly.

What Mao Tse-tung meant was that the vast majority of the teachers and cadres could correct their mistakes and make a significant contribution to the socialist revolution if they were properly led. In other words, they were friends, not enemies, and had revolutionary potential. Kuai regarded them as hopeless.

every weakness of the other side, blowing small errors to huge proportions in order to destroy the opposition politically.

All this, however, only came out later. At the time, what Kuai's comrades, the embattled rebels, saw in him was fearlessness, principled opposition to an oppressive Work Team, polemical skill of a high order, and extraordinary leadership ability. Kuai Ta-fu became a hero to the left, not only at Tsinghua but throughout the country, and his group published a large volume of his speeches and writings as a means of exposing the bourgeois reactionary line of Liu Shao-ch'i and rallying students all over the nation to rebellion.

If an extraordinary figure—Kuai Ta-fu—stood at one pole on the Tsinghua campus, at the other pole stood an unlikely figure—Wang Kuang-mei, Liu Shao-ch'i's wife. As the Work Team ran into resistance and came up against the formidable talents of Kuai and his "iron rods" (hard-core rebels), Liu Shao-ch'i sent Wang Kuang-mei in person to put down the rebellion. She was careful not to show her face in public or even to use her own name. She went by the name of Hou P'u, or simply Hsiao Hou (Little Hou). She arrived at night and left at night, wearing a cloak over her head and shoulders. When on the campus she stayed at House A, the creaking wooden-floored mansion that I have already described. It was well suited to her cloak-and-dagger style, for it was Wang Kuang-mei herself who pioneered the concept of the Work Team as a sort of undercover investigation group, slipping into a community behind the backs of its known leaders and taking depositions from all the dissatisfied and disgruntled elements in order to get the lowdown on the cadres in power before even talking to them. This, it seemed, was the essence Wang Kuang-mei had extracted from her Peach Orchard (T'ao Yuan) experience, her work in the Hopei village of that name, and was now extending to her work at one of China's most important university campuses.

If Wang Kuang-mei operated behind the scenes, the same could hardly be said of Liu Tao, her daughter, who stepped conspicuously to the front to take the lead among the student loyalists who supported the Work Team. Liu Tao paired up

with Ho Peng-fei, Marshal Ho Lung's son,* to carry out among
the masses the political directives coming from above. Did Liu
Tao have talent or leadership ability? Apparently not. She was
a spoiled young woman, a debutante type, interested in fashion
and personal pleasure, and could not make a coherent speech.
But she was Liu Shao-ch'i's daughter, she was loyal, and she
had some prestige among those students who remained impressed by her background. When the Cultural Revolution began no one thought that Liu Shao-ch'i might be a target—how
he became one is part of the whole Tsinghua story—and so to
be the daughter of the head of state gave one a lead in that
wing of the student movement that set out to protect Party
people in power.

Ho Peng-fei's leadership was likewise based on family prestige for he himself had no outstanding ability. Indeed, he had
done such poor work in school that he had slipped into the
University through the backdoor. In his entrance examination
he had received less than fifty points, at least twenty below
the minimum for admittance. He had been shunted off to
Tsinghua Middle School for a year of extra work, then quietly
included in a later first-year class. All of which showed, said
the rebel students, that before grades all were not equal, that
a high cadre's child found open doors where others found only
a blank wall.

Liu Tao and Ho Peng-fei also benefited temporarily from
the "five red" policy, according to which the early student militants admitted only the sons and daughters of "good" social
categories to their ranks. The five "good" or "red" categories

---

*Ho Lung was made one of the ten Marshals of the People's
Liberation Army in the 1950s. He is famous as an early guerrilla
fighter who repeatedly went into the hills in the 1920s armed with
a vegetable knife. He has always been something of an individualist
and a maverick. After Liberation in 1949 he headed the Central Sports
Commission. He was identified quite early in the Cultural Revolution
as a Liu Shao-ch'i supporter in the military establishment and this
designation has never been questioned or reversed. His line in sports
was typically revisionist, leading to the establishment of a sports elite
rather than promoting a mass movement useful to all.

were the workers, the poor and lower-middle peasants, the revolutionary cadres, the revolutionary soldiers, and the revolutionary martyrs. If your parents were none of these you were beyond the pale as far as the early Red Guards were concerned.* The theory of revolutionary inheritance that thus developed was expressed in a poem:

> A dragon begets a dragon.
> A phoenix begets a phoenix.
> The son of a mouse, from the day of his birth
> knows how to dig a hole in the ground.

With this as a theoretical base, the sons and daughters of high cadres often stepped forward very actively when the Cultural Revolution began. They found it easy to rebel against school authorities, for they resented discipline and any kind of restriction. Proud, privy to much inside information, they had always enjoyed privileges as compared to the children of the rank-and-file. They took it for granted that they were "revolutionary successors" and so found it easy to struggle against others. But once their own parents were attacked and overthrown, their status dropped drastically and their morale collapsed. Often they were expelled from the units to which they belonged or had even led, and they became extremely confused. To attack school authorities was one thing; to attack and expose one's own family, one's own parents, was another. As one high cadre after another was deposed, these "revolutionary successors" lost their footing completely. The inheritance theory on which they had based their ascendancy also collapsed; in fact,

---

*All mass organizations of middle school and university students that were formed once the Cultural Revolution began in 1966 can be lumped together under the designation Red Guards, which is what the first rebel units at the Tsinghua Middle School called themselves. There was no such thing as a nationwide Red Guard organization, but rather a plethora of diverse groups all committed to defending Mao Tse-tung, while in practice taking opposite sides on specific questions. The Red Guard designation became universally popular after Mao Tse-tung met with some of the early groups who went by that name and donned one of their armbands.

it was already under attack by Mao Tse-tung and his supporters on the Central Committee, who challenged the whole idea as undialectical and anti-Marxist. How, with such a theoretical base, could young revolutionaries ever unit 95 percent of the people and 95 percent of the cadres against the main enemy—the revisionists? Mao's wife, Chiang Ch'ing, took the original couplet that summed up the inheritance theory:

> Father a hero, son a great fellow.
> Father a reactionary, son a rotten egg.

and rewrote it in line with Mao Tse-tung Thought as:

> Father a reactionary, son turns the tables.
> Father a hero, son carries on.

Many of these young people, after wandering in political limbo for a while, picked themselves up and joined the rebels. This was true of Liu Tao. She later drew a clear line of distinction between herself and her family and worked to support Mao Tse-tung's line. But in the summer of 1966 she was riding high as the offspring of a celebrity, and she had support from below and from above. The latter came not only from her mother, but from other high cadre of the revisionist clique who visited the campus from time to time.

Liu Shao-ch'i himself came more than once to check up on the work, but it was always late at night and he wore a large face mask so that nobody could recognize him. Po Yi-p'o, chairman of the State Economic Commission and alternate member of the Political Bureau of the Central Committee, was more bold. He came in broad daylight on June 19 and July 3 and spent a long time looking at the posters that covered the walls. In the course of one of these visits this prestigious old cadre got into an argument with Kuai Ta-fu, who didn't know whom he was talking to. As the argument waxed hot, Kuai called Po a "fat old man."

"To be old is no crime," retorted Po, "and as for being fat, that can hardly be an issue. Suppose I were to call you a capitalist-roader because your name is Ta-fu [great wealth]?" Turning to the crowd that had gathered around them, Po asked,

"How many here think that Kuai Ta-fu is of the left? All those who think so raise their hands."

Only Kuai raised his hand. All the other hesitated.

"You see," said Po Yi-p'o. "You are the only one who thinks you are a leftist!"

Why was Tsinghua so important? Why was it important enough to Liu Shao-ch'i and Po Yi-p'o to require personal visits? Why did Liu send Wang Kuang-mei there in person? The answer seems to be, first, that institutions of higher learning were important nodal points in a Cultural Revolution that was primarily concerned with the superstructure, a revolution that was in essence a contest over which class would control culture in China. And second, that among the universities in China Tsinghua enjoyed a pivotal position as the central institution for the study and development of science and engineering. In the period of socialist construction, these studies took precedence over all others, and consequently the main single centers of science and engineering also took precedence. The crucial importance of Tsinghua was illustrated by the fact that its president, Chiang Nan-hsiang, was at the same time Minister of Higher Education. An additional factor, in so far as Liu Shao-ch'i was concerned, was the fact that his daughter, Liu Tao, was a student there. (At that time his other children were at the Normal College Middle School, where so many higher cadres sent their offspring that it was called the best school in Peking.) Wang Kuang-mei had created her Peach Orchard Experience in the countryside as a guide to the whole nation in the Socialist Education Movement. Now with the help of Liu Tao she would be able to create a "Tsinghua Experience" as a guide to the whole nation in the Cultural Revolution.

Once Wang Kuang-mei went to Tsinghua, of course, Liu Shao-ch'i's prestige was committed there. Tsinghua became a focal point of the struggle between the two headquarters in the Communist Party, and its importance in the overall battle over line and policy in China was sharply enhanced. In the end, in the course of counteracting Wang Kuang-mei's influence, Chiang Ch'ing, Premier Chou En-lai, and Vice-Premier Hsieh

Fu-chih all went to the campus. This intervention from the very top was the basis for the students' belief that the revolution in China as a whole would stand or fall on what happened at their institution. Later, when factional struggle escalated, each faction thought that the proletarian headquarters at the Central Committee level, and therefore Mao Tse-tung himself, could not hold out without a victory for its side.

The first big break in the offensive launched by the Work Team against Kuai's rebels came on July 18. On that day all students confined to quarters were suddenly released. Yeh Lin announced that the period of criticism was over and that henceforth everyone would join in repudiating the original target of the mass movement, the capitalist-roaders. Suddenly, almost as quickly as it had begun, the great campaign to "pull out Kuai" ceased.

This happened because Mao Tse-tung had returned from the south and had sharply questioned what the work teams were doing. On July 22 Chiang Ch'ing went personally to the Peking University campus and led a critical review of that work team's accomplishments which lasted four days. By July 26, Wang Kuang-mei (who the students said had a pipeline to heaven—i.e., access to information at the very top) was quite aware of the outcome at Peking University and quickly took steps to fold her tents before they were packed up for her.

On July 28 the Peking Party Committee ordered all work teams withdrawn, but at the same time promised the students that an important part of the leadership group of each team would stay on the campuses to receive criticism from the masses.

Late in the afternoon of July 29, Wang Kuang-mei suddenly showed up in the dining room north of the Quiet House and made an apologetic speech to the students eating there. This was her first truly public appearance on the campus. Dropping her pseudonym, Little Hou, she called herself Comrade Kuang-mei and said, "People have welcomed me here because I am linked to Shao-ch'i. This is understandable."

Concerning the order for the work teams to withdraw, she claimed that she had not seen it and didn't know the details but that she was fully in accord with it. "I have been here only a short time," she went on. "I've only been an ordinary member of the Work Team. Have we any achievements? Have we any shortcomings? I think we have some of both. Of course, I have my own opinions about this but it is hard to speak out. Since the people are rising up in rebellion, of course we welcome it, but some people are raising all these problems to much too high a level. Never mind. If you want to serve you I can join in the daily chores—I will gladly work in the kitchen, sweep the floors, clean the privies. Since coming here, it is true, I have not been close to the masses. I haven't done well in living with, eating alongside, and studying with the people. Since I have been criticized for this I am willing to change. I am willing to cook, sweep, and carry nightsoil. Then you may judge whether I am a revolutionary or not by my actions."

Thereupon she reported for work in the kitchen and was assigned to sell food at the counter. Potatoes, to be exact. But rebel students claimed that even as a potato server she was a rank opportunist, giving extra portions to those whom she hoped to influence while assuming a posture of false humility before the student body as a whole.

Posters immediately went up against her. "Expose Wang Kuang-mei's food-selling schemes!" "Wang Kuang-mei spreading potatoes, like an angel spreading flowers."* Not at all mollified by this famous lady's sudden surrender, the student militants insisted on going into the issues and raised them to the level of principle: what Wang Kuang-mei and the Work Team had carried out, they said, was a "bourgeois reactionary line."†

---

*This sarcasm was aimed at Wang Kuang-mei's somewhat pathetic efforts to dress and act as a beautiful young thing when already overweight and no longer young.

†What the students meant by a "bourgeois reactionary line" was a political line or set of policies that suppresses the mass movement and all effective criticism of those in power through political attacks on rebel leaders and on rank-and-file critics. The work teams of 1965 all carried out such a line. Individuals who came to power later de-

On the evening of July 29 a mass meeting was held on the campus. Representatives of the Peking Municipal Party Committee and the Central Committee officially announced that the Work Team would withdraw. Wang Kuang-mei repeated the gist of her dining-hall speech, and a Preparatory Cultural Revolutionary Committee was selected to carry on the work the Work Team had so suddenly dropped. The selection of this Committee, to which Tsinghua's official seals were turned over—thus putting it in power on the campus—was rigged by the retreating Work Team. Democratic forms were followed without the substance of democracy. What happened was that certain names of students and minor staff members were read off. If there was applause for them, they were confirmed as members of the Committee. Since the Work Team had mobilized a large portion of its campus supporters, the "loyalists," to come to the meeting, every name selected by the Work Team received some applause and the new Committee was quickly constituted. Liu Tao was chairwoman; Wang Jench'ing, a loyal Work Team supporter, and Ho Peng-fei were vice-chairmen. Yeh Lin then announced that the masses, through their elected Committee, now held power in Tsinghua.

"In fact," said my student informants, "we had a work team without the Work Team."

6
Two Lines Emerge

Up to this point the Cultural Revolution at Tsinghua could be summarized as falling into two main periods, the first from June 1 to June 10, ten days of rebellion as the students and staff rose up against President Chiang Nan-hsiang and the

---

veloped this technique in new forms. By attacking the many down below, they protected the few in power up above. In practice, what the bourgeois reactionary line means is to protect yourself and your position by attacking and even framing all rivals and their supporters.

other "capitalist-roaders" of the old administration; and the second from June 10 to July 31, or fifty days of "white terror," as the Work Team moved in to suppress the student rebels and made the most militant student leader, Kuai Ta-fu, the central target of attack.

In August a very confused period began, a period which saw the crystallization of two lines in the student movement and a sharp struggle between them. I say crystallization, because from the very beginning two lines were discernible. There were those students who from the start rebelled against the administration and went on to rebel against the Work Team, and there were those students who from the start defended the administration and later loyally defended the Work Team. These differences took organizational form when certain rebel forces gathered for a liaison meeting on August 8. They formed a loose coalition known as the 8-8s, which later turned into the Tsinghua Mao Tse-tung Thought Red Guards. Certain loyalist forces held a "liaison meeting" of their own on August 9 and formed a coalition known as the 8-9s, which later turned into the Tsinghua Red Guards. I have put this second liaison meeting in quotes because in fact the 8-9s already had an organizational center in the Preparatory Committee and it was hardly necessary for them to call a liaison meeting. What happened was that Liu Tao and Ho Peng-fei called their supporters together to rally them against the rebels who were organizing.

Neither the rebel nor the loyalist groups were fixed. Individuals moved both ways across the political spectrum from one camp to another before the organizations took shape, and continued to move both ways across organizational lines after the organizations were set up. In general, throughout the course of the summer and fall the rebel side gained strength and the loyalist side lost strength, until in December the latter collapsed altogether, at least organizationally. But in the course of the struggle there was a minor growth in membership for the loyalists whenever they went on the offensive, and they maintained considerable strength until very late in the year. In June loyalists were clearly in the majority, in August they were certainly as strong as the rebels, and only after October 6—when rebel forces from all over the country held a grand rally in Tien An-Men square which set exposure of the "bourgeois reactionary line" (the repression carried out by the work teams) as the main task—did the rebels really begin to sweep the field and the loyalists to crumble fast.

Of course, many students, staff, and lesser cadres at Tsinghua joined neither side in the struggle. Only a minority were consistently active as rebels or as loyalists. The bulk of the campus population of 40,000 tended to be drawn in during the high tides of the movement, only to fall into apathy or neutrality as the tides ebbed. Toward the end, when factionalism developed to the point of armed struggle, only a few hundred people actually took part. Thousands left the area altogether, to return only after order had been restored. Other thousands stayed home in the family quarters and set up patrols to keep factional "fanatics" out.

In August the rebel 8-8s, or Mao Tse-tung Thought Red Guards, did not include Kuai Ta-fu and his hard-core supporters (who had been placed in the fourth category, die-hard counter-revolutionaries, by the Work Team). Kuai had been so sharply denounced and so firmly labeled that most rebels, though they sympathized with him, dared not unite with him. The aim of their organization was to struggle for the rehabilitation of counter-revolutionaries ("removing the hats," or "reversing the case"), but until the main targets of the Work Team actually were rehabilitated politically they did not unite with them organizationally or invite them into their ranks. This made it necessary for Kuai and his group to set up an organization of their own, the Chingkangshan Regiment of Tsinghua University. But this didn't happen until September 24, almost two months after the Work Team folded its tents, and one month after the loyalists, with some measure of success, had mobilized a mass movement to smash the rebels of the Mao Tse-tung Thought Red Guards.

The political struggle that grew in intensity as the organizational lines were drawn revolved around the question of what the principal target of the mass movement should now be—should it be the work teams and their "bourgeois reactionary line," or the "party people in authority taking the capitalist road," against whom the whole mass movement had originally been directed. This issue took the center of the stage all over the country as soon as the work teams stepped down. At Tsinghua the Work Team formally withdrew and turned its powers over to the artificially created Preparatory Committee on July 29. On the very next day Premier Chou En-lai arrived on the campus to investigate the situation and after several days of talks called for a mass rally on August 4. This rally was attended by more than 10,000 rank-and-file people and by important members of the Peking Party Committee and the Central Committee.

In his speech, which was the main event of the day, Chou En-lai said that the work teams had made serious mistakes in line, had called revolutionaries counter-revolutionaries, and had suppressed the mass movement. Instead of uniting the broad masses of students and staff to expose the "capitalist-roaders" in power, they had turned the campaign inward against the students themselves and had protected the few by attacking the many. This was none other than a "bourgeois reactionary line," aimed at protecting the bourgeoisie in power at Tsinghua and suppressing the revolution. Chou En-lai went on to praise the student rebels for standing up to the Work Team and for exposing its repressive practices.

This speech, of course, amounted to "reversing the case." Chou En-lai said that revolutionaries had been called counter-revolutionaries and that the work teams had carried out a reactionary line. He said that these serious mistakes were the responsibility of the Peking Party Committee and of the comrades on the Central Committee who were in Peking during the period. In other words, he took some blame on himself while at the same time making it clear that Liu Shao-ch'i, the ranking Party leader in the city, also had to share the blame.

This speech encouraged the rebels tremendously and gave them a sound theoretical basis for continuing their struggle, but it did not entirely solve either the question of who the "revolutionaries" who had been suppressed were or the question of what should henceforth be the main direction of the move-

ment. Chou En-lai only "reversed the case" in general—he didn't
do it concretely, he didn't name any names. Consequently, since
it was generally conceded that there were some counter-revolutionaries on the campus, an official screening was necessary,
some higher authority had to take responsibility and remove
the "counter-revolutionary caps" one by one from all those who
were in fact genuine revolutionaries. Unless this was done hundreds of people still carried a "tail" others could grab whenever
it suited them, thus muddying the waters when the struggle
got sharp.

Furthermore, although Chou En-lai made it clear that the
work teams had made serious mistakes, he apparently did not
make it clear whether in the future the mass movement should
continue to expose these mistakes and seek their source or
should return to the attack on the "capitalist-roaders" who had
already been overthrown.

The rebels, who gathered together for their liaison meeting on August 8, felt that it was impossible to go on investigating the "capitalist-roaders" without first getting to the bottom
of the "bourgeois reactionary line" of the Work Team, which
was in effect a form of protection for the "capitalist-roaders."
They wanted to seek out those responsible no matter how high
this search led them. They also felt that unless their "counter-
revolutionary caps" were officially and specifically removed,
they coud not do effective revolutionary work. So they raised
the slogans, "Expose and repudiate the bourgeois reactionary
line" and "Reverse the case on the so-called counter-revolutionaries."

The loyalists, who were called together by the Preparatory
Committee on August 9, chose not to challenge openly Chou
En-lai's analysis of the work team period as wrong. Their strategy was to accept Chou's analysis, acknowledge the criticism of
the work teams, and call on everyone to get back on the track
—in other words, let bygones be bygones and let everyone
now unite in exposing and repudiating Chiang Nan-hsiang and
his clique of "capitalist-roaders" on the old University Party
Committee. The bourgeois reactionary line, they said, was just
a mistake made by loyal revolutionaries unfamiliar with the

twists and turns of the socialist period. What this amounted to was an attempt to block a line of inquiry and exposure which had to quickly lead right to Liu Shao-ch'i, with the danger that he would be exposed not only as the man responsible for the work teams' bourgeois reactionary line, not only as Chiang Nan-hsiang's behind-the-scenes supporter, but as China's leading "capitalist-roader."

Already the rebel students were hot on the trail. They had discovered that it was Liu's wife, Wang Kuang-mei, who had actually initiated the "pull out Kuai" movement. On the very day that they met to form their coalition, the "Sixteen-Point Decision of the Central Committee Concerning the Cultural Revolution" was issued and the phrase "Be on guard against those who brand the revolutionary masses as counter-revolutionaries" struck an especially responsive chord. Wasn't Wang Kuang-mei just such a person, and didn't Liu Shao-ch'i stand right behind her? On both occasions when Wang Kuang-mei had appeared in public at Tsinghua (June 19 and July 29) hadn't she said, "Comrade Liu Shao-ch'i has asked me to look into the movement at Tsinghua"? Wasn't this an admission that he was personally involved? On August 10, after the Central Committee had set up reception centers in the city,* Mao Tse-tung had met with a group of student delegates and called upon them to "pay attention to state affairs and carry the Cultural Revolution through to the end." By "state affairs" didn't Mao mean that one should look into the record of the head of state?

On August 19, when the 8-8s held their grand rally to demand that the Central Committee "reverse the case," fighting teams (one was called "Sunflower") prepared the way with bold posters that said such things as: "Wang Kuang-mei is the number one political thief of Tsinghua and behind her stands a big umbrella!" and, "Look where all the renegade threads lead to!"

---

*These centers were established to receive delegations from the people and to listen to complaints and suggestions from the mass organizations that sprang up everywhere following the publication of the "Sixteen-Point Decision."

Both posters pointed to Liu Shao-ch'i; the latter referred to the hundreds of young Communists who in the late 1920s had been released from Kuomintang jails after they capitulated by signing statements repudiating the Communist Party, and were then put to work as trusted cadres by Liu, who had arranged the whole deal.

The 8-9s, alarmed by this turn of events, packed the rally with "dare-to-die" fighting teams. They seized the microphones and tried to break up the meeting. When the 8-8s shouted, "Reverse the case on the revolutionary rebel spirit," the 8-9s responded with, "Only the left, not the right, is allowed to rebel." They challenged the class backgrounds of each speaker, shouting that only the offspring of revolutionaries could be revolutionary and asking every rebel who tried to speak, "Are you a dog's son [a reactionary puppy]?" When the meeting did break up, they mounted a huge parade and wound through the campus shouting, "We will never allow the Rightists to overwhelm the sky!"

On August 23 an editorial in *People's Daily* called for overthrowing anyone who opposed Mao Tse-tung Thought "no matter how high his position, no matter how great his prestige, and no matter how long he has worked for the revolution!" To the rebels this was obviously another reference to Liu Shao-ch'i. Hadn't P'eng Chen already been overthrown?* If the call was to overthrow people of still higher position, who could be meant other than Liu? Thus they argued more vehemently than ever and came into sharp conflict with the 8-9 loyalists, who once more denounced them as counter-revolutionaries and sons of dogs. The debate had no sooner ended than the rebels wrote in huge characters on the road: "Liu Shao-ch'i must be removed as head of state," and put up posters that made little

---

*P'eng Chen was the mayor of Peking up until May 1966. He was at the same time the secretary of the Peking Party Committee, a member of the Central Committee, and a member of its Political Bureau. He was allied with Liu Shao-ch'i and was exposed and removed from office before Liu became a public target.

attempt to disguise their target: "Liu Tao—Wang Kuang-mei —.?." "Liu Tao, your mother says . . . What of it? Even if your father said it, we'd still pull him off the horse!"

As soon as these posters went up the loyalists pulled them down, but as quickly as they pulled them down, other equally pointed messages took their place. Soon word spread through the whole city that at Tsinghua there were posters attacking Liu Shao-ch'i. Thousands came to the campus to see them and this intensifed the struggle between the student organizations. Those visitors who leaned toward the rebel side were delighted with the attacks on Liu, but those who supported Liu, or could not believe that a man of his prestige could be a capitalist-roader, were very upset. They said that the Tsinghua rebels had carried out a coup d'état.

Soon word spread that a counter-revolutionary incident aimed at splitting the Central Committee had occurred on the campus. In retaliation the 8-9 loyalists called a mass meeting of their supporters in twelve universities and schools. On August 24 thousands of people gathered at Tsinghua Middle School on the north edge of the campus, and, under the leadership of Ho Peng-fei, issued an important proclamation. It said that their newly organized Tsinghua Red Guards (the 8-9s) would take full power on the campus to prevent a right-wing take-over. As for the small handful of counter-revolutionaries—the Mao Tse-tung Thought Red Guards (the 8-8s)—who hoped to split the Central Committee, they deserved a thousand cuts and ought to die a thousand deaths. Outsiders were ordered to leave the campus, pickets were set up to patrol all roads, traffic was stopped, and a curfew imposed. Lest there remain any doubt in people's minds about the intentions of the loyalists, posters went up announcing a "red terror." Squads went around looking for anti-Liu posters. If any were found, they were pho-tographed and then torn down. If any student protested, or entered into a debate on the issues, he was driven away with the slogan, "Reactionaries have no right to speak." Anyone passing by on the roads or walks was searched for notes and posters in an attempt to prevent any new counter-opinions from going up on the walls and reed mats. A student from the Chemistry Department (Kuai's home base) was roughed up and his glasses knocked off.

The posters which the Tsinghua Red Guards were tearing down had not been signed by individuals. They had been put up by Mao Tse-tung Thought Red Guards organized in fighting groups called "Sunflower," "Monkey," etc., and were signed with the name of the group and an address in the dormitory where the group representative could be found. All these addresses were searched out that day by the Tsinghua Red Guards and anyone found was physically attacked.

The rebels of the Mao Tse-tung Thought organization, taken by surprise by the power and suddenness of this assault, had to retreat for a few hours. Some fled the campus and either hid out in the ruins of the Yuan Ming-yuan, an old imperial pleasure palace just to the northwest of the Tsinghua grounds, or found their way to Peking University nearby where sympathetic forces took them in. They reasoned that the intensity of the repression meant they must be on the right track politically. On August 19 their demand for "reversing the case" against Kuai had provoked attempts to break up their meeting. In the days that followed, their public accusations against Liu Shao-ch'i had provoked the "red terror." Having hit a raw nerve, the obvious thing to do was to press forward. Once they recovered their balance, they banded together more tightly than before and began to fight back. They organized safety patrols, flying squads, and an alarm-signal system. By evening they felt strong enough to take the offensive again. They broadcast a statement condemning the destruction of the posters and said that all those who had taken part had been "deceived." At the same time they put up signs quoting Mao Tse-tung: "The future is bright." To do this and to avoid arrest was not easy, however, for the Tsinghua Red Guards were still patrolling the campus and were arresting anyone suspected of opposition. Poster-makers had to dash from their dormitory doorways, quickly paste up their messages, and then duck for cover.

Those who made it back safely reported desolation from one end of the campus to the other. Everywhere walls and reed mats had been roughly stripped, leaving shreds and bands of torn paper that flapped aimlessly in the wind. Here and there the new slogans of the loyalists stood out in stark relief —"Long live red terror," "Only the left is allowed to rebel," etc. How different it was from the lively scene only one day earlier!

As this confrontation between loyalists and rebels mounted to a climax, the Work Team members who had stayed on to receive criticism and repudiation withdrew. Those who still did not recognize how much damage had been wrought by their oppressive line must have left with a smile. Weren't the loyalist forces they had left in power on the offensive? Perhaps their smiles were tempered a little by the traditional New Year's congratulation cards they received from the rebels. The characters on one side of each card read: "We welcomed with tears a rude nurse who dealt out daily beatings!" On the other side the message was: "Kick aside the obstructing rock! Overjoyed are we who have been set free!" Across the top of the card was written: "Make revolution on your own. We don't need a nurse!"

These slogans, so poignant and correct at the time, were to be used again and again during the Cultural Revolution, but not necessarily with the same meaning or the same political content, as we shall see.

The events of August 24 demonstrated that the rebels of the Mao Tse-tung Thought Red Guards were still in a minority. The Tsinghua Red Guards, backed up by the Preparatory Committee, still dominated the campus. In the days that followed it was difficult for the rebels even to put their arguments before the public because they could not get University money for paper, ink, or brushes. They had only limited access to the loudspeakers which the other side used day in and day out to denounce them, and they had no newspaper such as the other side possessed to use as a vehicle for a constant stream of polemics against "counter-revolutionaries." Even when the rebels found money for silk armbands, they could not get "Mao Tse-tung Thought Red Guards" printed on them because the print-

ing company would not do the work without authorization from
the Preparatory Committee, which was in no mood to give the
rebel organization any openings. The rebels donned red armbands without anything printed on them, but when they went
out to speak people asked, "Are you Red Guards?"

"Of course we are. Don't you see these armbands!"

"Yes, but there is nothing printed on them," replied the
skeptics in the audience, and so rebel words were treated with
suspicion.

In spite of these handicaps, the rebels gained support with
each passing day. The very suppression which they suffered
caused many people to rally to their cause. Furthermore, events
beyond the campus were in their favor. The Central Committee's "Sixteen-Point Decision" certainly argued for a free hand
for rebels everywhere and condemned those who, in order to
suppress the mass movement, called revolutionaries counter-
revolutionaries.

> Large numbers of revolutionary young people, previously
> unknown, have become courageous and daring path-
> breakers. They are vigorous in action and intelligent.
> Through the media of big-character posters and great
> debates, they argue things out, expose and criticize
> thoroughly, and launch resolute attacks on the open and
> hidden representatives of the bourgeoisie. In such a great
> revolutionary movement, it is hardly avoidable that they
> should show shortcomings of one kind or another; how-
> ever, their general revolutionary orientation has been cor-
> rect from the beginning. . . .
>
> Since the Cultural Revolution is a revolution, it in-
> evitably meets with resistance. This resistance comes chiefly
> from those in authority who have wormed their way into
> the Party and are taking the capitalist road. It also comes
> from the force of habit of the old society. At present, this
> resistance is still fairly strong and stubborn. But after all,
> the Great Proletarian Cultural Revolution is an irresistible
> general trend. There is abundant evidence that such re-
> sistance will be quickly broken down once the masses be-
> come fully aroused. . . .
>
> The only method is for the masses to liberate them-

selves, and any method of doing things in their stead must not be used.

Trust the masses, rely on them, and respect their initiative. . . . Let the masses learn to distinguish between right and wrong and between correct and incorrect ways of doing things.

Make the fullest use of big-character posters and great debates to argue matters out, so that the masses can clarify the correct views, criticize the wrong views, and expose all the ghosts and monsters. . . .

In certain schools, units, and work teams of the Cultural Revolution, some of the persons in charge have organized counterattacks against the masses who put up big-character posters criticizing them. These people have even advanced such slogans as: Opposition to the leaders of a unit or a work team means opposition to the Central Committee of the Party, means opposition to the Party and socialism, means counter-revolution. . . . This is an error in matters of orientation, an error in line, and it is absolutely impermissible.

A number of persons who suffer from serious ideological errors . . . are taking advantage of certain shortcomings and mistakes . . . deliberately branding some of the masses as "counter-revolutionaries." It is necessary to beware of such "pickpockets" and expose their tricks in good time.

Was not this directed squarely at the Tsinghua Work Team and at its immediate successors, the leaders of the Preparatory Committee?

If this was not clear enough, there was Mao Tse-tung's own big-character poster, which he wrote on August 5 but which did not become public on the Tsinghua campus until August 23. This poster read as follows:

China's first Marxist-Leninist big-character poster and the Commentator's article on it in *Jenmin Jihpao* [*People's Daily*] are indeed superbly written! Comrades, please read them again. But in the last fifty days or so some leading comrades from the central down to the local levels have acted in a diametrically opposite way. Adopting the reactionary stand of the bourgeoisie, they have enforced a bourgeois dictatorship and struck down the surging movement of the great Cultural Revolution of the proletariat. They have stood facts on their heads and juggled black and white, encircled and suppressed revolutionaries, stifled opinions differing from their own, imposed a white terror, and felt very pleased with themselves. They have puffed up the arrogance of the bourgeoisie and deflated the morale of the proletariat. How poisonous! Viewed in connection with the Right deviation of 1962 and the wrong tendency of 1964 which was "left" in form but right in essence, shouldn't this prompt one to deep thought?

Making use of these top-level documents, the rebels stood firm, beat off the counterattacks of the loyalists, insisted on a formal "reversal of the case" for almost everyone, and continued their research into the origins of the bourgeois reactionary line, a search every thread of which led right back to Liu Shao-ch'i.* This firmness on their part, together with the thrust of the documents from above, began to disintegrate the opposition, attract and pull individuals from the loyalist to the rebel side, and mobilize many who had up till then been passive.

One big factor in all this was the experience Tsinghua students had as they went out on liaison assignments to the far corners of the country. Students from all organizations went out, but everywhere they found that the mass movement was being suppressed by local authorities. Long after the work teams had been withdrawn in the Peking area they were still riding high in many regions and localities; and in some localities where work teams had been withdrawn local Party committees were still actively suppressing their left critics.

---

*On the question of "reversing the case," many still did not dare defend Kuai Ta-fu, or even demand that he be cleared. This temerity became a political issue later when Kuai emerged as the outstanding student leader.

7
Student Liaison

"On the Sinkiang train all that was coming over the loud-speaker was old music," said Tsu. "No study of Mao Tse-tung Thought, no political content. We were fed up and went to find the head conductor.

"'The Red Guards are going to take over your broadcasting station!' we said.

"The conductor saw us coming, so fresh, so brash! What could he do?

"'Okay,' he said. 'Run it as you like, but don't break the equipment.'

"He took us to the broadcasting compartment and showed us how to use everything. We organized three programs a day, reading articles on the Cultural Revolution in Peking, and on the revolutionary rebel spirit of the students at Peking's Middle School No. 36 and at Tsinghua University. The passengers supported us.

"Some funny things happened. We went through the records to find some that we could play. We found one entitled 'Sinkiang People Praise Mao Tse-tung.' We put it on the turntable but after a few notes the needle jumped the groove and made a loud screech. We stopped the record, replaced the needle, and started again, only to have the same thing happen all over again. It was the record that was damaged. It had long ago been set aside. But when the chief conductor heard those screeching sounds, he came running from one end of the train, while the assistant conductor came running from the other. They thought we had broken their precious machine. Even though we explained again and again that it was all due to a messed-up record, they wouldn't leave after that.

"Before we got off the train we demanded that the crew continue our type of revolutionary program. The conductor said, 'You have educated us. We will carry on and we will welcome you back anytime to handle the programs for us!'"

This story is typical of the way student rebels from Peking took charge, challenged authority, and shook complacency everywhere as they went out to rally university and middle school students to expose and repudiate the "Party people in authority taking the capitalist road" in distant provinces.

All of my informants had gone out, at one time or another, on such missions. Among the first to go was Tsu, who was elected by comrades in his department to join a group of twenty traveling to Tientsin University, where the rebel faction found itself hard-pressed in the second week of August. It is doubtful if the pressure on the Tientsin rebels was any greater than that felt at the time by the students at Tsinghua who went to their aid: the difference was that at Tientsin University the Party Committee was still in power, had thrown its support to a loyalist group which it had helped to set up, and was suppressing, by administrative measures, the activities of the rebel minority. The latter, grouping together as the August 13 Red Guards, decided to march to Peking to put their case before Chairman Mao.

They managed to break out of the loyalist encirclement on the evening of August 12. Then, before they had marched halfway to the capital, a special train sent by the Central Committee picked them up. The concern shown for the rebels by the Country's leaders convinced the Tientsin authorities to modify their attitude. This should have been an important lesson to people in power elsewhere but they were slow to learn it. Repression continued unabated in many places.

One of these was Honan. Jen Yen-sheng told about his experiences there in some detail. Jen was more dour than the other former students who came together each day to talk to us. He was a twenty-six-year-old Hopei middle peasant from Hsingtai, where an earthquake had wreaked such destruction in 1968. He had the height and lean frame typical of many northern peasants. His high cheekbones, square jaw, flat chin and crew cut gave him a military air. He spoke slowly, calmly, and rarely interrupted the others—though they often interrupted him.

"On August 26, 1966, I left Peking by rail and went to

Chengchow with a group from Tsinghua and Peking universities. At Chengchow University they were still debating the problem of work teams and the atmosphere was just as if a work team still held control. Each speaker had to be approved and each one spoke for an hour or more. The problem under discussion was whether T'ang Yuan-ch'uan [the Kuai Ta-fu of Chengchow] was a counter-revolutionary or not. When the Work Team was still at the university he had opposed it. They had called him counter-revolutionary and he had gone to Peking to appeal.

"We three students from Tsinghua were disgusted with all the long speeches. The next night another endless debate began. About halfway through the evening we couldn't bear it any longer and we demanded the right to speak. But we weren't allowed time. So we sent a note up: 'This is no debate meeting!' It was signed by the Peita-Tsinghua liaison group.

"When this note was read out it sent a ripple through the hall. People turned to each other saying, 'There are Peking students here to help us.' But we were dispersed through the crowd and didn't come forward.

"On the third night we decided to speak first, before the meeting got underway—Tsinghua first, Peita second—and to speak for ten minutes only. I hopped up and said, 'T'ang went to Peking! This was a revolutionary act. He trusts the Central Committee. Whoever calls him a counter-revolutionary is carrying out the bourgeois reactionary line.'

"Their system was to allow only one speaker at a time, but as soon as I said these words people jumped up all over the hall and the meeting became chaotic. Before I spoke the atmosphere had been relaxed. People were sitting there, smoking, fanning themselves. Some even sat in armchairs, half asleep. But as soon as I spoke everyone became excited, people rushed to the front and crowded around the stage. The masses shouted, 'Excellent!' 'Very good!'

"T'ang Yuan-ch'uan also ran up. He had been under such severe attack. He congratulated us and said, 'You gave me such support. You must come to my dormitory. There is much to talk over.'

"But when the meeting was over those who opposed us wouldn't let us go. They wanted to debate with us and defeat us. The Chengchow University Cultural Revolution Committee, the group that had welcomed us to town and had found rooms for us, was very upset. 'We welcomed you, but you gave support to the other side!'

"The crowd wouldn't leave. The minority faction of suppressed rebels issued all sorts of invitations for us to come and stay with them, to talk, and so on. T'ang said again, 'You'd better come to my place, you may be surrounded here and detained.'

"But we said, 'Never mind, we'll stay together.'

"That same night Ch'i Teng-kuei, vice-secretary of the Honan Party Committee, came to find us and asked what we thought about the issues. We thought him brave for even daring to come and speak to us.

"'You should support T'ang, not oppress him,' we said.

"Then Liu Chien-hsun, secretary of the Honan Party Committee, wrote a poster which he entitled 'My Poster.' It said that T'ang's trip to Peking was not bad. This poster went up the very evening that we spoke. The next day Liu met with all of us from Peking. The Honan Cultural Revolution Committee people broke in saying, 'You have T'ang's side represented here, why not let us join?'

"They plastered posters all over the room: 'Saving gods get out of here! Go back to Peking!' 'Blabbermouths, ten out of ten are wrong.'

"Liu told them they were very impolite. 'I have guests here from Peking. We are trying to have a serious discussion.'

"We complained that his attitude was not clear. Though he had gone so far as to say that T'ang's act was not counter-revolutionary, he wouldn't say it was revolutionary. We demanded something more clear-cut.

"Outside people were milling around shouting 'Bombard Liu.'* They were angry because he wouldn't let them in to disrupt the discussion.

---

*The phrase "bombard" means to attack and expose with publicity—not to fire artillery shells.

" 'You see,' he said. 'Just talking to you has enraged them. Work is very hard. I haven't slept for days.'

"After some discussion we left, but the loyalist faction surrounded Liu and wouldn't let him leave.

"Those of us from the Peking liaison group then split up according to plan. I went to the Chengchow Technical School. As soon as I got there the loudspeakers began to blare, 'The Peking Red Guards are here to make a report!'

"I was not prepared for that. My idea was to visit the campus, read the posters, and find out what was going on. But they thrust the microphone in front of my nose, so I had to say something. I told how Wang Kuang-mei oppressed us and how we fought back. I spoke about the rebel spirit and how important it was. Then the rank-and-file of the other faction crowded around to debate the T'ang question. We didn't want to debate this, so the situation got tense. Wherever we went people said they wanted to debate, but actually what they did was to surround and detain us. It was no debate at all.

"The Honan Party Committee then issued a statement: 'The attitude of the Peking Red Guards is revolutionary. No one should oppose their activities.'

"This was a great boost for us. The minority side, the suppressed rebels, all came to tell about what had happened to them, how they had not been allowed to leave Chengchow and travel to Peking. They couldn't get travel money from the administration and they were not allowed on the train free.

"So we said, 'We'll take your problem to the Honan Party Committee.' (Liu had said we were welcome to come and find him at any time.) But when we got to the Party Committee offices we couldn't get in. We demanded entry but the guards refused. Finally Wang Wei-chun, another vice-secretary, came out to face us.

" 'The Cultural Revolution is a movement,' we said. 'If you don't let these people move, how can it go well?'

" 'We are willing to let them go. Perhaps there are problems below,' Wang said.

" 'You must let them go!' we shouted in chorus.

" 'I'll write a note, then they will be allowed on the train,' he said. And so this problem was solved.

"Every evening the debate continued at the University. Liu had sent a work team that used oppressive tactics. When he was exposed he made a self-criticism and admitted that it was wrong to send the team, but he also said he thought the Honan University Party Committee had done a lot of good work. And that was why he had protected it.

"This upset many people. They attacked him for not taking a clear stand and the meeting dissolved in disorder.

" 'Now's the time to mobilize the masses, now's the time to let all the problems out!' we said.

"Nobody dared openly defend the Communist Party Committee, so both sides went to debate with Liu. That evening more Peking Red Guards arrived and the debate continued into the small hours of the morning. Liu was heavily criticized. He shook hands with us and said, 'It's good to bombard me. If I am a man the truth can do no harm, and if I am a devil I can't run away. I welcome your criticism.'

"We analyzed the crimes of the Chengchow Work Team according to our experience at Tsinghua and then wrote the whole thing out on a wall poster, citing facts and incidents about how they had carried out the bourgeois reactionary line. After these posters went up the other side, the loyalists, began to waver. They thought perhaps they had been wrong since *all* the people coming from Peking supported T'ang. So they asked us to come and talk. They wanted to talk it over, to hear the other side and get further explanations.

"What they couldn't accept was the idea that the class background of the members of the minority faction was generally as good as theirs. They told us how bad T'ang was; they presented all the information they had collected about how he had gone to Peking to appeal out of self-interest. But to appeal to the Central Committee, to appeal to Mao Tse-tung, how could this be bad? If people are denounced haven't they the right to appeal?

"They asked us many questions. We answered on the basis of our experience in the Peking struggle. After a morning's exchange the majority began to see our point and promised that in the afternoon they would take a different stand.

"From that moment on T'ang's organization grew very fast and became the nucleus for a big group called the Chengchow University United Committee. This soon turned into a majority movement and became the center of the Cultural Revolution in Honan."

Honan was apparently the only province where the established Party Committee came out in support of the rebel minority. It was also the first province to allow Red Guards, regardless of their politics, to travel free of charge. Mao Tse-tung praised the Honan leaders for this and approved Liu Chien-hsun, the secretary of the Honan Party Committee, as head of the new Honan Revolutionary Committee when it was set up in 1967. Ch'i Teng-kuei, vice-secretary of the Honan Party Committee, so impressed Mao and the other leaders that he was eventually called to Peking for high-level work. He is now an alternate member of the Political Bureau of the Central Committee.

If Honan was relatively easy to organize because of the enlightened attitude of its higher Party leaders, Sinkiang was the opposite. There the "Party people in authority" maintained tight control, suppressed the student movement, and mobilized the people against the Red Guard "agitators" from Peking.

Tsu, after he returned from his work in support of the August 13 group in Tientsin, went off to the Northwest on August 18. He went with an elected group of student militants similar to the one that had earlier visited Tientsin. At the time the Red Guards still adhered to the "inheritance theory," so that all those chosen for the trip were of working-class or poor-peasant background. They traveled first to Lanchow, in Kansu province, where a student rebel had been killed by a loyalist on the university campus. Stimulated by Mao Tse-tung's August 18 reception of Red Guards in Peking, the rebel movement was developing well in Lanchow, so on August 26 Tsu and twelve others boarded the train for Sinkiang. Ten girls from the Peking Middle School No. 36 went with them. Tsu described it this way:

"We traveled without tickets. We only had to show our

student cards. As for eating, we spent our own money. If we ran out of money we simply went to the local authorities, signed slips, and borrowed money. Those students who poured into Peking in September and October were fed free of charge. Peasants from country schools got food money for the road, they were subsidized by their school.

"When we arrived in Urumchi, we didn't talk to anyone. We just asked the way to Sinkiang University, even though we weren't sure there was such a place. We had our Red Guard armbands on, we formed into ranks and marched out of the station singing songs. All the people in the streets were curious.

"When we got to the University our arrival was immediately reported to the University Party Committee. These were all the same people who had led before the Cultural Revolution began. There had been no rebellion here at all.

"The vice-secretary of the Party Committee came out to meet us.

" 'Welcome, welcome,' he said.

"He led us into his office. It was a fine place with covered sofas all around. We didn't like the looks of it. We refused to go in. We sat out in the hall on our bed rolls and sent a few people out to arrange some place to stay, preferably an ordinary classroom. But when we were finally shown our quarters they had been fixed up with armchairs, spring beds, and woolen blankets. It was an attempt to co-opt us.

"Since we had no other place to go, we decided to move in for the time being. By that time our arrival had been reported to the Autonomous Region Party Committee and on August 28 a man came to see us. From our dormitory window we saw him get out of his big car and walk over. He was short and fat and had the bearing of a leader. It turned out to be Wu Kang, vice-chairman of the Autonomous Region and vice-secretary of the Party Committee. He was number three man in Sinkiang. We had already heard from students at the university about the bourgeois reactionary line in their school. This was one of the cadres responsible.

" 'I'm sorry I didn't come to welcome you yesterday,' he said. 'Maybe these quarters are not so good. Perhaps you should move to the People's Liberation Army reception center where things are more comfortable. We would like to show you some of the sights of Urumchi and also—have you tasted our melons? The melons of Sinkiang are very famous!'

"What a way to begin!

"We jumped up angrily. 'Now is not the time to talk crap like this. We came to discuss your class line and the bourgeois reactionary line you have been carrying out in Sinkiang. So don't give us any nonsense about scenic sights and sweet melons.'

"Then we told him about the problems we had heard about at the University. When we found he had been the Party secretary of the Aeronautical Institute in Peking, we realized he had once worked under Chiang Nan-hsiang. So we asked him if he had anything about Chiang Nan-hsiang to expose!

"He became very quiet. 'All these are important matters,' he said, and retired.

"We split up and went to all the middle schools in the city. We found that the repression had been serious. There were students in Middle School No. 1 who had written some posters critical of the provincial Communist Party. They had been called counter-revolutionaries. Their parents had been warned to break relations with them or lose their salaries or wages.

"Everywhere we went we were surrounded by people shouting, 'Long live Wang En-mao!'—Wang En-mao was chairman of the Sinkiang Autonomous Region and secretary of its Party Committee. We were in the heart of a little independent kingdom. Clearly the Party Committee of the region was not carrying out the decision of the Eleventh Plenum, which stated that the work teams should be withdrawn. Instead, liaison personnel had been sent out to all the schools and these people played the role of work teams.

"We decided we had to see Wang En-mao himself. We crowded, all twenty of us, into the reception room at the Party Committee offices. We demanded an audience with Wang.

" 'Who are you?' asked the clerk in charge.

" 'We are Red Guards from Peking!'

"This man checked in the halls outside, then led us to a second reception room. A bunch of people came out to shake hands. Among them we recognized Wu Kang. Opposite me was Wang En-mao.

" 'Our work is in accord with the directives of the Central Committee,' he said. 'The work teams have been withdrawn. Of course, many problems still remain. We welcome your criticisms and suggestions.'

"Then we brought up what we knew. We charged them with saying one thing but doing another. As we talked four secretaries sat behind us and took notes, jotting down everything we said. They also recorded our discussion on tape.

"At the beginning Wang En-mao had a smile on his face, but as we talked his face changed color. We demanded that he send people down to check up on the work and solve the problems of repression that had come to our attention. 'If you don't do this,' we said, 'you may turn into your opposite. From a revolutionary you will turn into a counter-revolutionary!'

"We went back to our quarters, but we no sooner got there than many people came to debate with us. They called us Rightists from Peking who stank so much at home that we couldn't stay there and so came all the way to Sinkiang to make trouble.

"In reply we wrote two posters: 'Bombard Wang En-mao,' and 'Support the middle school students who are in rebellion.' Then lots of rank-and-file people came to find us. The more we looked into the problems the more serious they seemed. Not only were the local rebels under attack, but the attack came down on our heads as well. No sooner did we put up a poster than we were surrounded by people demanding to debate with us; a vehicle with a loudspeaker followed us through the streets broadcasting continuous attacks. It even followed us to the dining room at the University.

"On September 3 we went again to Wang En-mao's headquarters to protest the attacks on us. We wanted to explain to him Premier Chou En-lai's line on the Cultural Revolution. Wang En-mao wouldn't even receive us.

"But many people who had been suppressed by him supported us. We went in front of Wang's office at noon and waited until late afternoon for him to come out. We announced that we would not eat until he came out to debate. There we sat in the yard of the Regional Party Committee and with us sat many Sinkiang students—two or three hundred. They joined us in our hunger strike. While we were waiting we held meetings to expose what we knew about Wang's reactionary line.

"To drown out these meetings the Party Committee rigged up two loudspeakers which blared out, 'Your action is counter-revolutionary. You are as bad as the Soviet representatives in India.' Since Sinkiang students were sitting with us, the authorities mobilized their parents, their sisters, and their brothers to speak over the loudspeakers.

"'I am your mother. You must not allow counter-revolutionaries from Peking to deceive you. If you persist in your wrongheaded action I will have to break with you.' So spoke the parents and family members.

"But we fought back. When the rank-and-file saw this oppressive way of doing things, more and more joined us. Disregarding our empty stomachs, we decided to send people out on the streets to lecture and to expose what was happening. As we told about the hunger strike, the reactionary acts of Wang, and the surging Cultural Revolution in Peking, more and more people flocked to join us. Our courage grew. But we hadn't eaten all day long and we were very hungry. That evening a cold front moved in. We had left Peking with only light clothing. Now we sat in the open, freezing and shivering. When the Sinkiang students saw our predicament they brought a cart full of sweaters, sweat shirts, and padded clothes. So we maintained our vigil and this incident grew bigger and bigger.

"Finally Wang En-mao became worried about what might happen and at 4 A.M. on the third day he finally came out. He came and sat on the platform in front of us. He was surrounded by bodyguards. The whole thing was a farce!

"'You had better call off your demonstration,' he said. 'Your attitude is all wrong. You want to see me. Well, here I am. Take a good look.' With that he went back inside.

"We decided that to continue the hunger strike was wrong.

We had already won a victory. After all, Wang En-mao had come out. So we decided to break up, find something to eat, and carry on the struggle in the streets.

"At our quarters there was a guard at the door at all times. They said this man was there to protect us, but actually everyone that came to see us had to register with him. Thus they controlled all who had contact with us, a form of intimidation. When visitors got home they had to explain why they had come to see us.

"In the beginning they fed us well, but as the struggle continued they offered us only a few boiled potatoes and navy bread—a very hard kind of bread that turns sour in water. Whenever we went out we were surrounded and shouted at. We no sooner offered an opinion than a large crowd gathered around and refused to let us go. All these people looked like cadres, not rank-and-file people, and they obviously did this in an organized way. After we had debated thoroughly with one, another stepped in to take his place, and so it went on endlessly. We learned that the Party Committee had divided its cadres into three groups which took turns following us and debating with us in order to drive us out of Sinkiang.

"After the weather turned cold, the Party Committee gave each of us an old sheepskin cloak. Wrapped in these old cloaks we sat on the ground and debated. But the cadres wouldn't let us leave to eat, to drink water, or even to go to the toilet. Once four of us were surrounded and held in debate for ten solid hours. Suddenly two middle school students pushed their way through the crowd and handed us some large cakes to eat.

" 'You people are going too far,' they shouted at our opponents. 'At least let them eat.'

"Others on the street joined in then, shouting, 'Let them eat, let them eat!'

"The cadres tried to restrict us in other ways too. We found it hard to get paper and we couldn't get the use of a mimeograph machine. We got together enough money to buy one but all the stores swore that they had none in stock. So we learned our lesson. We tried walking into a store, looking around casually until we saw what we wanted, and then saying, 'We want this machine!'

"At this point the clerk went to find the manager. The manager came in and said, 'This machine has just arrived. We don't have any price on it yet. We can't sell it.'

"So we were foiled again. In the end we went way out in the countryside to find a mimeograph machine and had to settle for a simple screen. With a strip of bamboo we scraped ink through the screen and made hundreds of leaflets one by one. But since their leaflets hit the street by the thousands we couldn't compete. Nor could we compete with their loudspeakers, for they had a sound truck while we had none.

"But we found a way. We wrote out clean, concise messages on posters, then stood by the bus station. As the buses came out we pasted our posters on their sides. Since the buses ran all over the city we got our points across to the whole population. We had trouble with the Uigur language, though. They write from right to left. We didn't know that and we printed their leaflets backward.

"We were so busy during these days that we got almost no sleep. When we got too tired we took catnaps in our sheepskin cloaks, and then woke up and went to work again.

"The authorities spread all sorts of rumors about us. They said we were the sons of capitalists and landlords, and on September 9 Security Headquarters prepared warrants for our arrest.

"But just at that time *People's Daily* called on the workers and peasants to support the revolutionary students. To arrest us would have been too brazen. They pulled back. The warrants were never used.

"We kept up the struggle until early October when we decided to come back to Peking to report to the Central Committee. I came back to Peking on October 4, together with several Sinkiang students. The Central Committee put us up in the Ministry of Commerce and let us hear tapes of speeches Premier Chou En-lai had made during our absence. The general secretary of the State Council, Chou Lung-hsin, also received us and told us what the premier had said.

"The whole idea was that it was correct to fight the bourgeois reactionary line, but that we must be careful of bad people who might take advantage of the situation in the border areas to create chaos. We should pay attention to policy and to tactics. We promised to read more of the material from the Central Committee and Mao Tse-tung.

"We felt that we had support but that the comrades in Sinkiang were still suppressed, so we went all the way back to tell them what the premier had said. We also reported on the big October 6 mass meeting in Peking where Kuai Ta-fu led the Red Guards in taking an oath of loyalty to Mao Tse-tung.

"By this time the Sinkiang students had awakened. They fought together with us. We organized all their people and set up a Red Second Headquarters in Urumchi. Wang En-mao felt constrained to write a letter supporting this and *People's Daily* printed it. Thus the Urumchi situation improved and large numbers of people began their attack on Wang En-mao's bourgeois reactionary line. Since the people were more and more conscious, we held a mass meeting to repudiate the line of the loyalist Red Guard First Headquarters. Three thousand activists joined our parade and people in the streets applauded.

"We decided that the masses were aroused and that Wang En-mao had to draw back. We decided that the situation was good, that the Sinkiang people could carry on their own revolution, so we got back on the train for Peking. It was already almost the middle of November."

8
Liu Shao-ch'i Exposed

By taking an active part all over the country in the kind of struggle that went on in Sinkiang, Tsinghua students learned to recognize and hate the "bourgeois reactionary line." In the outlying provinces the suppression of the left was often cruder and harsher than it was in the capital, and hence easier to understand. Since it also lasted much longer—there tends to be a marked lag between the capital and the hinterland in every political movement—Peking students were able to contrast the flourishing, often chaotic but always exhilarating mass movement where they came from with the stagnant repressive atmosphere of their destination. Since wherever they arrived they immediately called for rebellion, they also had a chance to live through for a second or even a third time the experience of being labeled counter-revolutionary, of being denied the right to speak, to organize, and to advocate, and consequently also the experience of standing firm, finding mass support, and fighting back.

"From all this," said Tsu, "we realized that the essential thing was to hold power. Without political power the people can do nothing. With power they can carry through the revolution. Seeing capitalist-roaders in power in so many places and watching them carry out the bourgeois reactionary line, we became enraged. We learned to hate Liu Shao-ch'i!"

Students like Tsu also learned a great deal about how state affairs were managed, how the real political framework of a province, a city, or a university should be investigated and if necessary exposed, and how a struggle for power should be conducted. What they did not learn was how to prepare themselves for holding power. The deference with which they were treated as Peking militants, the response their ever more radical slogans elicited from the masses, and the ease with which they moved onto takeover committees throughout the country when the movement to seize power began, gave them an exaggerated sense of their own skills and importance. They began to think that without them, without their particular faction or clique, the revolution could not succeed, for only *they* were really revolutionary, only *they* deserved to hold power.*

---

*To illustrate the prestige of ultra-left slogans at this time, Premier Chou En-lai told us about a student who changed his name from Hou Chou-chun (Hou Kicking Straight) to Hou Luan-chun (Hou Kicking Around Wildly). The Premier advised him to change it back again.

But in fall of 1966 the question of holding power had not yet come up. The rebel students and the masses whom they helped galvanize into action were still fighting for the right to organize and to make themselves heard. In this battle the mass meeting of October 6 in Tien An-men square marked a turning point. This was a rally of rebels from all over the nation. They came together to celebrate the "revolutionary rebel spirit," to challenge and overthrow the "bourgeois reactionary line," and to lay blame where it belonged no matter how high the persons or person involved might be. They also came to remove, once and for all, the counter-revolutionary labels that had been fastened by various Communist Party committees and work teams. How much the climate of opinion had changed by this time can be seen by the fact that Kuai Ta-fu was leader and chief organizer of this meeting. His own group on the campus, the Tsinghua University Chingkangshan Regiment, had been formed only two weeks earlier. It was made up of hard-core "counter-revolution-aries" of the fourth category, people whom the ordinary militants of the Mao Tse-tung Thought Red Guards had not dared unite with organizationally because the Tsinghua Work Team had made their names "stink." Now this group functioned as the nucleus of the nationwide rebel movement. Because they had stuck to their guns, had refused to retreat even one inch, and had turned out to be right, their prestige was very high and their fame spread far and wide.

Whether to repudiate the "bourgeois reactionary line," whether to "reverse the case" against the "counter-revolution-aries," whether to expose the sources of the Work Team's power —these had been the issues throughout August and September. The October 6 meeting marked the climax of this struggle, the victory of the rebel line over the loyalist line. After this meeting rebel organizations, morale high, went on the offensive every-where and loyalist organizations began to retreat. Toward the end of November a section of the loyalist Tsinghua University Red Guards formed a rebel regiment and broke away from the parent organization. This triggered an increasing number of individual defections and group withdrawals.

Die-hard loyalists, fearing complete collapse of their line, shifted tactics. They turned their fire from the student rebels down below to the Cultural Revolution Group of the Central Committee up above,* accusing it of carrying out an ultra-left line, a line left in form but "right" in essence, a new "bourgeois reactionary line."† This was the political basis for the offensive launched by T'ao Ch'u, who had been brought to the Cultural Revolution Group from South China only a few weeks earlier. T'ao Ch'u's line was "suspect all, overthrow all," including the comrades of the Cultural Revolution Group of the Central Committee. "Let the masses liberate themselves," shouted the former loyalists. "Kick aside the Cultural Revolution Group, we don't need a nursemaid." Unable to maintain themselves on the right they suddenly launched an attack from the left. It was a plea for anarchy which, if successful, would have decapitated the whole rebel movement. On the Tsinghua campus the spokesmen

---

*The Cultural Revolution Group of the Central Committee was a group of Communist cadres working directly under the leadership of the Central Committee but not necessarily members themselves. The Group was responsible for leading the Cultural Revolution, which in practice meant guiding or trying to guide the many-faceted mass movement which the Cultural Revolution unleashed. The composition of the Group changed many times. Particularly prominent were Ch'en Po-ta, Political Bureau member and Mao's secretary in Yenan days; Chiang Ch'ing, Mao's wife; Chang Ch'un-chiao, a Shanghai Party Committee member now a member of the Political Bureau; Wang Li, during the Cultural Revolution acting editor of *Red Flag*, acting director of the Propaganda Department of the Central Committee, and acting director of Hsinhua News Agency; Kuang Feng; and Ch'i Pen-yu, who along with Kuang Feng was a co-editor of *Red Flag* during the Cultural Revolution. Wang Li, Kuang Feng, and Ch'i Pen-yu were later deposed as members of the May 16 Conspiracy.

†An ultra-left line is a line or set of policies that attacks friends as enemies and isolates working-class revolutionaries, an adventurist line that tries to do today what can only be accomplished tomorrow, a sectarian line that depends on a few activists to accomplish what only masses of people can do. Such a line is "right" in essence because it leads to defeat for the revolution and compromises it just as surely as does right-wing collaboration and betrayal.

for this line were Ho Peng-fei and Li Ch'eng-chiu's son, Li Feng.*
These young men were carrying out at the grass roots a struggle
that was simultaneously going on in the Central Committee—a
last ditch attempt to maintain Liu Shao-ch'i in power.

At this point Chiang Ch'ing, Mao Tse-tung's wife and a member of the Central Cultural Revolution Group, stepped into the
fray to combat the "kick-aside" theory and rally the rebels to
continue the revolution. With her help all the left groups on the
Tsinghua campus formed an alliance. Dissolving their old organizational forms and names, they merged into one United
Chingkangshan Regiment. Simultaneously, the loyalist organizations collapsed. The rump Tsinghua Red Guards publicly burned
the seal of their group and then merged as individuals in the
new Regiment. All this took place at a grand rally on December
19, the high point of the rebel movement on campus. With all
the politically active students and staff united in one organization, the opposition forces were completely routed.

"The loyalists were crushed ideologically and organizationally. Power was seized back from them," said Tsu.

The spearhead of the whole movement then turned directly
on Liu Shao-Ch'i. At a grand rally on December 25, the president of the republic was named by name and denounced as a
capitalist-roader. From that point on it was official both in
China and abroad that the "chief Party person in authority
taking the capitalist road" was Liu Shao-ch'i.

The events at Tsinghua in the fall of 1966 must be seen
against the background of a developing mass movement that
was nationwide in scale. It engaged almost the entire university
and middle school population in political action and then spread
to the working population in factories and on the land. Mao's
meeting with the early Red Guards in Tien An-men Square on
August 18 and his poster "Bombard the Headquarters," which
became public on August 23, sparked a tremendous upheaval.
As fast as rebels organized Red Guard groups to challenge the

---

*Li Ch'eng-chiu was the secretary of the Szechuan Party Com-
mittee.

people who held power over them, power holders organized loyal Red Guards in the name of upholding revolution. (Often, of course, the loyalists organized first in hopes of pre-empting the field.) As the struggle grew sharper, both sides saw the need for contact. Mass organizations everywhere began to send delegates to other places to link up with those of like mind, and also to send investigators to uncover the past records of administrators with whom they were in conflict, or the past records of movement leaders they hoped to expose. Peking students went out, as we have seen, to mobilize young rebels against the "bourgeois reactionary line," and young rebels and loyalists alike came pouring into Peking to make contact with the student organizations they most admired, to read the lively posters on Peking campuses, and to carry back to their home communities the spirit of the Peking struggle. After Mao met with a million or so Red Guards on August 18, the demand for trips to Peking increased many-fold, not only to establish contact and study revolution but to see Chairman Mao himself. Since young people, if only they showed a student card, could ride trains and buses free, over 11 million of them poured into the city during the next three months. The resources of the whole community were sorely taxed to house, feed, and care for them. All campuses and schools were temporarily converted into guest houses; Tsinghua alone at one time played host to 40,000 young visitors. The overall political effect of this extraordinary travel was to stimulate rebellion, strengthen the left, and expose the right. But a trip to Peking alone was not enough to make the issues clear, especially since the Peking student movement was split at least three ways, and since the struggle between the bourgeois reactionary line and the proletarian revolutionary line—as the struggle against the work teams came to be known—had to be fought anew in every locality.

When the weather turned cold in the fall, and after the great student migration slowed down, the Central Cultural Revolution Group called on everyone to return home to make revolution in their own backyards. The offer of free transportation for wandering youth was withdrawn. Many students obeyed this call, but many others continued to roam about, this time on foot, making long marches instead of taking long train rides. Their goals—to establish liaison, contact the masses, spark revolution in out of the way places, and visit famous historical spots. Tsu Hung-liang walked from Tsunyi in Kweichow to Shaoshan in Hunan, following in reverse the route of the Red Army on its Long March in 1935. The distance covered was 650 miles.

Kao Hung-chin, a student in the Chemical Engineering Department at Tsinghua, whose father had long been a pedicab operator in Foochow, Fukien, walked with thirteen others from Foochow to Chingkang Mountain in Kiangsi, a trip of 350 miles. His group was particularly interested in talking to old peasants who remembered the civil war days when the Workers and Peasants Red Army, led by Mao Tse-tung and Chu Teh, had made this region its base. Local authorities, nervous about the final outcome of the student rebellion, were glad to see their most militant young people depart on extended treks through the hinterland and offered them stipends of as much as 80 fen a day for as long as they might stay on the road.* With the militants out wandering, the situation at home would naturally be much more stable. Of course, if one's own young people marched away, other young people were sure to march in asking embarrassing questions and trying to mobilize those who remained at home for rebellion. The best thing to do was to treat these "outside agitators" as honored guests, give them good hotel or guest house accommodations and good food, thus co-opting them to one's own side rather than driving them to rebellion with condemnation and suppression. But if the established authorities learned fast, the young people on the move also learned fast, and on the whole they rejected the "silver-coated bullets" of the capitalist-roaders and the diversions of the Long Marches in favor of returning home to carry the revolution through to the end. It was because the majority of the Tsinghua student militants had returned to their own campus by mid-December 1966 that it became possible to form the "big al-

---

*The yuan is divided into 100 fen. One yuan today is worth about $.45.

liance" of rebels and launch the public movement for the exposure of Liu Shao-ch'i.

Since Tsinghua had been a stronghold of the capitalist-roaders in the educational field prior to 1966, and since, once the Cultural Revolution began, Tsinghua had been chosen by Liu Shao-ch'i as a concentration point for suppressing the mass movement, it also became a concentration point for the exposure and repudiation of Liu and his line once the mass movement broke free. In practice this took the form of direct confrontation with Liu's wife, Wang Kuang-mei. From the moment that Wang Kuang-mei abandoned the campus in August, the students she had oppressed demanded that she return to face criticism. After the United Regiment was founded in mid-December this demand was renewed with vigor. Again and again the students asked the Central Committee and the Central Cultural Revolution Group to send Liu's wife to the campus to face charges. Kuai Ta-fu even organized mass sit-ins in front of the Central Committee headquarters at Tungnanhai in the Forbidden City to dramatize this demand. But, so our informants told us, Mao Tse-tung and Chou En-lai did not consider the time ripe or the preparations sufficient so they did not respond.

On January 6, 1967, on the eve of the seizure of power by workers, students, and revolutionary cadre in Shanghai, Kuai and his close comrades took matters into their own hands. They persuaded Liu's daughter, Liu Tao, who had by then begun to question her past role, to prove her new revolutionary ardor by "drawing a clear line between herself and her parents." They demanded that she call her mother and say that she had been run over by a car and badly hurt. This call not only brought Wang Kuang-mei to the campus, but it brought Liu Shao-ch'i as well. Both were seized by Kuai's group. Liu himself was released and allowed to return to the city, but Wang Kuang-mei was held and brought before a mass meeting.* Bowing to a *fait accompli,* Chou En-lai went along with this confrontation on three conditions: (1) that reason and not violence be used; (2) that the students not personally humiliate their captive;

---

*Presumably Chou En-lai intervened to insist on Liu's return.

(3) that they give her adequate food and lodging, hear her self-criticism, and then send her back to Tungnanhai immediately.

Kuai reported the first two points to his followers but not the last one. The mass meeting was a fiasco. The students had not done their homework. They did not have enough facts about past line and policy to truly expose either. Only a few people spoke up and when Wang Kuang-mei answered back in refutation they became discouraged. Many left the meeting before it was over. Wang Kuang-mei was very clever. When questions touched on matters which she preferred not to discuss she claimed that they violated security: "In regard to this I can only tell Mao Tse-tung or the Central Committee. I cannot reveal state secrets," she said.

Thus she frustrated her questioners. Unable to beat her down with facts and arguments, Kuai finally took her off the stage; but instead of sending her back to the city he held her incommunicado while his lieutenants grilled and threatened her in private. It was all to no avail. This whole affair violated Central Committee directives, violated Mao Tse-tung's policies, and exposed in one ominous flash what the future might hold in store once students came to power.

By April the movement for the repudiation of Liu Shao-ch'i had matured. A vast amount of information had been gathered from all over the country. Mao Tse-tung and Chou En-lai apparently felt that the time was now ripe and so, when the Tsinghua rebels again asked for a confrontation with Wang Kuang-mei, they agreed. On April 7 an editorial on the "bourgeois reactionary line" of the Tsinghua Work Team entitled "Hit Hard at Many in Order to Protect a Handful" was printed in *Red Flag*, the Communist Party theoretical magazine that circulates nationwide. This article attacked Wang Kuang-mei by name and detailed her mistakes on the campus. On April 10 she was turned over to the United Chingkangshan Regiment and brought before a huge mass meeting—a meeting of approximately half a million people, some of whom came from as far away as Paoting and Tientsin in Hopei. This time the preparations had been thorough and the masses had been mobilized: a sound truck had crisscrossed the city announcing the confrontation, posters had been distributed far and wide, and over three hundred organizations, including schools and factories, had been invited. Some of them had sent delegations, others had simply declared a holiday, closed their doors, and sent everyone out to the campus. Buses blocked the roads for miles and the sea of people overflowed the University grounds and out into the surrounding area so that loudspeakers had to be set up beyond the campus gates.

Thousands of Tsinghua students and teachers had worked day and night to sum up Liu's record both before and during the Cultural Revolution. All possible material had been brought together, sifted, organized, and then written out. In the center of the campus the repudiation posters dominated everything. Both sides of the main road were completely lined with them. In addition, all over Peking special reed mats had been erected for posting anti-Liu material and they were hung with statements, cartoons, pictures, and rhymes, giving the whole city a festive air.

Behind this huge effort lay the special Headquarters to Direct the Struggle Against Wang Kuang-mei. It had many teams—teams for posters, teams for handling outsiders, teams for physical arrangements, etc.

"When we saw Wang Kuang-mei standing there with her head down, listening to us, and we remembered the previous summer when she had pressed us down so hard, we thought we really had stood up!" said Tsu.

At the meeting Wang Kuang-mei was asked to stand on a platform made of four chairs. She stood high enough so that tens of thousands could see her. On her head she wore a ridiculous, wide-brimmed straw hat of the kind worn by English aristocrats at garden parties. Around her neck hung a string of ping-pong balls painted bright yellow to simulate gold. A tight-fitting formal gown clung to her plump body and sharp-pointed high-heeled shoes adorned her feet. The whole outfit was grotesque, designed to mock the fine clothes she had worn while on a state visit to Indonesia a few years before.

"This was not a good thing," said Tsu. "It was a violation

of policy. It was designed to humiliate her personally, and it undermined serious struggle against her ideology. The important thing was not to ridicule her bourgeois appearance, but to expose her wrong line and her methods of work."

Behind Wang Kuang-mei stood six leading cadre who had played an adverse role in the history of the University—P'eng Chen, former mayor of Peking; Lu Ting-yi, former head of the Propaganda Department of the Communist Party; Chiang Nan-hsiang, former Minister of Higher Education and President of Tsinghua; Po Yi-p'o, chairman of the State Economic Commission; Liang T'ien-feng, former Minister of Forestry and a vice-leader of the Tsinghua Work Team; and Yeh Lin, leader of the Work Team. All six spoke during the meeting, criticizing their own past mistakes and criticizing Wang Kuang-mei. But before they spoke several victims of Liu's busy wife spoke out against her.

The meeting was opened by two Red Guards who had been called counter-revolutionaries of the fourth category. One of them had been so hard pressed that he had tried to commit suicide on a railroad track. His leg was badly mangled. He was followed by one of the "set-aside" cadres,* and then by a peasant from the Peach Orchard brigade where Wang Kuang-mei had removed honest revolutionaries from office in favor of incompetent sycophants.

The masses, aroused by the accusations made by Wang Kuang-mei's victims, shouted angry slogans. "Down with Liu, Teng, and T'ao!† Down with cow-devils and snake-gods! Carry

---

*A "set-aside" cadre is a cadre suspended from office by a work team (acting from above) or by a mass movement (acting from below). "Set aside" does not mean dismissed, but simply suspended pending investigation. Such a cadre could be restored to office, or, in rare cases, could be permanently demoted or transferred.

†"Liu, Teng, and T'ao" refers to Liu Shao-ch'i; Ten Hsaio-p'ing, secretary of the Communist Party and Liu's most important collaborator; and T'ao Ch'u, who came up from the South China Party Committee to join the Cultural Revolution Group of the Central Committee—only to initiate ultra-left, "overthrow-all" policies which supported Liu.

the revolution through to the end!" These shouts from tens of thousands of throats rolled through the campus and the surrounding Haitien district like sea waves. They pounded the plump figure of Wang Kuang-mei in her straw hat and her ping-pong ball necklace until it seemed she could no longer stand, but stand she did and the meeting went on—P'eng Chen . . . Lu Ting-yi . . . Yeh Lin . . . There was even an American speaker, Sidney Rittenberg, who spoke for the rebels of Radio Peking and brought international greetings and support.

The chairman and chief organizer of this huge demonstration was Kuai Ta-fu. All the threads of authority led to him as the leader of the Tsinghua University Chingkangshan United Regiment, the most famous and the most prestigious Red Guard detachment in the whole of China. If Kuai's name was not already a household word, this meeting helped make it so.

The mass confrontation with Wang Kuang-mei marked the high point of the repudiation of capitalist-roaders in Peking. The apparent unity and enthusiasm of the participants left everyone with a sense of power, purpose, and accomplishment. But, in fact, serious friction had already arisen inside the Chingkangshan Regiment, frictions that were eroding the unity, the purpose, and the accomplishments of the rebel students even as they consolidated their newly won positions of prestige and power at the University.

9
Split

What the rebel left seized in December 1966 was not power to run the University, but only the right to lead the mass movement. When the Tsinghua Red Guards broke up and burned their official seal, the left, united as the Chingkangshan Regiment, won a guarantee that its posters would go up, that its voice would be heard, that the printing presses, speaking halls, and microphones would be available to its spokesmen. This was not administrative power, still less Party power, but it was effective power over the mass movement, power to lead the rank-and-file of the students, the lower cadre, and the staff.

The January Storm in Shanghai* raised the whole national struggle to a new level. The question of real administrative power, full control of Party and state, came on the agenda at every level and in every institution in the land. And often it was Tsinghua Chingkangshan Regiment rebels, who maintained liaison stations in every major city, who put this issue forward most actively and made sure that it was acted on. Wherever Chingkangshan Regiment people appeared they were listened to with respect, even with awe, and when revolutionary committees later came to power all over the country, seats were either held by Regiment delegates or seats were set aside for them, when and if they should appear. Tsinghua Chingkangshaners helped seize power in Shanghai and co-sponsored the famous seize-power proclamation of Revolutionary Rebels that shook the whole nation on January 6. When Liu Ke-p'ing set up his new government in Shansi province a few weeks later, a Tsinghua Chingkangshaner sat on his committee.

Back on the Tsinghua campus the Regiment did not fare so well. While it held de facto power for brief periods, it never was able to set up a legitimate University administration. In January the Chingkangshaners seized and burned the official seal held by the Preparatory Committee and set up a new administrative committee to run things. But this was only an interim committee. It could not be the final organ of power because the Peking Municipal Committee and the Central Committee of the Communist Party would only recognize as legitimate a revolutionary committee based on a "three-in-one combination"—that is, on a combination of representatives of mass organizations, of the armed forces, and of the old revolutionary cade.† The Tsinghua administrative committee that crystallized

---

*When workers, students, and revolutionary cadre seized state power in China's largest city.

†"Three-in-one combination" has three meanings. It can be, as here, a combination of popular leaders, old cadres, and army men;

in early 1967 was really only an arm of the Chingkangshan Regiment. Since it represented only one mass organization it could not possibly be called a three-in-one revolutionary committee. Before a viable committee could be set up it was necessary to await the return of large numbers of students still away on Long Marches or manning distant liaison centers, the active involvement of "good" or "comparatively good" cadres, all of whom had been "set aside" by the Work Team, and the selection of some cadre from the armed forces, possibly from the navy work team that had come to help transform education. By April these conditions could all be met, but just when the coalition became possible the Chingkangshan Regiment split.

The split came over the old cadre—which of them could be trusted, which could be called revolutionary, which could be drawn into the new ruling committee to help transform Tsinghua into a "proletarian" rather than a "bourgeois" university.

One group of students held the view that Tsinghua was the rottenest spot in the whole education set-up and had been under a bourgeois dictatorship for seventeen years; hence *all* the old cadre were rotten to the core—hopeless capitalist-roaders. To find honest revolutionary cadre one had to seek out those who had been isolated, oppressed, and attacked in the years prior to 1966. In other words, only those known as rightists and counter-revolutionaries in the past had some reason to rate as revolutionaries today. In coming to this conclusion, the students were reasoning from their own experience during the fifty-day "white terror," when those students who had then been called revolutionary were really conservative or reactionary, while those who had been called counter-revolutionary were really the revolutionaries. Students who took this position rejected all cadre who had held power before; they reached out a hand to the misfits, the targets of past cam-

---

or it can be old, middle-aged, and young; or it can be workers, technicians, and cadres, as in the scientific research groups set up as a result of the Cultural Revolution. "Three-in-one" is most often used in the first sense.

paigns. This position was reinforced by a rebellious group of teachers and staff called the Red Teachers Union, which was led by just such a group of former misfits who had brought together a questionable assortment of malcontents for the purpose of completely overthrowing the old Tsinghua.

Another group of students considered the wholesale rejection of old cadre to be an ultra-left position, one which violated Mao Tse-tung's policy of curing the disease to save the patient and uniting all those who could be united to oppose the main enemy. They did not agree that Tsinghua's history since 1949 had been nothing but seventeen years of bourgeois dictatorship; nor did they agree that all the targets of previous movements had really been revolutionaries framed under right-wing attacks. Some of those "targets," they thought, really *were* rightists and antisocialist elements. This group of students was ready to rehabilitate and unite with most of the cadres who had been "set aside" by the work team. Their position found support in a Central Committee directive of March 1, 1967, which said in part:

> It must . . . be soberly recognized that most of the cadres are good, and that the alien class elements who have wormed their way into the ranks of the cadres are very few in number. . . . To refuse to make a class analysis of persons in authority and instead to suspect, negate, exclude, and overthrow them all indiscriminately is an anarchist trend of thought.

That two lines in the Chingkangshan Regiment emerged on the question of cadres was no accident. Those lines could be traced back to the original positions of many of the participants. It was Kuai Ta-fu and his hard-core Chingkangshan rebels, the former "counter-revolutionaries" of the fourth category, who rejected most if not all of the old cadres; and it was, in the main, former loyalists of the old 8-9s, later the Tsinghua Red Guards, who wanted to rehabilitate most if not all of the old cadres. The former 8-8s, the Mao Tse-tung Thought Red Guards, split on this issue, some going along with

Kuai and the extremists, some joining the 8-9s in their support of the majority of the cadre.

These differences over old cadres might not have been enough by themselves to split the Regiment if its members had been firmly united in other ways. But in fact the original Chingkangshan militants had never accepted the old 8-9s as revolutionaries. They considered them opportunists who jumped on the anti-Liu bandwagon only when to do otherwise made them politically suspect. Whenever differences arose they called the 8-9s "Liu supporters" and hardly listened to what they had to say. Furthermore, the Chingkangshan rebels also attacked the former 8-8s because they had not fought hard enough to "reverse the case" on Kuai and his "fourth category" people. Kuai attacked them as waverers, and some of his supporters said they were "nothing but little landlords with red strips of cloth hanging around their arms. They're even worse than the 8-9s!"

This kind of attack drove sympathetic 8-8s away. Some of them stuck with Kuai, but others joined up with former loyalists to oppose him. The struggle escalated on April 14, when all those who favored a policy of uniting with the majority of the old cadres met to caucus for their position under the slogan, "Thoroughly repudiate the bourgeois reactionary line on cadres." At this meeting they formulated an independent policy and asked Regiment headquarters for time on the campus loudspeakers to publicize their view. But the leaders of the Chingkangshan Regiment, dominated by its chairman Kuai, told them: "You are only a part of the Regiment. You can't air minority views over the loudspeaker. You can't express an independent position." This angered the caucus group and drove them into one coherent faction. When Kuai and his supporters tried on April 30 to set up a revolutionary committee which contained only cadres they trusted, the whole issue came to a head. The opposition left the Regiment and set up a separate organization which they called the Tsinghua Chingkangshan April 14 Regiment. It came to be known, for short, as the 4s. Kuai's group retained its original name, Tsinghua University

Chingkangshan Regiment, and became known simply as the Regiment.

To the young militants on both sides who quarreled over this issue, it seemed very real, very basic.

"We were involved in serious struggle over the old cadres," said Tsu, who was one of the 8-8s who chose to stick with the Regiment. "They said setting up a revolutionary committee with only the cadres we liked on it was equivalent to capitalist restoration. But we thought, if we can't set up a revolutionary committee this month, when we die we won't be able to shut our eyes. We thought if we accepted their nominations, the old Tsinghua would be restored for sure, and we wept as we debated among ourselves."

"As for us," said Jen Yen-sheng, a former 8-8 who joined the 4s, "Lin Chieh, the editor of *Red Flag*, gave us support. He said, 'I think you 4s are acting according to Mao Tse-tung Thought.' So we assumed that we had the support of the Central Committee. One of the cadres whom we trusted, Li Kang—his case has not been settled, at a minimum he committed some serious capitalist-road mistakes—said at our meeting that the cadres supported by the Regiment were all rotten, they were nothing but leftover landlords, rich peasants, rightists, and bad elements who had hated socialism for seventeen years. For them to come to power would indeed be a restoration. Then he pointed out certain ones: 'See, he's the bad one, he's the one who is spreading all the rotten ideas'—thus he mobilized us for a showdown struggle."

If Lin Chieh and Li Kang urged the 4s on, Ch'i Pen-yu, of the Central Cultural Revolution Group, and the cadres in the Red Teachers Union urged the Regiment on. Said Ch'i, "You Regiment people are the real revolutionaries, you are the core." Cadres of the Red Teachers Union said, "You are the red flag of the whole country. Look how many 8-9s there are on the other side. If you ever allow them on the stage the Cultural Revolution will be defeated. On this issue you must struggle to the end!"

Once the Chingkangshan Regiment split organizationally, the rift grew steadily wider. Even though at the bottom, among the rank-and-file, there always existed a desire for a united movement, the leaders on both sides denounced each other ever more vehemently. The members of each leading group thought that only they were revolutionary and that only they should wield power.

"We are famous throughout the country as staunch, hard-core 'iron-rod' rebels," shouted the Regiment adherents as they cursed the 4s.

"We are the true proletarian revolutionary rebels of the Tsinghua campus," shouted the 4s as they cursed the Regiment.

Later, when Mao Tse-tung issued his famous directive that the Cultural Revolution was the continuation of the fight between the Kuomintang and the Communist Party, each side quickly denounced the other as the Kuomintang of today, and each was convinced that its struggle at Tsinghua was a reflection of the life-and-death struggle between the bourgeoisie and the proletariat then underway in the Central Committee. In this atmosphere every small disagreement was soon elevated to an important question of principle and was seen as a part of a showdown struggle between revolution and counter-revolution. The students involved were even receptive to those who said, "Yes indeed, this is a struggle between the Kuomintang and the Communist Party and such a struggle cannot be settled by words, it must be settled by arms, it must be settled with guns!" Among those who spoke like this were a number who were consciously provocateurs.

About a year after the split, armed struggle did break out between the Regiment and the 4s, but in April 1967 no one anticipated such serious escalation. The leaders on each side, anxious to seize and wield power in the name of revolution and Mao Tse-tung Thought, only wanted to expose and defeat the other side politically. Once convinced that the opposition was indeed counter-revolutionary, they threw principle out the window and held that all means were justifiable if they led to victory. Each side tried hard to lead the other into making political mistakes and then to seize on these mistakes. In order to do this, each tried to unite into a very tight fighting team, vigorously denying all its mistakes and weaknesses while exaggerating and holding up to ridicule and scorn the mistakes and weaknesses of the other side.

Each side adopted an opportunist attitude toward Mao Tse-tung Thought—if any formulation or directive aided them they would proclaim it to the skies, but if it was against their interests they would ignore it. When Mao Tse-tung criticized all those who thought only they were the "center," that no one else could possibly be as revolutionary as they were, both the Regiment and the 4s held a mirror up to the other side asking, "How can you think only you are the center?" while failing completely to hold the mirror up to themselves and ask, "Why do we think that only we are the center?"

When Mao Tse-tung said that it was important to make a class analysis of factionalism, each side grabbed at the idea. The 4s said the Regiment had an ultra-left position because their class base was petty bourgeois, while the Regiment said the 4s had a right opportunist position because they were not just petty bourgeois but bourgeois . . . period! From this it was an easy step for each side to claim—and to believe, as we have seen—that the other represented the Kuomintang.

This developing factionalism also made it easy for each side to distort the other's position, especially with regard to cadres. The 4s were not, of course, in favor of rehabilitating all the old cadres: they were for making distinctions, for repudiating mistakes, for bringing back into the political arena only those who recognized their mistakes and wanted to take the socialist road. At the same time, the Regiment was not for rejecting everyone: they too wanted to unite with the best of the old cadres. But since the 4s stressed *rehabilitation* and the Regiment stressed *repudiation,* the two positions were counterposed and simplified until they seemed to be in direct opposition. What it amounted to in practice was that any cadre proposed by the Regiment for inclusion on the revolutionary committee was automatically rejected by the 4s, and any cadre proposed by the 4s was automatically rejected by the Regiment. The cadres picked by each side were not chosen on the basis of any careful analysis, any thorough investigation into their records, but only because they expressed support for one

side or the other. "If you support me I will back you; if you
support the other side I will attack you." Thus each side built
cadre support in an unprincipled way and each side, as was
later revealed, brought into its ranks very questionable people
—class enemies, former Kuomintang officials, wreckers, and
counter-revolutionaries, along with many "good" and "relatively
good" revolutionary people.

Those national leaders on the Central Cultural Revolution
Group who concerned themselves most with student affairs
did nothing to overcome this burgeoning factionalism. On the
contrary, men like Ch'i Pen-yu, then a hero to the rebels, encouraged it. He told the 4s, "Your position is in accord with
Mao Tse-tung Thought, you should persist in it." At the same
time he told the Regiment, "You are the real revolutionaries
and you should be the core of the power structure at Tsinghua."
With this kind of encouragement from above the divisions
could only grow deeper and sharper.

"We developed three interlocking mistaken viewpoints,"
said Tsu. "First, we misjudged ourselves. We thought, 'We are
perfect flowers and the others are garbage.' Second, we misjudged the masses who held different views. We cursed them
either as loyalists or ultra-leftists. Third, we liked those cadres
who agreed with us and disliked those who disagreed—whoever disagrees with me is bad!

"The result? Each side tried to crush the other, to 'stink
it out' politically. We picked what we found useful in Mao
Tse-tung Thought and disregarded what was not so useful.
What a change in attitude! When we had been rebels suppressed
by the Work Team we had studied Chairman Mao with tears
in our eyes and valued every sentence. But when we came to
power in the mass movement all that changed. We suddenly
became very jeolous of our power. We only chose things from
Chairman Mao that would support our position and not things
which would show it up as false. We were afraid other people
would take away our power, but we didn't really consider how
to use our power to serve the people!"

Once the split occurred the two organizations on the
Tsinghua campus conducted parallel activities that were very

similar in political content, but they refused to unite in carrying them out. Instead, each sought to be the vanguard in the struggle to carry on the revolution and each ignored or attacked the activities of the other.

"What sort of activities did we undertake? Well, at first there was a mass movement for the repudiation of Liu Shaoch'i's book *On the Self-Cultivation of Communists*," said Tsu. "This followed the April confrontation with Wang Kuang-mei. Later many students went out into the countryside to promote revolution and grasp production. We also had a movement to repudiate the revisionist educational line at Tsinghua. All of these movements could have been carried out together by the rank-and-file of the two organizations, but power remained in the hands of the leaders and they never allowed any activity to unite the factions.

"Take our movement to repudiate revisionist education. Each faction held separate meetings. The content of the study might be the same, but we didn't sit together. Both groups marched in parades and rallies, but we didn't march along the same routes, or depart and arrive at the same time. Sometimes we even raced to see who could get to mass meetings in the city first. Many of these things seem like jokes now, when we look back on it. There were so many silly things! Whenever a new directive of Mao's came out we rushed to put up posters celebrating it. If the other side had a very nice poster in a prominent place before we got there, we would paste paper over their signature and write our signature on it. We also raced to see who could read new directives over the loudspeaker first and thus prove the greatest loyalty. The side that spoke last was either less loyal or not loyal at all. Thus we labeled each other anti-Maoist! We also sought to serve our factional interests with each new Mao Tse-tung quote, racking our brains to think how it could be used against the opposition.

"Even physical defects and small personal quirks became grist for our mill. For instance, Shen Ju-huai, the head of the 4s, had one eye that was fixed in a permanent squint. Even though he had good 20-20 vision in both eyes, we called him 'slant-eyed Shen' or 'dead-eye Shen.'"

Underlying this intense rivalry there was, in fact, one level at which the two organizations cooperated—the financial. Divided as they were on political issues, they were still able to get together to sign the vouchers which the State Bank demanded before issuing funds. Prior to June 1966, the Financial Department of the University had handled disbursements approved by the administration. When the Work Team came, its leading cadres decided such matters. After the Work Team left, the Preparatory Committee took over the task—with the result that the rebels were unable to get money for paper, ink, or loudspeakers. When the United Chingkangshan Regiment replaced the Preparatory Committee as the real power on campus, the Regiment leaders won the power to direct financial expenditures; but after the United Regiment split, a split which divided the cadres and staff of the Financial Department into two hostile camps, the State Bank did not dare play favorites. Its cadres demanded papers stamped with the seals of both sides before disbursing funds. Since no one could live or carry on any struggle at all without the money provided by the State Bank, the two sides got together each week long enough to arrange for their living allowances and other necessary funds. In everything else they went their separate ways.

The factional split at Tsinghua was by no means unique. Similar cracks in the mass movement appeared at about the same time at all the major universities and in industrial, commercial, and government units as well. The underlying cause for this is difficult to understand, but in general, as the mass movement developed in the course of two-line struggle in China's socialist society, it tended to split and bog down into an unprincipled struggle for power between factional leaders. Mao Tse-tung has called this "bourgeois factionalism." The unprincipled struggle was definitely linked to the latent bourgeois ideology of the various contenders for power, who started as rebels in legitimate struggle against reactionary oppressors and ended up quarreling over personal prestige and position. In the process they degenerated from honest revolutionaries into scheming careerists, while conscious reactionaries left over from the old society stepped into the fray waving false red

flags and sometimes ended up as leaders of the whole movement. This latter phenomenon was summed up by Mao Tse-
tung when he said: "Factionalism shields counter-revolutionaries
and counter-revolutionaries make use of factionalism."

Another general characteristic of this process was that the
contending forces always reduced themselves to two. At the
start, many trends appeared and vied with one another, but
sooner or later they joined, merged, or dissolved until only
two were left. Third forces, middle forces, could not stand.
They either distintegrated, their membership going as individuals to opposite sides, or they split and went two ways, or they
fell as a block to one side or the other. The most striking parallel
to this in the Western world is the American two-party system,
which could surely be aptly called a system of "bourgeois factionalism." Here third forces arise over and over again and,
unable to stand, are sooner or later absorbed into one side or
the other.

A third characteristic of the mass movement seemed to be
that the factions sought outside support and teamed up with
like forces elsewhere. Here the matter got complicated, because
in practice the link-ups did not always follow any obvious
political logic. In Peking the militant rebels of the Geological
Institute, led by Wang Ta-ping, were much closer ideologically
to Kuai Ta-fu's Regiment than the New Peita Commune, led
by Nieh Yuan-tzu, who throughout the work team period was
a functioning member of the Peita Work Team. Yet in part
because Wang Ta-ping was critical of some aspects of Kuai
Ta-fu's program, he linked up with the 4s on the Tsinghua
campus and thereby earned the undying enmity of Kuai and
the Regiment. They, in retaliation, linked up with Nieh Yuan-
tzu's New Peita Commune and Han Ai-ch'ing's Red Flag
Regiment to form the "Heaven" or "Sky" Faction (so named
because its main center was the Aeronautical Institute). The
other famous student rebel was Tan Hou-lan, from the Normal
College. She linked up with Wang Ta-ping to help form the
"Earth" Faction (so named because the Geological Institute's
East Is Red Commune was its main center).

Gradually all the other factional organizations in the Pek-

ing area linked up with either Heaven or Earth and bitterly
attacked one another, even though they were often closer to
individual organizations on the opposite side than they were to
many of those on their own side.* Temporary alliances on some
overriding issue of the moment led to permanent alliances with
either Heaven or Earth that completely obscured the original
splits that had brought the factions into being. The underlying
basic disagreements—*Pao* and *Ke* (protect and rebel)—which
had set the students, cadres, and workers at loggerheads in the
first place, got all mixed up as groups crossed lines for temporary advantages. In the end the only consistent principle was,
"The friend of my friend is a friend and the enemy of my friend
is an enemy." After a few sharp fights enough bitterness was
generated to keep these feuds going indefinitely.

At the core of both Heaven and Earth stood "good" rebels
who had fought hard against the work teams and their bourgeois reactionary line. Yet they fought each other endlessly
until Mao Tse-tung intervened in ways that will be described
later.

Where in all this did the Red Guard First, Second, and
Third Headquarters, so prominently reported in the Western
press, enter in? First Headquarters was set up by loyalists who
worked with and defended the work teams in the summer of
1966—that is, by the likes of Liu Tao and Ho Peng-fei. Second
Headquarters was set up by groups like the Mao Tse-tung
Thought Red Guards (the 8-8s) at Tsinghua who opposed the
teams but were not willing to go to bat for those denounced as
"counter-revolutionaries." Third Headquarters was set up by
Kuai Ta-fu and others like him who had taken the brunt of
the bourgeois reactionary line in 1966, only to emerge victorious
in the fall. The Red Guard Representatives Congress that was
established in Peking in February 1967 was conceived as a
merger of all three of those headquarters, but actually the ma-

---

*Two important units of the Earth Faction were the Peita Ching-
kangshan Regiment and the Normal College Chingkangshan Regiment, both originally inspired by Kuai Ta-fu's Tsinghua Chingkangshan Regiment and close to it ideologically.

jority of its leaders were from Third Headquarters because by that time the other two had lost most of their support.

All five of the most famous Red Guard leaders—Kuai Ta-fu, Tan Hou-lan, Wang Ta-ping, Han Ai-ch'ing, and Nieh Yuan-tzu, each the leader of the mass movement at a large university or institute—were top cadre in the Red Guard Representatives Congress. Of these all but Nieh had been early rebels. Yet they fought each other on opposite sides as Heaven and Earth throughout 1967 and most of 1968, and helped spark similar factional strife throughout the length and breadth of China.

10
Pay Attention to
State Affairs

For Tsinghua students concerned about revolution the big events of 1967 did not take place on the campus but out in the streets of Peking and in the other big cities across the nation where Peking students on liaison sparked massive political upheavals that often ended in armed clashes.

The most important of the many demonstrations and actions in the capital in which students played a major part were the "pull out Liu" sit-in and the sacking of the British Mission. On a nationwide scale, the campaign to "pull a handful out of the army" overshadowed all other actions. These three movements overlapped and were interrelated. The "pull out Liu" sit-in took place outside the Central Committee offices at Tungnanhai from July 18 to August 5. It had hardly got ten underway when the Wuhan incident broke out in the triple cities of Hupei on July 20.* The Wuhan incident served as the trigger for a wide-ranging attack on the commanders of military regions

---

*The Wuhan incident was a warlord-style revolt of the local military commander, Ch'en Ts'ai-tao, who defied Central Government directives and emissaries in July 1967.

throughout the country which was still going strong when the assault on the British Mission in Peking occurred on August 22.

The two common threads that ran through these three events were defiance of central leadership—as embodied in Premier Chou En-lai, who appears to have had Mao's backing throughout—by large numbers of student radicals backed up by some mass organizations of young workers and cadres, and the collusion of Wang Li, Kuang Feng, and Ch'i Pen-yu of the Central Cultural Revolution Group in instigating and mobilizing this defiance. Their goal was to break the power of the leading group around Mao Tse-tung, especially the power of Chou En-lai, and to break the unity of the People's Liberation Army. It was a formula for seizing power from Mao Tse-tung in the guise of protecting the Chairman and his line. Most of the people involved, however, were completely unaware of the larger aims.

The "pull out Liu" affair began, apparently innocently enough, on July 10 when the Old August 1st Regiment of the Civil Engineering Institute (a student faction) went to Tung-nanhai to protest the fact that Liu Shao-ch'i, who had directly suppressed all the students of the Institute during the work team period, had sent a self-criticism only to the New August 1st Regiment (an opposing faction). The Old August 1st members decided to confront Liu in person and went to camp in the street outside Tungnanhai, where he was living under the protection of—and simultaneously as a prisoner of—the Central Committee. At first only four other organizations joined in, forming a small but raucous knot of people who blocked a side street and shouted, "Pull out Liu."

Premier Chou En-lai, Vice-Premier Li Hsien-nien, and the commander of Mao Tse-tung's bodyguard, Wang Tung-hsing, had all made clear again and again that Liu should not be criticized and repudiated face-to-face, but back-to-back—that is, not in person, but in society, through speeches, rallies, articles, broadcasts, and cartoons. But Kuang Feng and Ch'i Pen-yu (Wang Li was then traveling in the South) saw in this small demonstration a chance to mount a major offensive and so spread the word through a nationally known student leader, Kuai Ta-fu, that Liu was not sincere, that he would not admit his errors, that he accused the Central Cultural Revolution Group of framing him. They urged mass action to put pressure on the former head of state and force him to speak honestly.

This call was all that was needed to bring the students of Peking and their allies among the masses into the streets. At Tsinghua the Regiment and the 4s vied with one another to see who could mobilize the largest contingent to repudiate Liu, who could get to the city first to command the most strategic location near the West Gate of Tungnanhai, and who could set up the most powerful loudspeaker to blast forth its condemnation. Since the 4s were not nearly as well known as the Regiment, they tried especially hard to gain fame through this action. They cut through the grounds of the Geological Institute on their way to the city to get ahead of their rivals and even sent a truck with poles and reed mats to Tungnanhai to occupy a favorable spot with a permanent "Pull Out Liu" headquarters, which they manned day and night for almost three weeks. The Regiment, confident of its nationwide reputation, joined in the first day's parades and speeches but camped only one night in the streets before retiring to the more comfortable quarters of the Tsinghua campus.

The Regiment's lukewarm attitude did not suit Ch'i Pen-yu. He telephoned Kuai on July 26 and told him, "'Pull out Liu' is the central task of this period. How can the Regiment fall behind?" Thereupon Kuai hurriedly organized a contingent to return to the city to see the affair through to the end.

Indeed, the Regiment youth returned to a most remarkable scene, unprecedented in the history of Peking or any other capital. Hundreds of thousands of people were permanently encamped in the streets around the Central Committee headquarters. Banners and streamers flew overhead, slogans were plastered on every available wall and mat, loudspeakers blared from a hundred locations, and cooking fires sent up their smoke and aroma from as many makeshift kitchens. The people, most of them young, had sat through heavy rain, cold dawns, and hot noons. They were browned, dirty, tired, but enthusiastic, each day thinking that this day at last Liu Shao-ch'i would be delivered over to them to be thoroughly repudiated, once and for all.

The din created by this huge crowd, and especially by the competing loudspeakers, made it impossible for Central Committee members behind the red walls to sleep. Desperate, the leaders of the nation finally negotiated for silent mornings so that they could catch a few hours of rest. But once the agreed time had elapsed each day the loudspeakers blared forth with more vigor than ever.

The responsible leaders of the Central Committee, including Chairman Mao, had no intention of turning Liu over to the masses, for obviously what might happen to him under the circumstances could hardly be controlled. Instead they sent emissaries to urge the people to decamp. But Ch'i Pen-yu whipped up the crowds again and again by saying that Mao's strategy was not to give in right away, since that would end the affair, but to hold off until the movement mounted to its highest pitch of numbers and enthusiasm. "If you mobilize more people and repudiate Liu more profoundly, in the end you are bound to succeed," said Ch'i.

When August 5, the anniversary of Mao Tse-tung's "Bombard the Headquarters" big-character poster, came around, the people in the street thought surely this would be the day. The various factions decided to take turns holding meetings in front of the West Gate. But since each wanted to be sure to be there to grab Liu when he came out, those adhering to the Earth Faction began to physically assault those belonging to the Heaven Faction, hoping to drive them off and take their place. What began as a unified movement to confront Liu looked as if it might end in a major street brawl with hundreds hurt.

At 1 P.M. the West Gate opened, but instead of Liu Shao-ch'i, Vice-Premier Hsieh Fu-chih, head of Peking's Revolutionary Committee, emerged. In the name of the Central Committee and Chairman Mao Tse-tung, he urged everyone to go home. Finally convinced that their demonstration would not be successful, some factions left right away. Others caucused and left the next day. By the evening of August 6 the "pull out Liu" movement had collapsed completely.

What most of the participants never knew was that under cover of this unprecedented demonstration a small group of ultra-left rebels had been mobilized to seize and hold Chou En-lai, should he come forth. Their theory was that if the demonstration was big enough and lasted long enough Chou would have to come out to calm things down. Then the militants would seize him. In the ensuing chaos others on the Central Committee, probably meaning Ch'en Po-ta, could make their move toward the seats of power.

In the meantime the Wuhan incident occurred in the south. This gave the militant rebel movement a new *cause célèbre* around which to rally the nationwide struggle. Ch'en Ts'ai-tao, commander of the Wuhan Military Region, had backed a mass organization primarily composed of workers called the Million Heroes, and had used Independent Division 8201 to suppress several left factions of students and workers who were calling for his overthrow. Hundreds had been wounded and dozens killed by the time Hsieh Fu-chih and Wang Li arrived in the name of the Central Cultural Revolution Group to try to settle the affair. When these two told Ch'en that his support for one side against the other was wrong and that his use of troops was unconscionable, the regional commander, in the tradition of the warlords of old, arrested the representatives of the central government and held them for questioning. They were roughly handled by the troops that took them in, and rumor had it that Wang Li's leg was broken. Chou En-lai had to fly down to effect the release of his representatives. Reluctant to land at the Wuhan airfield when he found that it was surrounded by tanks and large numbers of the Million Heroes, and concerned that he himself might be kidnapped, Chou landed at a field that was held by loyal air force contingents. He proceeded overland to negotiations which eventually brought about the release of Hsieh and Wang and the surrender of Ch'en, who returned to Peking for criticism and presumably punishment.

That Ch'en, a capitalist-roader notorious for his suppression of the left, would dare defy the Central Cultural Revolution Group confirmed the worst fears of the student rebels such as Kuai Ta-fu who had long believed after discussions with Wang Li, Kuang Feng, and Ch'i Pen-yu, that the country was in imminent danger from a right-wing coup d'état spearheaded by reactionary army commanders. As early as April 1967, Wang Li had made an analysis of the overall situation in which he claimed that once Liu Shao-ch'i and Teng Hsiao-p'ing had been overthrown, other Liu's and Teng's with guns (Party people in authority taking the capitalist road in the army) would try to take their place. Mao Tse-tung and the proletarian headquarters at the center were threatened by a multilayered encirclement, Wang Li averred; the first layer was the conservative peasant organizations in the countryside, the second layer was a right-wing trend backed by the army in Shansi,* the third layer was the capitalist-road commanders holding power in various military regions, and the fourth layer was the ring forged by the reactionaries on Taiwan, their imperialist backers in Japan and the United States, and the social imperialist power on the northern borders. Without increased vigilance and an energetic mobilization of the masses, Mao's line was in danger of defeat and the Cultural Revolution could end in a counter-revolutionary triumph.

As a first step in avoiding these possibilities, Wang Li advised the well-known rebel factions to set up a network of correspondents to concentrate on gathering information on the doings of the military throughout the country. Acting quickly, Kuai Ta-fu set up, with Regiment command, a Military Information Group which reported directly to him and sent out personnel to such important military regions as Peking, Nanking, Chengtu, Shenyang, Wuhan, Canton, and Foochow.

These correspondents went out under the auspices of the Regiment and carried with them letters of introduction not only from their own commander Kuai, but from Wang Li, Kuang Feng, and Ch'i Pen-yu of the Central Cultural Revolution Group,

---

*One Shansi faction then thought to be conservative was led by the commander of all provincial armed forces, Chang Er-ching.

and from Yang Ch'eng-wu, the acting chief-of-staff of the People's Liberation Army (PLA), or from Hsiao Hua of the General Political Department of the People's Liberation Army. The credentials helped these brash students gain entrance into regional military headquarters, and to gather vital intelligence about the armed forces all over the country. Summaries of their findings were sent to Kuai, who correlated the material on a big military map in his Tsinghua headquarters. To ensure systematic coverage, Kuai developed an "Outline for Military Investigation" which was printed up in 200 copies. This outline called for investigating the important leaders of each military region and sub-region, including commanders of security forces and fighting troops—their appearance, history, political statements, and activities during the Cultural Revolution. It also called for learning how each regional command was organized, how its troops were transferred and deployed, what military installations it controlled, and what bridges, airports, rail lines, and highways served it. Complete lists of the names of army cadres were sought and successfully copied for at least four of the main military regions—Canton, Nanking Shenyang, and Foochow. Figures on the total number of military personnel in the army, navy, and air force were also compiled. Kuai's master map was soon crowded with military data, much of it hitherto secret.

The Military Information Group and its intelligence effort was thus established as a serious effort on the part of revolutionary students to prepare for any lethal challenge to the revolution on the part of sworn enemies of Mao Tse-tung. If in order to defend Mao they had to seek out and correlate secret military information, so be it. If in order to defend Mao, they had to take up guns clandestinely and prepare for battle in the hills, so be it. They were prepared to make any sacrifice, including that of their lives, for Mao Tse-tung and the socialist revolution. It is unlikely that at this time any of the young militants seriously considered the possibility that their actions might later be used in a provocation against the PLA at a time when the PLA had become the main piller of Chairman Mao's strategy for ending factional fighting. As they saw it, they were rallying to defend Mao Tse-tung in the midst of a very dangerous crisis.

Ch'en Ts'ai-tao's mutinous behavior seemed to lend substance to this whole thesis. If Ch'en Ts'ai-tao in Wuhan could defy Mao's proletarian headquarters, were there not "Li Ts'ai-tao's" and "Chang Ts'ai-tao's" elsewhere prepared to do the same? Wang Li told them that there were, and at the huge reception organized to welcome him home from Wuhan on July 26 he spoke privately to Kuai Ta-fu about it.

"Have you been badly hurt?" asked Kuai, who had heard about a broken leg.

"No, but my toe is broken," answered Wang Li.

"Is it true that some PLA commanders do not listen to Chairman Mao?"

"Yes," said Wang Li.

"Is this the time to confront this question?"

"Yes," said Wang Li. "The central task of this coming period is to pull out of the army a small handful of capitalist-roaders who have usurped military power."

"And who are the most dangerous of these?" asked Kuai.

Wang Li named Hsu Shih-yu of the Nanking Military Region, Han Hsien-chu of the Foochow Military Region, and Ch'en Hsi-lien of Shenyang as people who must be overthrown.

11
Pull a Handful from the Army

When Wang Li, then at the pinnacle of his fame and influence, urged Kuai Ta-fu to launch a campaign against key leaders of the People's Liberation Army, Kuai went quickly into action. He called joint meetings of the rebel heads from other schools to clarify the "pull out" task, and reorganized the Regiment in order to turn its face outward. A Department of External Affairs was set up with Jen Ch'uan-chung as head, backed up by ten vice-heads. The Military Information Group's correspondents already in the provinces turned their headquarters into liaison stations (altogether the Regiment set up forty-seven), and over 2,000 students went out to man them. By the time of the August 1 *Red Flag* editorial,* calling on the revolutionaries of the whole nation to pull a handful from the army as the central task of the day, the Regiment forces were already in position to take the lead.

Kuai, sitting in front of his military map like a commanding general at staff headquarters, sent a stream of cables and letters to the far corners of the land, naming targets, suggesting strategies, prodding laggards, and praising activists. At this time Kuai's prestige was such that his words carried as much, if not more, weight than those of many members of the Central Committee, which most militants assumed he was defending, and Kuai had only to suggest an issue or a campaign to stir enormous activity in any region.

In order to enrich his knowledge of military affairs, Kuai authorized a raid on the home of Hsu Hsiang-ch'ien, one of the PLA's ten marshals and a vice-chairman of the Military Commission, a man whose great revolutionary record went all the way back to 1935 when he commanded the First Regiment of the North China Workers and Peasants Red Army. The guards at Hsu's house refused to let Kuai's "iron rods" in. They went over the wall in secret and seized four big and three small safes full of material, much of it classified. All this they took back to the campus to study.

When members of the Central Committee heard about the raid they sent troops from the Peking Garrison Command to reclaim the safes. They ordered Kuai to return everything and copy nothing. But Kuai delayed as long as possible, locked the door to his headquarters, refused to come out himself, sent others to negotiate, and in the meantime urged his people to

---

Red Flag is the theoretical organ of the Central Committee of the Communist Party of China. *Red Flag* editorials often initiated key developments during the Cultural Revolution. In the summer of 1967, *Red Flag* was in the hands of the ultra-left, May 16 forces who used it to launch a nationwide campaign against the leadership of the People's Liberation Army.

copy as much as they could as fast as they could. Before the soldiers recovered the material students had copied such sensitive sections as the complete list of Fourth Field Army cadres and portions of Hsu Hsiang-ch'ien's wartime diaries. They later used some of this material in communications that were sent far and wide across the country, thus exposing vital military secrets.

In the provinces Kuai's forces went into action swiftly. On July 27, one day after Kuai's meeting with Wang Li, P'eng Wei-ming, head of the Regiment's First Department, arrived in the Northeast to mobilize an attack on the military region headquarters there. Charging the local PLA with supporting a faction of conservatives, P'eng Wei-ming's Northeastern allies attacked the army's reception station in Shenyang, took over the building, drove the army personnel out, and even threw some of them bodily out the windows. Then they nailed up the doors and barricaded themselves inside.

This led the next day to a sharp fight with the opposing student faction, in the course of which four middle school students were killed. When PLA fighters stepped in to stop the bloodshed, P'eng accused them of supporting the conservative side. He tried to create a big incident by taking the bodies of the four dead students in their coffins to the military region headquarters for burial. When this did not bring the PLA commanders out, P'eng ordered an assault on the headquarters building. He himself, wearing a military helmet, took the lead as dozens of trucks filled with student and worker rebels converged from all sides. Once they took over the building they raised the flag of the Tsinghua Chingkangshan Regiment on the roof.

These violent acts in Shenyang brought criticism from the Central Committee, but Wang Li, Kuang Feng, and Ch'i Pen-yu praised the young rebels for their militancy and said their main direction was correct. Soon after, Kuang Feng called Kuai and announced that he planned a personal tour of the Northeast and wanted two members of the Regiment headquarters to go with him. T'an Chien-lung and Ma Hsiao-chung were chosen. In order to ensure a tumultuous welcome for Kuang Feng in the

Northeast, Kuai cabled his people there to enlarge the incident and sent Jen Ch'uan-chung to prepare the ground. Jen, head of the Regiment's Department of External Affairs, was a skilled organizer. He soon brought fighting to many other areas of the region, including Fushun. There he personally stole a tank from a PLA repair shop and led the rebel forces into the streets with machine-guns, tanks, and artillery all seized from the PLA. Not only were many fighters on both sides killed, but hundreds of innocent bystanders lost their lives in the battle. The casualties in the Fushun incident were unprecedented in the whole Cultural Revolution.

While Jen was doing his utmost to mount an offensive at the scene, Kuai, in Peking, called a conference of Northeastern rebel heads, denounced the PLA commanders in the Northeast as Ho Lung men,* and urged his listeners to hurry back and pick up their guns. Those who returned to Changchun, capital of Kirin province, put 60 millimeter cannon in position to fire on the headquarters there. But the Red Ninth Company of the local PLA rushed its soldiers to the scene. They stood right in front of the gun muzzles and dared the rebels to fire. This so moved many rank-and-file members of the rebel forces that they defected and took the cannon away from those who would turn them against the army.

Before he could actually depart for the Northeast, Kuang Feng was exposed as a "May 16 Conspirator." His plan for a new Liao-Shen campaign† in the Northwest went bankrupt and the fighting there was brought under control.

In the Southeast, across the strait from Taiwan, Kuai's liaison cadres spread a rumor that Commander Han Hsien-chu was against Chairman Mao. They issued leaflets which asked, "Which headquarters does Han belong to?" When Kang Sheng

---

*Since Ho Lung was Liu Shao-ch'i's chief military collaborator, to call these commanders "Ho Lung men" meant in effect to call them Liu Shao-ch'i men.

†The Liao-Shen campaign, which liberated the whole Northwest, was fought in 1948. It was planned by Mao Tse-tung and carried out by Lin Piao.

of the Political Bureau of the Central Committee saw these leaflets he said, "People without hate for the revolution could never write such things." Chou En-lai's reaction was, "These people cannot be revolutionaries, they must be counter-revolutionaries!"

But Wang Li and Ch'i Pen-yu supported Kuai. "If Han has made mistakes you can bombard him," said Ch'i. PLA chief-of-staff Yang Ch'eng-wu said, "If you want to overthrow Han, I support you." So slogans such as "Down with Han Hsien-chu" filled the air over Quemoy and Matsu. When the Kuomintang troops on the island heard this they immediately took up the cry, for it called for the overthrow of the military commander most dangerous to them. Then, of course, the revolutionaries on the mainland, hearing their own words thrown back by the Kuomintang, gave the matter second thought, and many of them opted out of the whole campaign. Obviously, as the premier said, "to oppose Han is to help Chiang Kai-shek."

Kuai's lieutenants sparked major campaigns in the Northeast and in Fukien, but the heart of their drive against the army centered on Nanking, where Hsu Shih-yu commanded the military region. The vice-commander was a man named Tu Fang-p'ing. He had earlier established ties with Wang Li, Kuang Feng, and Ch'i Pen-yu, and he led a large rebel movement which unilaterally seized power in the city and then went on to demand the overthrow of Hsu. The Tu Fang-p'ing group was called the Excellent Faction because after it seized power its members declared that the situation was "excellent." The opposition, which had been defeated and driven from the city, was known as the Make Wind (or Fart) Faction because its members had responded in disgust to the cries of "Excellent, excellent!" with "You're worse than a bunch of dogs making wind!"

Late in July, after Wang Li said that Hsu Shih-yu must be overthrown, Kuai Ta-fu himself went to Nanking to confer with Tu Fang-p'ing. He then assigned several hundred Tsinghua Regiment stalwarts to the region. They urged the Excellent Faction to study the spirit of the Peking masses who were surrounding Tungnanhai. Then, with the help of Kuai's "rods," the Excellent leaders launched a campaign against the Military Region headquarters. Several hundred thousand people went into the streets and stayed there for several weeks. Vanguard detachments actually broke into the headquarters yard and occupied it for a whole month. They also broke into the head-quarters building and beat up PLA soldiers and staff.

Intensive research into Hsu Shih-yu's record unearthed no serious problems which could be used as a basis for the attack, so the young rebels concentrated instead on trying to provoke an armed reaction to their incursions. The Nanking PLA could then be accused of unwarranted suppression of the mass move-ment. But Hsu Shih-yu failed to respond. Fighting began, but not between the Excellent Faction and the PLA; it began be-tween the Excellent Faction and the Make Wind Faction, which Tu Fang-p'ing accused of preparing a counteroffensive in the countryside where the majority of its members had earlier been driven. Claiming that the Make Winds were about to lay siege to the city, the Excellents attacked with machine-guns and hand grenades. Armed struggle raged for several days, but in the end, due to energetic intervention on the part of Chou En-lai and Chiang Ch'ing, who opposed the campaign to oust Hsu and sharply criticized Kuai for centering his attack on the PLA, fighting died down and the masses in front of the military head-quarters were dispersed.

Kuai had planned a huge mass meeting against Hsu Shih-yu for the latter part of August, but it was called off at the last minute. Then, on September 1, the Regiment liaison station in Nanking received a telegram from Kuai that said, "Hsu Shih-yu is a good comrade. Our liaison station should withdraw from the city. Please publish this widely."

Kuai's request for publicity was hardly necessary. The tele-graph operator who took the message was from the Make Wind faction and Kuai's message was all over the city before the liaison station or the military region headquarters even received their copies. When it became clear that Mao Tse-tung and the Central Committee actually stood behind Hsu, large numbers of people moved to support him and posters went up all over

the city announcing adherence to Hsu and to the Central Committee.

During July and August the Tsinghua 4s competed with
the Regiment in the campaign to "pull a handful out of the
army." They too sent hundreds of activists out to man more than
a dozen liaison stations in various parts of the country. As part
of this effort Wang Yung-hsien went to Nanking on August 5
as head of the East China liaison station.

"After all the speeches and editorials, I went to Nanking
determined to pull out Hsu Shih-yu," Wang said. "But the
Regiment crowd had already pre-empted the field. They had
posters everywhere proclaiming, 'Down with Ch'en Ts'ai-tao!
Down with Hsu Shih-yu!' And their newspaper was filled with
attacks on Hsu. Each new telegram from Kuai stimulated a new
high tide of activity, posters, and reinforcements for those surrounding and occupying the military region headquarters.

"Kuai's first telegram read, 'Wang Li says there are at least
three commanders who oppose Mao Tse-tung: Hsu Shih-yu,
Han Hsien-chu, and Ch'en Hsi-lien!' It came at midnight, and
by dawn the whole city was covered with posters repeating
this message.

"Tien P'u, Hsu's wife, went to Peking to appeal on behalf
of her husband, but Wang Li refused to hear her, saying, 'The
case is clear.' Kuai sent a second telegram that spelled this out
and stimulated a new outburst of anti-Hsu feeling and action.

"We 4s tried to do our part, but the Regiment 'rods' attacked
us, saying that we were only against Hsu on the surface, while
we really supported him in our hearts. So wherever we went
people resented us and treated us coolly. Excellent Faction
people even grabbed us, beat us, and demanded that we confess
our real thinking. When we refused to respond they put us in
trucks, drove way out in the country, and dropped us off, one
by one, in out of the way places.

"Finally we decided that since everyone seemed to believe
we really supported Hsu, maybe we had better turn around and
support him in fact. We debated this for a while and then came
out on Hsu's side, thus linking up with the Make Winds. When

Kuai's pro-Hsu telegram came on September 1 we were very happy, for we were already on the right side! But it wasn't a matter of principle, we only did it out of factionalism, because we found it hard to agree with the Regiment on anything."

When it came to the sacking of the British Mission on August 23, it was the 4s and not the Regiment who played the major role. This was because the key group responsible for the affairs, the Anti-Imperialist Anti-Revisionist Liaison Station in the Foreign Ministry was linked not to the Heaven Faction but to the Earth Faction, and the 4s were part of the Earth Faction. The Anti-Imperialists were left-leaning cadres with ties to Wang Li. With the help of thousands of rebel students from the Foreign Language Schools, they had effectively ousted Ch'en Yi as Foreign Minister and placed Yao Teng-shan, a returned military attaché from Djakarta, in command of foreign affairs. Yao Teng-shan had issued an ultimatum to the British authorities in Hongkong, giving them forty-eight hours to release several imprisoned Chinese journalists or face the consequences. On the day that the ultimatum was to expire the Tsinghua 4s received a phone call asking them to mobilize for a demonstration in front of the British Mission. Over the loudspeaker all 4s supporters were called together for a meeting. A cadre from the Anti-Imperialist, Anti-Revisionist Liaison Station told them, "Tonight we are going into action to show the British how tough we can be. After the tempering of the Cultural Revolution our rebels are strong and angry! During the Cultural Revolution the British seized and spread a lot of unauthorized information. If they don't answer in time, we'll seize it all back. Bring screwdrivers and pliers. When we get in there we'll open up the files. Wear black clothes. They might shoot at us. Don't give them a clear target. All those who can read English should strive to be in the vanguard. Bring flashlights."

The speaker then brought out a map showing where the Mission was situated, and where the fuse boxes, water pipes, and water tank were.

"We were enthusiastic," said Kao of the 4s. "We sent one big contingent into the city and then decided that wasn't enough,

so we sent another. Our forces helped surround the whole place.
At first we were well disciplined. We sat down in orderly rows
and listened to five rules set down by the Premier. He said
we could protest, protest in writing, hold meetings, etc., but
must not break into the grounds.

"Our protest meeting began at 9 P.M. with denunciations
of British oppression broadcast over the loudspeaker. 'What
are you going to do?' we asked again and again. At 10 o'clock
the ultimatum expired. What would happen? We only knew
we would show them! Then PLA men came and surrounded the
place. The Premier had said we should not break in. I asked
what we should do. The answer I got was that the Premier has
to say things like that, but if the masses take revolutionary
action who can prevent it?

"Actually, the break-in had long been planned by people
who hoped to overthrow the Premier. The activists of the Anti-
Imperialist Anti-Revisionist Liaison Station came up from behind
with loudspeakers blaring. Some individuals in front jumped up
and threw bottles of ink at the walls and windows of the building. This was a diversion. As the ink flew out front, others
found their way inside the building from the back. They began
throwing chairs and sofas out the windows. The loudspeakers
behind us urged us to action. We pushed against the PLA lines
shouting, 'Back up! Let us in! People over there have already
gone in!' There were eight lines of soldiers. Some youngsters
tried climbing over their heads but they were thrown down.
The soldiers' lines finally broke at one spot. We rushed through
to climb the fence. Soldiers pulled some of us down but others
got over.

"At 11 we saw flames. First the oil barrels in the garage
burned. Then the main gate opened. People rushed in. The cars
began to burn, three Mission-owned cars burned. Fire engines
came but armed people stopped the firemen. They had to withdraw. The flames rose higher. Fire engines returned, lots of
them. The firemen pushed through the crowd to get near the
building. About the time the fire started Chou En-lai and
Chiang Ch'ing sent an order to all of us to stop the assault, but
it was not broadcast. We didn't hear it until later, but as soon

as we did we all left the area. By then it was too late. We felt very bad.

"When the PLA lines gave way the British ran into the basement and locked themselves in. But people broke in and pulled them out. Police intervened and took the British across the street to the Albanian Embassy, but even as they crossed the street some of our people tried to tear their clothes off.

"Actually, most of us thought this action was not so good. Why should we mount this kind of violence in China? When we dispersed after the Premier's directive, we all felt that something had gone wrong. How had the building started to burn? We 4s had participated from the beginning in what came to be known as a counter-revolutionary incident. After that many people opposed us, criticized us, and put a lot of pressure on us. We had to criticize ourselves many times. But the Regiment was not involved, so they used our mistake to gain ground and put us in a bad light."

If the 4s made a serious mistake in joining the attack on the British Mission, Kuai Ta-fu and the Regiment made a few of their own that may not have been so world renowned but still damaged them politically. One of these was giving unqualified support to Ch'en Li-ming, the "madman of the modern age."

Ch'en Li-ming first came to public attention as the protegé of the Red Teachers Union, whose members discovered him confined in an insane asylum when they went to liberate a colleague named Fang Tien-hsien who, they claimed, had been committed as a dissident. They were looking for premature anti-Liuists, people who had been persecuted for their politics during the years Liu Shao-ch'i held power, in order to lend credence to their theory that the "revolutionaries of today must be sought among the dissidents of yesterday."

Ch'en Li-ming fit the bill much better than Fang. A landlord's son who had been a revolutionary cadre in Hsiangtan City, he had written a long critique of Liu Shao-ch'i many years before, only to be hounded from his job and finally incarcerated in an asylum for his pains. The Peking Secuity Police told the Red Teachers Union that Ch'en had written more cogent polemics against Marx, Lenin, and Chairman Mao than he had against Liu. They claimed that he was a reactionary who should be indicted for counter-revolutionary agitation if he ever became well enough to leave the asylum. But Sung Ch'ing-ying, a former Kuomintang district leader now established as the most radical of the Tsinghua teachers, responded by leading an assault on the headquarters of the Security Police. With the support of hundreds of United Regiment students (this was in January 1967, before the split), the Red Teachers Union had broken into the police offices, seized the telephones, made speeches over the loudspeaker system, urged the prisoners in the municipal jail to rise and break out, ransacked secret files, and made off with a complete dossier on Ch'en Li-ming.

The Red Teachers Union then took the material on Ch'en to Wang Li and Ch'i Pen-yu of the Central Cultural Revolution Group. These two "reversed the case" for Ch'en, declared him to be a revolutionary hero, a "madman of the modern age,* and approved the action of the teachers in liberating him and all his files.

According to Wang Li, Ch'en Li-ming's attack on Liu Shao-ch'i was detailed and well organized enough to constitute a theoretical contribution to the revolution, whereas his fulminations against Mao Tse-tung were an irrational product of his recurring mental illness. Wang Li therefore gave the Red Teachers Union a green light to suppress Ch'en's questionable writings while they compiled his anti-Liu material into a new "Diary of a Madman" and issued it in various forms, including popular comic books. On the basis of this published material, some students in Tientsin wrote a play called "Madman of the Modern Age" which won acclaim from Wang Li and Ch'i Pen-yu and was widely performed in the spring and summer of 1967, first in Tientsin, then at Tsinghua, and then all over Peking and North China. Sidney Rittenberg, an American work-

---

*This name is based on the famous "Diary of a Madman," in which the author, Lu Hsun, lays out a brilliant critique of Kuomintang rule and China's crisis of the twenties in the form of the writings of a "madman," in order to avoid persecution.

ing for Peking Radio, even raised money among the foreign nationals in the city to put on two performances especially for foreigners.

After the play had made him famous as a political prophet, Ch'en Li-ming appeared in the flesh on the Tsinghua campus to recount his long heroic struggle against Liu Shao-ch'i. He was thereupon launched on a public career as a lecturer rallying antirevisionist sentiment at political meetings all over the country.

At Tsinghua, Kuai Ta-fu became very active in promoting Ch'en Li-ming. Kuai honored Ch'en by including him in the Kuai faction and said that he had been a Kuai faction man for seventeen years. "By definition a Kuai faction man is a rebel oppressed by Liu Shao-ch'i. Any attack on Ch'en is an attack on me," said Kuai Ta-fu in his usual bold and defiant style.

But other forces, including certain members of the Peking Security Police, kept chipping away at Ch'en's reputation, reminding all who cared to listen that Ch'en Li-ming was a polemecist against the whole socialist system and not just against that revisionist aberration, Liu Shao-ch'i. To prove their point they published some of Ch'en's anti-Maoist writings. In February 1968, six months after Wang Li had been exposed as a "May 16" plotter, and about the same time that Ch'i Pen-yu was finally removed from office as part of the same conspiracy, the Central Committee declared that Ch'en Li-ming was a counter-revolutionary and that the play "Madman of the Modern Age" was a counter-revolutionary work.

This decision put Kuai and the Regiment in an awkward spot, but its impact was softened somewhat by the fact that Ch'i Pen-yu, aware of the way the wind was blowing in the fall of 1967, had backed away from "Madman" Ch'en, had eased him off the public platform, had sent him to the Hsingshen Sanatorium in the Western Hills for a rest, and had finally assigned him to a minor research post in the Academy of Sciences. In the meantime the play had quietly been dropped. By February 21, 1968, when the Central Committee made its damaging announcement, Kuai Ta-fu had already set up an investigation group to look into the true nature of Ch'en Li-ming. Thus Kuai could make a case for the idea that he had been fooled all along and that he was as anxious as anyone else to get at the truth.

Even as Kuai Ta-fu backed away from Ch'en Li-ming, he took the offensive against the new revolutionary committee at the Normal College and linked up with another unsavory character, one Fan Li-yao, who was trying to overthrow the committee from the inside. On the surface, what Kuai and the Tsinghua Regiment had against the Normal College revolutionary committee was that it had been set up by Earth Faction forces. Acting together with Han Ai-ch'ing of the Aeronautical Institute and Nieh Yuan-tzu of Peking University, Kuai helped bring all the Heaven Faction forces from the schools and colleges of Peking out to the Normal College campus to demand the overthrow of its new leading body. Tens of thousands of people showed up. As they demonstrated, Kuai directed them from the front seat of a jeep that sped from place to place according to the needs of the moment.

Mao Tse-tung and his headquarters group, recognizing this as a test case in a nationwide campaign of ultra-left overthrow attempts, took drastic action. The Peking Security Police intervened, arrested three key people—including Fan Li-yao, who was designated a counter-revolutionary—and upheld the revolutionary committee. Kuai was severely criticized by Central Committee members for his provocative role.

Under attack for this and similar extreme acts, Kuai finally made a public self-criticism. He spoke before a mass meeting at the University, pretended to be sorry, and left the stage weeping. A few minutes later he showed up backstage, all smiles. "A politician must be a good actor," he said to Ts'ui Chao-shih of Regiment Headquarters. "Don't you think I put on a pretty good act?"

12
Big Alliance

Competition for public prestige as militant revolutionaries helped sustain and widen the split between the Regiment and the 4s, but the fuel that kept the factional fires burning day in and day out was the continuing repudiation of cadres back on the campus. Each week both factions found cadres to criticize and expose and thus generated successive meetings. Without such meetings the leaders could not have held their followers together. These repudiations did have some positive results. Some of the cadres were educated; they were forced to think through their past acts and their class stand in the light of the two-line struggle that was emerging. But as for the students, the meetings rarely touched their "souls" because they were used, in the main, for partisan purposes. A primary goal was to expose a cadre who had won the support of the other side and thus condemn that side's politics. Secret investigations were carried out. If damaging material was unearthed it was quietly compiled and held in reserve until the right moment for sudden public exposure—the right moment being the one that would most deeply embarrass and confound the other side. Then the faction under attack would be accused of protecting a counter-revolutionary, which implied counter-revolutionary intent on the part of its leaders. Did they not then deserve "a thousand lashes and a thousand deaths"?

None of this really helped misguided cadres to reform or young rebels to get at the truth. The real motto was not Mao's, "Cure the disease and save the patient!" but "Do the other side in!" As a result the prestige of both factions fell among the masses. Sensitive to the charge that they only repudiated cadres adhering to the opposite side, each faction occasionally held a meeting to criticize one of their own. After this members would shout, "Who says we don't look into the problems of our own side? See, here's an example!" But such token self-criticism could hardly cover up the partisan nature of most of the activity.

Late in the year some people on both sides got tired of this in-fighting and started a campaign for the transformation of the old education at Tsinghua. They looked up material about Resistance University in Yenan and made suggestions for applying that experience to their modern university. Realizing how divorced they had been from working people and from production, the civil engineers worked out plans to carry on designing at various work sites where the workers too could be drawn in. They also sent out teams to investigate the graduates of their department—how they had done on actual jobs since leaving the University and what ideas they or their workmates had for changes in the educational system. The whole admissions system, which recruited students like "Little Tito," and the special regulations that treated girls like debutantes (girls were not allowed to carry more than 55 pounds on construction sites) were also investigated.

But only a minority of the students took part in this effort. The factional leaders were not interested. They maintained that without their "proletarian" faction in power all this work would be lost. Since power was the crux of the whole question it was idle to talk about specific reforms. "Let's make sure the University is in the hands of the working class [i.e., our hands]. Then we'll transform it," they said.

Other students, growing sick of politics, took advantage of the confusion to retire to the library and read. The theory of "technique in command" thus showed up again as scores of people dropped out of political action and began pursuing careers on their own. Some studied mathematics. Others studied foreign languages. They were "voting with their feet" against the senseless trend of events.

In September 1967, after the high tide of attacks on PLA headquarters had abated and the Foreign Ministry had returned to Chou En-lai's control, a powerful movement in favor of "big alliances" and an end to factionalism swept the whole nation. Mao Tse-tung returned from an extended southern trip and stated unequivocally: "There is no conflict of fundamental interest within the working class. Under the dictatorship of the proletariat there is no reason whatsoever for the working class

to split into two big irreconcilable groupings." Everywhere
rank-and-file people, sick of factional struggle, seized on this
directive to demand unity. In Nanking the whole city was
covered with reconciliation posters. Members of the Make Wind
Faction who had been driven beyond the city limits were welcomed back. Meetings were held in every work unit and school
to dissolve splits and create a single revolutionary organization
of the masses. A similar tide of unity swept Shanghai, Hankow,
Canton, and Peking.

Tsinghua University could hardly ignore the trend. The
factional leaders, meeting separately in urgent sessions, felt
great pressure from below. Mao Tse-tung himself had initiated
the January Storm in Shanghai; now he was calling for "big
alliances."* If a group did not go along, how could it maintain
a position of leadership?

Strong pressures came from above. The Central Cultural
Revolution Group called in the Tsinghua student leaders and
told them: "The whole country is forming alliances. How long
can you go on quarreling? If you don't get together and decide
on some form of coalition, we won't let you join in the National
Day celebrations."

After this the 4s Headquarters Committee decided in favor
of alliance. But they did not know how to proceed. Kuai Ta-fu
had never recognized the 4s as a legitimate organization. How
could they make an alliance with him? The Regiment leaders,
rising to the occasion, finally put out a statement that they recognized the 4s as a legal organization. They suggested talks
and a coalition headquarters.

"Since Kuai had taken the initiative, we too had to seize
the time," said Wang Yung-hsien of the 4s. "As Kuai walked
over to negotiate we beat drums and cymbals to welcome him
and invited him in with enthusiasm. We held the talks in the

---

*Mao called for "big alliances" between the opposing factions.
A big alliance was a formal agreement, usually written, between the
leaders of two contending factions. It set up a new organizational
structure that included representatives of both sides at the top, while
the rank-and-file merged down below.

Agricultural Engineering Building, not far from the big campus statue of Chairman Mao. The masses lined up on both sides of the road to welcome them. Our negotiations lasted two days and all the time the people outside cheered us on.

"We agreed on a coalition headquarters without too much trouble. Since Kuai, as a nationally known student leader, was already on the Standing Committee of the Peking Revolutionary Committee, we decided to be generous and let him hold first place on our committee. But we stipulated that if the Regiment held the chairman's seat, then the 4s had to hold the next post and so on in alternation. We insisted on complete balance and equality between our two sides. As for the name of the new coalition, it was to be called the Chingkangshan Regiment General Service Station.

"When the masses outside heard that an agreement had been reached, they held a tumultuous celebration, cheering, shouting, and dancing in the street. But when we returned to our headquarters certain 'rods' among the 4s were very upset. 'How come you have called it a Regiment Service Station? It seems as if we 4s have been completely dissolved! Where's the coalition here?' They convinced Shen Ju-huai that the new organization should be called General Headquarters, not Service Station. So in the afternoon we went to find Kuai and asked him to change the name before we made any final declaration or held any public ceremony. Already people from far beyond the campus had come to take part in our unity celebration and the masses of both factions had assembled in front of the main building impatient for the proceedings to begin.

"Right then and there we quarreled. Kuai said the agreement had already been signed, how could it be changed? We said what's in a name? Why not change it to show that this is a real alliance? There is no question of principle involved here. This argument delayed the meeting. Many people jumped onto the stage to ask why nothing had started. The radio had already broadcast the news of Tsinghua's 'big alliance' and reporters had come out from the city to write it all up—and not only reporters but photographers as well.

"In the end Kuai relented. He made a concession. He

agreed to call our new organization the Coalition Headquarters. So the meeting began. But the atmosphere was not good. When one side spoke the other side would not applaud. Some who had planned to speak refused to do so. The masses could clearly see from the long delay and from the ill-will expressed that the two sides were still at odds. In the end the meeting broke up leaving a sour taste in the mouth.

"Of course, we 4s were to blame. It was we who insisted on changing the name at the last minute and thus created resentment all around. But if we were bad, the Regiment was no better. They said, 'Whoever tears up the agreement is Chiang Kai-shek. Shen Ju-huai tore up the agreement, therefore Shen Ju-huai is Chiang Kai-shek!' "

Thus on September 21 the Tsinghua "big alliance" got off to a shaky start. A period of uneasy truce followed during which there were no more big quarrels or fights. Rank-and-file members of the two factions joined the National Day celebrations together, formed real alliances in the University departments, and went off en masse to join the fall harvest. Joint offices and working committees were set up and some of them worked together without incident for months. No public statements were made which were not signed by both sides. But for a long time the leading committee of four, two from the Regiment and two from the 4s, could not be expanded because no agreement on personnel could be reached. Finally, under great pressures from below, a standing committee of thirty was chosen. Under it joint classes for political study were started and the transformation of the University was discussed.

But factional activity simmered dangerously just below the surface and now and then broke into the open. A constant source of friction was the 4s' support of the cadre T'an Hao-cheng. T'an was an officer of the Communist Youth League at the University who, after the Cultural Revolution began, had compiled one hundred examples of Liu Shao-ch'i's statements opposing Mao Tse-tung. These selected quotes showed Liu saying the opposite of what Mao was advocating at the same time. They were reviewed by the Central Committee and finally approved, making T'an very well known. When the time came to end the isolation of the cadres and pull good ones back into the struggle, both sides wanted to win T'an's support. T'an himself preferred the 4s. As soon as T'an took this step, the Regiment began to attack him. They singled him out for particular attention since he was more important as a public figure than the others. Kuai wrote him an open letter making fun of his stand and ending with the message, "If you go on like this you will end up as a die-hard capitalist-roader!"

The attack by the Regiment was all T'an needed to win all-out support from the 4s. The 4s not only recruited him into their faction, but they made him a member of their Headquarters Committee. When the Coalition Headquarters was set up in September they wanted him on that headquarters group as well. Kuai, speaking for the Regiment, agreed to the 4s' list with one exception—T'an. The 4s replied that T'an was the man they wanted. "This demand we will not drop!" The two sides quarreled bitterly and the quarrel went on and on. It was finally settled by an agreement that T'an could sit on the committee if he made a self-criticism before the masses and if his self-criticism was accepted. Later he did go before mass meetings more than once, but the listeners were not satisfied with his self-criticism and his status was never officially settled. Nevertheless, the 4s brought him along to Coalition Headquarters each time and each time the Regiment challenged his right to be there. These challenges continued until the headquarters broke up. The issue never was settled.

Even more serious than the chronic dispute over T'an was the action taken by a group of "iron rods" from the Regiment who quite illegally set up a Fight Self, Repudiate Revisionism liaison station dedicated to fighting the self-interest of Kuai Ta-fu and repudiating the revisionism of the 4s. And what was Kuai's self-interest? The compromises he had made in order to get agreement on a coalition headquarters! The charge was that in order to be elected leader of the united movement Kuai had sacrificed principle!

Kuai himself, not long after National Day, had met with Ch'i Pen-yu. Ch'i had asked him about the alliance. "Can this be a real alliance? How can you unite so quickly? One hundred years ago Marx called on the workers to unite, but it hasn't happened yet. Is it all so easy?" Mao had said that if two student factions are revolutionary then they should unite on the basis of revolutionary principles. Ch'i raised questions concerning the basis of the new student unity. He implied that the Tsinghua alliance was based not on revolutionary principle, but on expediency.

When Kuai got back to the campus he initiated a wide discussion among the Regiment militants around this issue. The majority decided that what they had formed was a political monstrosity, an alliance for alliance sake. So they set up their Fight Self, Repudiate Revisionism Liaison Station and factional struggle broke into the open with renewed vigor.

Soon some of the joint offices and united working committees broke down. Among the first to go was the joint office of records. Soon after the coalition was formed both sides had pooled their files and records in one building and had put a single person in charge. The man selected for this job was a member of the 4s. When the Regiment militants decided that the big alliance was unprincipled, they also decided that they could not trust one of the 4s to handle the records. What if he should deny Regiment people access while allowing the 4s unlimited use of his office? They decided to regain control of their files and records clandestinely.

One evening two young men from the Regiment went into the record keeper's office and asked if they could use his phone. He, of course, had no reason to object. What he did not know was that they had already removed the receiver from the phone they were calling, so that each time they dialed they got a busy signal. While waiting for their line to clear the two Regiment stalwarts engaged the record keeper in conversation. And, since the phone at the other end continued to be busy, the conversation went on for a long time. While the record keeper was thus engaged in an apparently innocent conversation, another group of Regiment "rods" crept upstairs with pliers and screwdrivers, picked the lock on the records room, broke the locks off the filing cabinet drawers, loaded all the papers into twenty book bags, and made off with them—this after carefully sweeping the floor and replacing everything in such good order that the room appeared undisturbed.

When, on the following day, the record keeper discovered the papers were gone, including those belonging to the 4s, the Regiment was ready with a poster expressing indignation at this "serious stealing incident." The 4s Headquarters Committee, knowing that none of their members had had a hand in it, suspected the Regiment and filed a strong protest. They demanded a thorough investigation. But the Regiment responded with another strong statement denouncing the "criminal act." To outsiders the wording made it apparent that they suspected class enemies, perhaps hidden among the 4s, perhaps coming in from off the campus.

This trickery fooled many ordinary people who were quite ready to believe that counter-revolutionaries had chosen this method to try and break up the big alliance. But it didn't fool the leaders of the 4s. They knew the Regiment had made off with the papers and the Regiment leaders knew they knew it. It was a major disruptive blow.

13
Split Again

As if the alliance at Tsinghua was not shaky enough, on December 17 Ch'i Pen-yu stepped in to fan the flames. The occasion was a meeting of student leaders from several Peking universities who had been called together to discuss educational transformation. Here Ch'i not only threw his support to the Regiment, but he simultaneously attacked the 4s for their choice of a song.

"The big alliance at Tsinghua," said Ch'i, "must have the Regiment as its core. This has been decided by history, by the reality of the current struggle. Of course," he went on, "Regiment people should be modest and avoid arrogance. As for the 4s, they should admit the leading position of the Regiment. This is not my opinion. It is not something that was decided by me or by you. It is simply an objective fact."

By stating the matter thus Ch'i Pen-yu implied that the Central Committee and Chairman Mao concurred in this view.

Delighted by Ch'i's open support for her faction, the Regiment delegate at the meeting, a young woman named Ch'en Yu-yen, asked Ch'i for an opinion about the 4s' battle song, the words of which, according to the 4s, came directly from Lin Piao. According to the Regiment, no such words had ever been spoken by Lin. The controversial verse went like this:

> Sometimes one must face sacrifice
> One must even sacrifice one's life!
> If I get finished off, I'm finished.
> When the shooting starts on the battlefield
> I make a resolution,
> "Today *lao-tze* dies in this place!"

To refer to oneself as a *lao-tze* (literally, your old man) is a form of oath. It implies that you are the father of everyone who is listening—hence you are calling them all bastards. It is a tough, devil-may-care way of speaking about oneself quite typical of soldiers in battle, but quite shocking to the ordinary civilian listener. An English equivalent might be, "Today your motherfucking uncle dies."

When asked if this was really a quote from Lin Piao, Ch'i said, "There is no such quote. Analyze it with Mao Tse-tung Thought. How could Lin Piao have used such words?"

"That's what we have been saying," responded Ch'en Yu-yen, delighted. "But they say we are spreading rumors and slandering them!"

"No," said Ch'i, "they are spreading the rumors. They are the criminals."

When Ch'i's words reached the campus they created a great stir. Ch'en Yu-yen, coming home exhausted, told her comrades briefly about what had been said, then went to bed. When Kuai Ta-fu returned much later in the evening and heard the news he was overjoyed. "We must broadcast it right away!" he said.

"But Ch'en has gone to sleep and so has everyone else," said the headquarters personnel. "Why don't we wait until morning?"

"Good news from on high can't be delayed," Kuai insisted. "Such good tidings must be spread at once."

He sent a car out to bring Ch'en back and immediately went on the air himself shouting, "Good news! The best news! An important speech by central leaders! Pay attention everyone!"

After Ch'en reported the details, Kuai took the microphone once more. "This is the Central Committee speaking, this is history, this is the proletarian headquarters backing us up!"

The Regiment people among his listeners all clapped and cheered. They clapped till their hands hurt. "Mao Tse-tung stands behind us! We must follow him to the end!"

The 4s, on the other hand, had been taken by surprise and felt betrayed. Although they too had had a delegate at the meeting, they knew nothing about what had happened until they heard Kuai filling the night air with his exultation. They immediately rushed out to find their delegate and ask him if it was true.

"Did Ch'i Pen-yu say that?"

"Yes," said the bewildered youth. "He said all of that."

This made the 4s very angry. They were angry at Ch'i's words and they were angry because the man from the 4s who had been invited to attend the meeting was such a strange, withdrawn person. He had invented a kind of brush for painting posters. When posters were being produced he always appeared, laid his tools out on the ground, and helped everyone with their writing. A queer duck! Now he had let them down. The Regiment was on the offensive in the middle of the night and the 4s had prepared no countermove.

The 4s Headquarters Committee called an emergency meeting then and there. As for the Regiment being the core, they decided that was easy to rebut. Had not Mao Tse-tung said that to think you are the center is childish? Anyone who calls himself the center is in violation of Mao Tse-tung Thought. And as for the Lin Piao quote, they had certainly not made it up and they resolved to track it down. Sure enough, after an intensive search they found it printed in a booklet put out by one faction in a People's Liberation Army school.°

Having made sure of their position, the 4s mounted a counteroffensive against the Regiment. They put posters all over the campus and all over the city saying, "What do you mean, 'I am the core'? What a stupid, anti-Mao statement!" And they called a big meeting for December 18 to hammer this point home and to defend their battle song.

At this meeting Ch'en Chu-san, an articulate leader of the 4s, said: "Some accuse us of spreading rumors. Who dares say that now? Here is a book printed under the supervision of the chief of staff, printed in black and white, and it contains the words of our song."

This really upset the people who were listening. Obviously the Regiment militants had spread lies and slander. Now was the time to "let them suffer a thousand lashings, let them die a thousand deaths!"

But the Regiment did not take these charges passively. As soon as Ch'en had finished speaking, they denounced him for attacking the proletarian headquarters of the Central Committee, for attacking Ch'i Pen-yu. Then on December 20 they seized Ch'en Chu-san, held him prisoner, and called a mass meeting to repudiate him as a counter-revolutionary. Of course the 4s could not allow such a meeting to proceed unchallenged. They rallied their ranks, showed up in force, and occupied the meeting site, hoping to prevent the proceedings from ever getting under way. A struggle began over control of the microphones. Soon fist fighting spread to the audience.

While the rank-and-file fought it out, Kuai whisked Ch'en away to the city and turned him over to the Security Police. The police held him for investigation on the strength of Kuai's

---

°Certain PLA institutions—its drama school, for instance—had the same rules as civilian organizations with regard to mass mobilization, political action, big-character posters, etc., even though in the army as a whole such activity was forbidden.

accusations, and the big alliance broke up for good, which was, of course, what Kuai wanted.

When the 4s heard that Ch'en was under arrest they were very angry. "How can anyone just grab people like that?" They mobilized several thousand supporters who marched into the city shouting, "Give us back Comrade Ch'en!" They gathered first in front of the Security Bureau, then left 200 to negotiate Ch'en's release while the rest marched on to Tungnanhai to find Ch'i Pen-yu. They never found Ch'i, but they did find some leaders of the Security Bureau. They confronted them with strong demands for the release of Ch'en, and set up a liaison station outside the Bureau's main gate to handle the protesters who continued to show up. Angry crowds gathered in such numbers that police work was disrupted.

The Regiment responded with a mass meeting and a huge demonstration to celebrate the anniversary of the great anti-Liu parade of December 25, 1966. It was advertised as a movement to overcome obstructions to the Ninth Congress of the Communist Party which everyone thought would soon take place. On posters and at the meeting Regiment writers and speakers denounced "the adverse current that is trying to make us rebels stink, and so slander us that Ch'i Pen-yu cannot get elected to the Political Bureau and young rebels of merit cannot get elected to the Central Committee." One noon broadcast openly said, "People are slandering us. They want to prevent our being elected to the Central Committee!"

This made the 4s laugh. How could Kuai be elected to the Central Committee? He wasn't even a member of the Communist Party!

On December 26, Vice-Premier Hsieh Fu-chih received delegates from both factions at his office in the city. In the audience sat Ch'en Chu-san, who had been released unconditionally. Ch'i Pen-yu stepped forward with a written speech. "This time," he said, "I'm going to read my speech so that none of you can grab a single straw for factional purposes."

Among the topics which he then took up was the 4s' battle song. "Lin Piao did once say those words," he said, reversing his opinion of a few weeks before. "The fact that the 4s used them for their battle song shows their great love for Lin Piao and for Chairman Mao!"

Now it was time for the 4s to celebrate.

"Our leaders called me from the city and informed us that Ch'en had been released," said Wang Yung-hsien of the 4s. "So I organized a welcoming crowd that stretched far beyond the school grounds. Our gathering was as big as the one that had assembled to| hear Ch'i Pen-yu's remarks when he praised the Regiment. So now we had our turn. Now we drew the crowd!

"But after this the conflict between us and the Regiment grew sharper and sharper. The sinister hand of Ch'i Pen-yu had caused both sides to make mistakes. He led us into head-on collision."

The speech in Hsieh Fu-chih's office was Ch'i's last official act. Early in 1968 he disappeared from public life, exposed by his own manipulations as an ultra-left troublemaker.

The unstable coalition between the Regiment and the 4s broke up completely after the Regiment seized Ch'en Ch'u-san and turned him over to the Security Police. Ch'en Ch'u-san's release did not repair the breach. On the contrary, it sharpened the antagonism between the two factions because it put the Regiment on the defensive politically, a position that for Kuai Ta-fu was both unusual and intolerable. Kuai was already on the defensive at this time because of his close ties with Ch'i Pen-yu and his all-out support for Ch'en Li-ming, the "madman of the modern age" who was under investigation at the Central Committee level. In order to recoup prestige, the Regiment took the offensive. In January 1968 its forces kidnaped two former University cadres who were active in the 4s organization and held them prisoner. The two cadres, Lo Chung-chi and Li Kang, were charged with counter-revolutionary activity and were tortured by their captors in order to obtain confessions that could be used to expose the 4s. Regiment "rods" made Lo and Li stand against the wall of a room each holding a stool at arm's length in his right hand. They had to stand until they agreed to sign attacks on Mao Tse-tung and the proletarian headquarters which had been drafted for them. If the prisoner's hand should sink, even slightly, he was beaten with a stick until he either raised the stool to horizontal position again or collapsed on the floor. Under this kind of treatment, repeated day after day, the two cadres finally signed the material forced upon them, and their "confessions" were then used to prove that the 4s harbored a counter-revolutionary clique at its very center.

Believing the "confessions" of Lo and Li insufficient to prove their case, on April 14 the Regiment kidnaped two more cadres from the ranks of the 4s, a man named Wen Hsueh-min and a woman named Jao Wei-tsu. These two they held and tortured in the same way and in due course extracted "confessions" even more damning than the revelations attributed to Lo and Li. Thus the myth of the "Lo-Wen-Li-Jao counter-revolutionary conspiracy" was born.

The 4s retaliated on April 20 by seizing a cadre who belonged to the Regiment, one Tao-seng. This so angered the Regiment militants that they issued an ultimatum: "Return Tao-seng within forty-eight hours or suffer the consequences!" The consequences were to be a general attack on the buildings held by the 4s.

Fearing the attack, the 4s began to fortify the Science Building, their main stronghold. At the same time they broadcast an announcement that anyone coming within fifty meters of this building would be seized. When a Regiment fighter inadvertently crossed the line he was captured and held prisoner. This was the incident the Regiment had been waiting for. On the next day, April 23, the Regiment launched an offensive against the Meeting Hall, a strategic location at the north end of the central oval that had until then been frequently used— but never permanently occupied—by the 4s.

As excuse for their action the Regiment claimed that four hundred spears had been stored there. This was a lie to which the Regiment lent credence by sending a very small student through the utility tunnels into the building. When he came back he reported spears everywhere. Morally buttressed by the alleged warlike preparations in 4s territory, Kuai Ta-fu ordered the Regiment to attack.

Post mortems in Peking in 1971 tended toward the conclusion that the escalation of the factional struggle into open warfare in April 1968 could not be explained in terms of campus issues alone. It was not a spontaneous development of the student movement. Kuai Ta-fu's attack was planned and carried through after the exposure of the Yang-Yu-Fu clique at the central command level in the Peoples Liberation Army. Yang Ch'eng-wu had been chief of staff of the army, Yu Li-hsin had been political director of the airforce, while Fu Chung-p'i had commanded the Peking Garrison. They were removed from their commands in March 1968 because they were members of the ultra-left May 16 Group, just as Wang Li, Kuang Feng, and Ch'i Pen-yu had earlier been removed from the Central Cultural Revolution Group. This put the May 16 forces in a desperate position. It was necesary to create a diversion, if possible even a provocation, which would put Mao Tse-tung's proletarian headquarters on the spot, force it to intervene in the student movement, expose it to attack, and thus give the May 16 Group a chance to re-group. Kuai Ta-fu was apparently chosen as the one to do the job.

Whether Kuai was a conscious member of the May 16th Group or only an ambitious rebel with ultra-left politics remains unclear.* Whatever his subjective state, objectively he seems to have colluded in a plan to provoke violence and to have carried it through systematically. Starting in March he made several attempts to persuade the Regiment to take up arms, but though he carried most of his "iron rods" with him, he failed to persuade the rank-and-file and his plans were therefore rejected. On April 22 at a special meeting in the Aeronautics Building, he tried once again. This time he made sure no objectors came to the meeting by inviting only those he was sure of and by personally standing guard at the door. After calling the meeting to order he said that the exposure of Yang, Yu, and Fu proved that there were counter-revolu-

---

*See Chapter 27, p. 275.

tionary conspirators at the highest level.* Their campus equivalent was the 4s.

"Now reason no longer works," declared Kuai in his persuasive oratorical style. "We have to move on to armed struggle. Once the fighting starts, if a 'red' hand intervenes it will support us, if a 'black' hand intervenes we will expose it." (By a 'red' hand he presumably meant Ch'en Po-ta, later exposed as a leader of the ultra-left; by a 'black' hand he meant Chou En-lai.) "This is a struggle between the Kuomintang and the Communist Party. It can never be settled with mere words."

When several of his stalwarts objected that it was almost May 1, an important national holiday, and that they would be severely criticized for starting any fighting at such a time, Kuai replied, "Never mind, the fighting will only last three days. We'll wipe them out and it will be all over before the festival. The Central Committee will support us."

These arguments carried the day. The rest of the meeting was devoted to specific plans for seizing the Meeting Hall and for laying down a propaganda screen that would win sympathy for the Regiment. The propaganda was issued from the Aeronautical Institute, where a small group of Regiment militants met to write an appeal to the Central Committee. "The Lo-Wen-Li-Jao clique has forced matters to a head," they proclaimed. "Faced with this intolerable situation, we have taken up arms."

There is an old Chinese saying that "The devil makes the first appeal." The Regiment, having decided to take the offensive, bombarded the public with material that put all the blame on the 4s. Meanwhile Kuai, having set everything up, left the campus. In case the fighting backfired, in case the Central Committee blamed the Regiment, Kuai would be in the clear. He could not be held responsible for events that occurred in his absence.

---

*In the in-fighting of the Cultural Revolution it was common practice to turn things inside out or upside down to suit the purposes of the moment. Though allied with Yang, Yu, and Fu, Kuai could use their fall as clear demonstration of a threat to Mao in order to mobilize people for an action that in fact threatened Mao's position and policy.

14
Armed Struggle

A Regiment commander with one hundred "troops" occupied the Meeting Hall shortly after midnight on April 23.
At dawn the Regiment loudspeakers blared forth the news
that four hundred spears had been found, that the action had
been taken in the nick of time, and that it had frustrated a major
offensive planned by the 4s.

Thus began the violent fighting which lasted through July
and steadily escalated from fists, sticks, and stones, through
"cold" weapons like swords and spears to "hot" weapons like
revolvers, rifles, hand grenades, and rockets.

The 4s, taken off guard at the Meeting Hall, immediately
began to prepare the weapons they were accused of already
possessing. Crews worked through the small hours cutting pipe
in spear-like lengths with angled points and making shields of
aluminum sheeting. Not long after the Regiment's victory announcement the 4s' hastily armed forces occupied the Generator
Building, just to the east of the Meeting Hall and across the
central oval from the Science Building.

When the Regiment leaders discovered that the 4s had
occupied the Generator Building, they launched a massive attack
aimed at taking it back. A People's Liberation Army Propaganda
Team made up of navy men had arrived on the campus some
time before.* Hearing that a violent fight was about to take
place, Team members rushed to the scene and tried to dissuade
the Regiment "rods" from continuing. Key leaders from both

---

*Propaganda teams were actually work teams sent in to various
cultural and production units to solve problems. They were called
"propaganda teams" because the designation "work team" had been
in disrepute ever since the work teams sent in by Liu Shao-Ch'i suppressed the masses of the students all over China. Also, since the key
solution to most problems was deep study of Mao Tse-tung's policies,
they made propaganda—the propagation of Mao Tse-tung Thought—
the heart of their work.

sides signed an agreement to stop fighting and to evacuate what each had seized. But even before the ink had dried, Regiment forces launched a second assault on the Generator Building. Losing control of the ground floor, the defenders retreated upstairs. Regiment spearmen using ladders forced several second-story windows, stabbing all who got in the way. The retreating 4s had to leap to the ground to escape. Some got away. Some were injured as they landed. An ambulance driven by a soldier from the Peking Garrison Command removed the stabbed and the maimed who managed to escape, but quite a few were captured.

When Kuai learned that an ambulance under orders from the Propaganda Team had rescued his enemies he was furious. The Regiment loudspeaker cursed the driver and accused him of supplying the 4s with weapons. When the vehicle returned to the scene Regiment fighters surrounded it, pulled the driver from his seat, and took him to a quiet spot in the grounds of the Summer Palace where they stripped and beat him. They wanted an admission that he had orders to support the "reactionary" 4s. When he refused to comply, they put him in the sidecar of a motorcycle and drove him (hung with signs) around the campus as an object lesson to all who would interfere in student affairs.

Tsu, of the Regiment, had this to say about that first battle: "I was asked to lead the assault on the Meeting Hall but I refused. I was not prepared for violent fighting that night. But the next day I took an active part in the assault on the Generator Building. In fact, I helped carry a ladder. I was the third person through the second-story window in the attack that defeated the 4s. What brought me into the fight? It was the meeting in the middle of the night. I was convinced that the Lo-Wen-Li-Jao clique was real and that the 4s represented the Kuomintang. Since this was the same fight between two headquarters that had split the Central Committee, we had to fight for the right of Mao Tse-tung and the proletarian headquarters to speak. How could we let evil schemers succeed? The time had come to shed blood for the Central Committee and for Chairman Mao!"

After the first battle the campus was quiet for a few days as both sides, entrenched in the buildings which they had seized, made weapons, fortified their positions, and tried to bring in supplies.

A second battle, on April 29, began as a clash over rice. Just before noon on that day, two truckloads of rice arrived from the city and proceeded toward a campus warehouse to unload. The 4s, anticipating a protracted struggle with the Regiment, sallied out in force to seize the trucks and bring the grain back to the Science Building. Too late, the Regiment commanders realized what had happened. They sent troops to seize the trucks but they were driven off by the 4s, who not only came out of the Science Building in force but threw rocks and heavy objects from above. The Regiment forces failed to get the rice but they did capture two prisoners.

Having lost the new rice, the Regiment sent a truck to one of the dining halls to seize the rice stored there. The truck was loaded with spear-bearing fighters. En route it ran into a hail of rocks launched by a detachment of 4s. As it swerved to avoid the rocks the truck tipped over, spilling its armed occupants in a heap on the ground. They all crawled out unhurt, but the truck had already run over a hapless 4. He was dead.

Crowds of uncommitted campus people and peasants from nearby villages turned out to watch the fighting. Children, excited by the violence, joined in the rock throwing. But after a while the battle subsided without a decisive victory for either side. The shock of one student dead under the wheels cooled the ardor of both sides and their "rods" retreated in disorder.

A third battle took place in the pre-dawn hours of May 2, when the Regiment launched a surprise attack on the 4s who held the Civil Engineering Building at the south end of the central oval. The Regiment, aping central government announcements concerning the fighting in the straits of Taiwan, had broadcast that they would only fight every other day and would never attack on holidays. The 4s, taking them at their word, went to sleep exhausted on May 1, a holiday. They were totally unprepared for the miiltary action that occurred after midnight, hence technically not on the holiday. Regiment fighters gained the second floor of the building before the 4s awoke. Jumping out of their beds in their shorts, the defenders seized on anything handy to throw at their attackers, but it was too late. A few escaped by jumping out the windows. Twenty were captured. One of these had a deep spear gash beside his eye, another had a badly sprained ankle. Expensive electric meters and other items of equipment in the building were smashed.

Though the casualties were light, the damage to the 4s was great because all twenty of the people captured were militants, hard-core "rods." Without them the 4s' fighting capacity was seriously weakened. Fortunately for the losers, two days later they captured a vice-leader of the Regiment, the assistant director of its Eastern Fighting District. This gave them a certain parity in regard to prisoners. The Regiment already held a 4s Headquarters Committee member and a director of one of its fighting districts. Since both sides wanted their leaders back, negotiations began for a wholesale prisoner exchange. The 4s had the most to gain from this since they held only fourteen Regiment people while the Regiment held twenty-four 4s. The talks took place in the middle of May.

"I was the head of the negotiating team for the 4s," said Wang. "We held our first talk in front of the Mao Tse-tung statue between the First Classroom Building, held by the Regiment, and the Agricultural Engineering Building, held by the 4s. It was safe because the main forces of each faction could gather on the roof of their fortress and keep watch on the other side.

"First we agreed on the spot for the exchange, which was the ground in front of the statue where we were negotiating. The date, it was decided, would be May 16 and the time 10 A.M. The 4s would concentrate their prisoners in the Agricultural Engineering Building and the Regiment would concentrate theirs in the First Classroom Building.

"When the great day arrived the 4s were lined up to the east of the statue, the Regiment to the west. Each side sent a delegation of three accompanied by a doctor into the building held by the other to see the prisoners. No prisoner would be accepted whose injuries endangered his life, for we were interested in effective fighters, not casualties. The injuries that concerned us included not only those received in the fighting, but those inflicted during the beatings and rough treatment afterward as each side tried to make its captives confess to counterrevolutionary activity and sign papers repudiating their past loyalties.

"As the prisoners, under escort, simultaneously passed the dividing line in front of the statue, the crowds of peaceful campus inhabitants who had come to watch clapped and cheered. Was this not a first step toward peace? What the onlookers didn't know was that each side had played tricks on the other. We 4s held back two prisoners who did not appear on our name list and the Regiment held back three. Both sides knew that the other had cheated but neither admitted it or made a public issue of it at the time. We saved our accusations for the bitter debates that followed."

Altogether the 4s gave up twelve of the fourteen prisoners they held while the Regiment gave up twenty-two out of twenty-five. Far from being a step toward peace, this prisoner exchange only stimulated further war. Each side was reinforced with loyal troops angry over mistreatment at the hands of their captors and determined to fight on.

The fourth and final battle with cold weapons took place on May 30. Again it was the Regiment that took the offensive, this time against the Bathhouse in the northeast sector of the campus, which was still held by the 4s even though the Regiment had for some time held the Old Dining Hall adjacent to it.

Kuai Ta-fu chose May 30 for this action as a political ploy. It was the anniversary of the Regiment attempt, one year earlier, to set up a revolutionary committee for the whole University. In 1967 a name list, comprising only Regiment people and close allies, had been submitted a few hours in advance to the Central Committee. Since it was blatantly factional and since there was no time to modify or expand the list, Chou En-lai rejected it, saying that it was impossible to approve a partisan list of this sort for the organ of power that would run China's most important university. The rejection had wrecked Kuai's hopes for taking power at Tsinghua, and had angered all the Regiment "rods." They thought they had earned the right to lead their institution. Now they wanted to mount a violent demonstration aimed at showing up the Premier's action and placing all blame for the continue disunity and chaos on the campus on him. The attack on the Bathhouse was set for the exact day, hour, and minute that Chou En-lai had rejected the Regiment's 1967 list.

What Kuai had planned for May 30, 1968, was not just an attack on the Bathhouse, but a general offensive that would finish off the 4s and leave the campus in the hands of the Regiment. He hoped that by attacking the Bathhouse with a small unit he would draw out the 4s' main forces in a rescue attempt. The Regiment's best units would then leap from hiding along the road and decisively defeat the 4s—whom they outnumbered almost two to one. This plan did not work. The alert 4s discovered the Regiment ambush in time and refused to walk into the trap. The fighting at the Bathhouse also went awry.

The Regiment first tried to take the two-story building with assault ladders. But the second-floor windows were narrow. Only one man at a time could mount for entry. The defenders easily held the attackers off with long spears. Kuai, after studying the situation, decided to throw a bridge across the gap between the Old Dining Hall roof and the Bathhouse roof. To make sure that no defenders manned the Bathhouse roof, mobile "artillery" was assembled in the form of hand carts loaded with stones and equipped with slingshots made of bicycle innertubes. This "artillery" kept the roof under such a devastating hail of missiles that the 4s could not prevent the laying of the ladder across the gap between the two buildings. Planks laid over the ladder rungs made a walk across which a courageous contingent of Regiment "rods" then charged.

When the full weight of the assault group pressed down upon the ladder, it bent just enough to cause the far end to slip off the edge of the roof. Down came the ladder bridge, the planks, the assault platoon, and all its weapons, down in a heap between the two buildings. Fortunately, Kuai had prepared for the worst by piling straw under the bridge. His men fell into the straw and no one was badly hurt.

After the bridge collapsed Kuai concentrated his fighters at the north end of the building, where they tried once more to storm up ladders to the second-story windows. By concentrating a great hail of rock artillery on the windows, the Regiment fighters hoped to drive the defenders back and thus make entry possible. But their tactics failed again and again. One brave warrior fell or was pushed from the top of a ladder and landed head first on a rock, crushing his skull. He later died.

Unwilling to call off the attack, Kuai transferred his ambush contingent to the Bathhouse, leaving only twenty stalwarts to block the road against the 4s' uncommitted troops. When they saw this opening the 4s pushed forward with a formidable contingent of spear bearers behind a "tank." The tank was made out of a tractor welded over with steel plate. When the twenty Regiment fighters saw this monster coming they formed a line across the road, but what could they do with spears against its steel plate? As the tank came close they broke ranks and fled, only to be charged by the 4s' spearmen, who turned the retreat into a rout. One of the Regiment fighters, run through by a spear, bled to death.

To stop the 4s who were advancing from the south, Kuai ordered his "Flag" bow-and-arrow team into the fray. They fired a hail of arrows point blank at the opposition, killing one and wounding several.

The tank, invulnerable to arrows, kept going, but a little further down the road the Regiment defenders had buried what looked like a mine. "If you come any further you'll be blown up," they shouted to the tank driver.

Not knowing whether the mine was real or not, the tank driver hesitated. Several Regiment fighters took advantage of this pause to rush forward and set the tank on fire with Molotov cocktails. Its crew had to abandon it before it blew up. One of them was so badly burned that three years later his face had still not healed.

With their tank out of action, with its crew scorched, with one man dead from an arrow and several others wounded, the 4s' main force gave up the assault and retreated into an old dormitory building to the west that had long been one of their strongholds. There they took up defensive positions in the basement.

At this point Kuai became desperate. So many had been wounded and several were already dead or dying on both sides, yet nothing had been won. Far from taking power, it looked as if the Regiment might even have to retreat. Kuai ordered his "rods" to pour gasoline on the Bathhouse. Molotov cocktails were quickly made and thrown against the gas-soaked walls. Flames shot up around the building. The 4s were trapped inside.

The defenders had had nothing to eat or drink since the night before. With their throats parched and their clothes scorched, they called out that they wanted to surrender. But Kuai would not listen. Instead of putting out the fire, he ordered more fuel. When the Haitien fire department arrived, he tried to prevent the firemen from going anywhere near the building.

This angered the peasants who had gathered from far and near to watch the battle.

"Don't burn people to death! How can you go to such extremes? Put up a ladder! Let the students out!" they shouted.

Finally Kuai relented.

As the scorched and suffocating 4s crawled down the rescue ladder, they were arrested as prisoners of war. The 4s lost a major fighting force—over thirty of their best people, the main troops of the Generator Building fighting team.

15
Siege

The bloody battle of the Bathhouse made no sense at all to any but the hard-core leaders of the two quarreling factions. Uncommitted people who watched from the sidelines became angry and embittered but they could find no way to stop the slaughter. The next day many people left the campus with their bedrolls on their backs. Tsinghua, they said, was no longer safe for anyone. Students, staff, family members alike began a general retreat, leaving a shrinking core of "activists" to fight it out.

Those who remained in the family quarters established their own self-defense units. They didn't care what faction a student belonged to, they wouldn't let any partisan into the residential area. And this in spite of the fact that the staff and their families were divided in their loyalties, almost everyone being sympathetic to, if not a member of, either the Regiment or the 4s. But whatever their allegiances, they had no use for the violent fighting. When Regiment "rods" came to their quarters, people linked to the Regiment would come out to drive them off saying, "We already hold this place so why don't you go away?" When the 4s came they got the same treatment from their cohorts inside the family quarters. Thus adherents of both factions united to keep the students out and prevent the fighting from spreading to their homes. This protective reaction on the part of the only remaining permanent residents on the campus resulted in almost complete isolation for those students still committed to the political battle. They barricaded themselves inside the buildings they held and sallied out only for sporadic raids on the other side.

The taking of the Bathhouse was the last big battle fought face to face. With one dead on each side and many wounded or badly burned, factional leaders shied away from new direct confrontations in favor of a strategy of protracted siege and countersiege, where few if any were exposed to hostile action and the contest became one of who could outlast whom. There were at least two objective reasons for this change in the character of the fighting. First, the original jigsaw relationship where the factions held alternate buildings and found themselves face to face throughout the campus had been altered by the four major battles. Now, in the main, each faction held a solid section of the campus—the 4s were entrenched in the south and east while the Regiment was entrenched in the north and west. With their forces thus separated and concentrated, it became extremely difficult for either side to dislodge the other and so a stalemate was reached on the military front. An exception to this general pattern was the Science Building, held by the 4s and surrounded on all sides by Regiment territory. Cut off from their fellows in the southeast, the 4s in the Science Building could only hold out as long as possible and in the meantime find some way to break free. The Regiment countered by laying siege to the building, containing all breakout attempts and trying to force a surrender.

A further reason for avoiding face to face battles after the debacle at the Bathhouse was the escalation of weaponry. Once the 4s had entered the fray with a tank, the Regiment countered with an armored car. Both sides then brought rifles into use and began manufacturing hand grenades. The Regiment, hoping to blast the 4s out of the Science Building, experimented with several small cannon, one of which had such a fierce recoil that it drove itself into the campus creek when fired and never was recovered. The 4s, in control of a fine machine shop in the Agricultural Engineering Building, actually made a rocket. When test fired it soared high into the northern sky and fell into a commune field, giving the hard-working peasants a scare. Since the rocket carried no warhead, it did not explode. Nevertheless, the peasants did not appreciate bombardment from the skies and protested vigorously in writing to the student leaders. It is doubtful if the guilty engineers were in any frame of mind to listen, however.

A major complaint about the education in pre-Cultural Revolution Tsinghua was that its theory was divorced from practice and that its graduates were incapable of designing or producing anything useful. That may have been true then, but as the warfare on the campus developed students on both sides of the battle lines showed a remarkable capacity for creative engineering, at least where weapons of destruction were concerned, and they rapidly applied what theory they had to the practice of producing armaments and explosives of all kinds. It seemed that their technical education had not been entirely wasted. They passed this test with good, even excellent, marks . . . and tragic results.

The development of protracted positional warfare and the escalation from "cold" to "hot" weapons which occurred in June were, of course, not simply parallel, but definitely linked. Once the enemy holed up in fortress-like seclusion, "cold" spears and arrows became quite ineffective and "hot" weapons of greater range and destruction were called for. Thus the fighting at Tsinghua leaped to a new, more sophisticated, and more dangerous level.

To enforce their siege Regiment snipers took up permanent concealed positions around the Science Building with orders not to let anyone enter or leave. One of these positions was behind a little hill west of the building, a second was in the small temple besides the Meeting Hall, and a third was maintained at one of the windows of the First Classroom Building, the Regiment's headquarters, situated 100 yards or so to the south.

Chang Hsing, a Regiment "rod," held the hill position with an automatic rifle. When he asked Kuai if he should use his gun on people Kuai said, "Either don't shoot or shoot to kill!" Many times Kuai had proclaimed that, "Headquarters will be responsible for any deaths." A few days later Chang shot and killed a 4s student who ventured outside.

A second member of the 4s, Yang Chih-chun, was shot from the window of the First Classroom Building. He managed to stagger back inside the Science Building but the medical care there was inadequate. When his comrades found that in spite of their best efforts Yang was dying, they attempted to negotiate with Kuai Ta-fu by loudspeaker for permission to send him to the hospital. But Kuai would not allow this unless the 4s put up a surrender flag. This they refused to do. Finally some women members of the 4s offered to disarm themselves completely and carry Yang out. But when they tried to leave the building they were fired on. Yang finally died for lack of medical care. His father, a former guerrilla fighter, wanted to see his son's body. He made a special trip to Peking with his wife, but Kuai Ta-fu demanded that they too wave a white flag in order to cross the no man's land in the Regiment's field of fire.

"Under Japanese bayonets I never waved a white flag. Why should I surrender to you today?" countered the elder Yang. He and his wife finally left Peking in anger without seeing their son's corpse.

The Regiment's efforts to enforce their siege resulted in another death when a second tank made by the 4s tried to run vegetables through the blockade to the Science Building. An armor-piercing shell seized in South China from a shipment of supplies bound for Vietnam, penetrated the tank's armor plate and killed the driver.

Altogether, once "hot" weapons came into play, four people died of bullet wounds and one leader of the 4s, Sun Hua-t'ang, was beaten to death by the Regiment captors. Since five had been killed in the earlier fighting, a total of ten students died between April 23 and July 27 when the Workers Propaganda Team brought the fighting to an end.

That so few were killed can only have been due to luck, for once the violent fighting began neither side gave the other any quarter. Time and time again lives on each side were brought into serious jeopardy. There was, for instance, the famous incident of the tunnel, when the 4s, hoping to break out, dug an underground passage from the southeast corner of the Science Building across the central oval toward the Agricultural Engineering Building, which their own fighters still held.

They had tunneled several hundred yards toward their goal when the Regiment guards, with the aid of a pipe buried upright in the ground, discovered from the strange noises underground that digging was in progress. The Regiment forces then dug their own tunnel in at right angles to the escape route. At the proper moment, when several 4s were busy at their digging, the Regiment men blew the tunnel behind them with dynamite. A large section of the roof collapsed. As the 4s crawled out from underground spitting and gasping for breath they were captured.

Having foiled this last, desperate escape attempt, the Regiment, on July 8, tried to finish off the 4s in the Science Building by burning them out. With a high-pressure pump they sprayed gasoline on the walls and roof of the four-story structure, then set it afire with incendiary bombs. To make sure that no one escaped, they set up machine-guns covering all exits. When the local fire department rushed to the scene, Kuai personally cut off the electricity to the whole campus so that no water could be pumped for fire fighting. He also set up pickets to prevent the firemen from entering the building, while Regiment fighters disguised as firemen and armed with hand grenades stormed into the ground floor hoping to blow up the building from below. An alert PLA man on one of the fire trucks saw through this plot and sent firemen inside to drive the Regiment people out.

It was a very hot day. The eighty-odd people in the building had barely enough water to drink, to say nothing of dousing the flames. The best they could do was to throw all the furniture and other combustible matter out the windows in hopes of confining the fire to the fourth floor. This strategy worked. Though the whole roof and fourth floor of the building burned completely, the other floors were saved. The heat was so intense, however, that large cracks opened up in the concrete floors and walls below.

This huge fire, visible for miles, blazed from 7 A.M. until 10 A.M., when the firemen, overcoming the resistance of the Regiment, finally put it out.

Once again, a major effort at annihilation had failed. The war continued as a stalemate, with neither side able to defeat the other.

How could the 4s hold out so long in the isolated Science Building? Only because of their ingenuity and foresight. Wang Yung-hsien, who was in charge of the defense of the building, had foreseen a long struggle and had arranged to haul in large quantities of rice and coal while this was still possible. In a sheltered spot behind the building he had led the group in planting vegetables. In the cellar they had all pitched in and dug a well so they had their own internal water supply. After the electricity was cut off they operated the blower on their cooking fire by means of a propped-up bicycle linked by a belt to the blower pulley.

When Regiment snipers made communication by hand or flag signals on the roof too dangerous, the besieged forces kept in touch with the other 4s' units by flashing signals at night, changing their code every so often so that the Regiment could not crack it. Since snipers fired at the light whenever they saw it, the 4s' engineers worked out a remote-control system for flashing their lights. Thus they were nowhere near when the bullets flew.

Fortunately, the 4s had a doctor with them in the building from the very beginning and also a small store of medicine. The doctor established a well-run clinic and took as good care as he could of the wounded. Though he was unable to save Yang, the student who was shot from the First Classroom Building window, he did save the lives of many others. Without him the 4s could not have held out as they did.

And why did the Regiment fighters maintain their siege with such persistence?

"At that time," said Tsu, "what seemed the most important thing in the world was to take over another building. We studied works on guerrilla fighting and we studied Mao Tse-tung on tactics, prisoner policy, and every other aspect of war. With regard to the Cultural Revolution, Chairman Mao had made it clear over and over again that violent fighting was not correct. But we reasoned that this prohibition applied only to issues between factions of the people. Anything could be done to the class enemy and we were fighting class enemies! We saw ourselves as only one front in. a much larger national struggle, a struggle between two headquarters on the Central Committee, but we thought we were the focal point of this struggle. Elsewhere in the country factions had formed big alliances. The whole trend throughout society was the formation of alliances, but we thought that Tsinghua was special because at Tsinghua we were fighting the Kuomintang. Outside, where there were mainly contradictions among the people, violent fighting was wrong, but here, where we stood face to face with the enemy, violent fighting was correct."

But even Tsu left the ranks of the fighters before the end. "I found that I had been deceived," he said. "I thought I was fighting for Chairman Mao and I was convinced that once we suppressed this bad opposition clique the Central Committee could stand up and speak out without fear. But gradually I began to doubt this. The number killed and wounded increased with each battle and among the dead were people who had been good friends of mine—poor peasants of my own class. Why should we kill class brothers?

"Furthermore, it didn't turn out as our leaders had said. The Central Committee didn't support us. On the contrary, they sent people to criticize us and demand that we stop the fighting. Vice-Premier Hsieh Fu-chih himself came and criticized us severely. I realized that if we went on with our war we would be making even bigger mistakes, and that I would be making the biggest mistake of all because I had been in the militia at home. I knew how to make explosives and mines. I knew about war.

"So finally even I drifted away. Toward the end of July there were only about 400 people involved in the battle on both sides. Of these, only about 300 were students—200 with the Regiment and not much more than 100 with the 4s. The other 100 were outsiders who had joined on opposite sides. They were pretty bad people on the whole, people who couldn't get along with the revolutionary committees in their home villages or institutions. They had run away. They found empty rooms here on the campus and moved in without anybody's permission. At meal time all they had to do was take their bowls to the student kitchen and eat. Most of them loved brawling and so both sides welcomed them, they were so good at it. But they were also without principles—sadists, some of them: it was they who beat the 4s' leader to death; and it was mainly outsiders, torture specialists, who mishandled the Lo-Wen-Li-Jao group.

"None of these bad eggs was killed or wounded. They were always urging us to greater extremes, but it was the good young brothers who died—not the hooligans.

"After the fire failed to drive the 4s out of the Science Building, Kuai's men worked to develop a cannon powerful enough to knock the building down. If the Workers Propaganda Team hadn't come when it did, no telling what would have happened or how many people might have died."

In regard to Kuai Ta-fu and his steady deterioration from a rebel hero into an autocratic factionalist, Tsu said, "We intellectuals are inept. We thought, 'We'll smash the other side.'

But we found that we couldn't do it. Kuai began with a campaign of political suppression. When that didn't work he tried violence. When that failed he gradually changed from a revolutionary rebel into a leader carrying out the bourgeois reactionary line—he turned into the opposite of what he had been, he became an oppressor.

"Today we understand Chairman Mao's directive that one must lead petty-bourgeois radicals onto the proletarian track. But when Mao Tse-tung went south in 1967 and returned with a warning for us young people that this was a time when we would be prone to make mistakes, we were puzzled. We looked hard for the mistakes we might make, but we actually thought we were immune. Kuai Ta-fu said, 'I have thought and thought, but I can't think what mistakes I might make.' Yet within a month, influenced by the advice of Ch'i Pen-yu, he led us full cry ahead down the road of violent confrontation.

"In 1968 Chairman Mao met again with us young rebels and again he warned us against serious mistakes of sectarianism, anarchism, and self-interest, but we forgot those warnings almost at once.

"Before the Cultural Revolution Kuai Ta-fu was famous for his arrogance. He looked down on everyone. When suppressed by the capitalist-roaders he showed a revolutionary side, but after he 'turned over' and became a renowned leader his true world outlook began to show. His world outlook found full expression in the Cultural Revolution—especially at the middle and the end. The poison of the old system, all the feudal and the bourgeois leftovers, were exposed in him and in us and we showed the destructiveness of petty-bourgeois intellectuals."

"But," I said to Tsu, "you poor peasants really cannot be called intellectuals."

"Well," he replied, "by family background many of us are poor peasants. But although our families influenced us in a good direction, all around us society pushed us to climb up. Once we got into middle school and went on to higher schools the traditional force of Chinese culture had a great influence and it was patently careerist.

"Just look at me. I got accepted at Tsinghua through an examination. Then I was called in by the leaders of my middle school. They told me I had gained glory for my school by doing so well. They said Tsinghua was not an ordinary place but one where only the highest technical people are trained: 'We hope you will study your chosen field hard and make a great contribution to the motherland in the field of science.'

"They also said that Tsinghua's teaching methods were the best. 'Make comparisons, write us constantly what you learn there, help us improve our methods.'

"They didn't say a thing about world outlook, about Mao Tse-tung Thought, about learning from the workers and peasants —all they said was try hard to be a famous scientist!

"And once I got here all the professors bragged about their special fields and about the great engineers they hoped to turn out. They competed in boasting about the glory of their work. Liao Szu-ching said, 'My profession is to train engineers, the engineers who will carry along all the other engineers.'

"A typical slogan in civil engineering was, 'A 100,000-foot tower raised from the earth—it all depends on the pen and the hand of the architect!' In physics it was, 'Without Newton no physics!' All this causes one to look down on labor. When we first came from the countryside we had the habit of labor, but our school authorities told us our thinking was too simple. 'What can you learn from peasants?' asked Chiang Nan-hsiang. 'Can you learn illiteracy from them?'

"When we suggested that we sweep and maintain our own buildings, the leaders said, 'No, concentrate your full energy on your studies. After you graduate you can then make a better contribution.' All this influenced us. Without our knowing it, it went deeper and deeper into us. In our minds we thought engineers and scientists were great and the work of peasants and workers was not for intellectuals! So it is not by accident that intellectuals think only they are revolutionary. Really, our world outlook after coming here was petty-bourgeois!"

16
People Set Aside

Throughout this long period—as the student movement grew, overthrew the Work Team, split, united, split again, and finally bogged down in armed struggle—the leading professors and higher cadres of Tsinghua remained under suspension, with no voice either in the running of the University or in the development or disintegration of the mass movement.

Many staff members and most of the ordinary teachers took part at one level or another in major political developments, but the professors, considered to be "bourgeois academic authorities," and the higher cadres, considered to be capitalist-roaders, continued as targets, not motive forces, of the Cultural Revolution. They adjusted as best they could to each successive constellation of power. To get a picture of what these people thought and felt, we talked to both professors and cadres about their role after the Cultural Revolution began. The most vocal was Professor Ch'ien Wei-ch'ang, who taught mechanical engineering and who had done research in rocket propulsion at Berkeley. After his return to China in 1949 he had become an important figure on the Tsinghua campus, in the city of Peking, and in the national government. Due to his great reputation as a theoretician, he had simultaneously held twenty-seven different government positions—advisory, honorary, and active—among them the post of vice-president of Tsinghua under Chiang Nan-hsiang. He was lumped with Chiang as an unreconstructed Rightist by the student rebels once the Cultural Revolution began.

But there were important differences between Professor Ch'ien and Chiang Nan-hsiang. Chiang was a Communist, a known revolutionary who flew a revisionist "red flag" to oppose the "red flag" of Mao Tse-tung. Ch'ien was a "bourgeois academic authority" who flew a "white flag" to oppose the "red flag" of Mao Tse-tung—a "white flag" that everyone could see. Both Chiang and Ch'ien believed that the professors should rule the school, but they went about achieving this in different ways. Chiang Nan-hsiang recruited professors into the Communist Party and promoted young Communists to professorships in order to create a professors' Party branch at the University that could rule the school clothed in a "red flag." Ch'ien was more direct. He simply declared that science has no politics and that the professors, as masters of science, should run the University— period. For this he was denounced as a Rightist in 1957. He was under a political cloud throughout the Great Leap period, but afterward, when Chiang Nan-hsiang reversed Mao's Great Leap policies, practice at the University returned to the road advocated by Ch'ien, his "Rightist cap" was removed, and he again assumed a prominent role on the campus and in the country.

In 1966 Ch'ien was again set aside as a Rightist. This made him a target of the mass movement, but not so important a target as the capitalist-roaders who had actually wielded Party power. During the first weeks of the movement large numbers of critical posters appeared around his house. He was called before mass meetings for special repudiation more than once, and whenever Chiang Nan-hsiang faced the people Ch'ien Wei-ch'ang accompanied him because everyone considered them to be two of a kind.

After the rebel movement broke into irreconcilable factions in April 1967, there was at least one thing beside finances that both sides agreed on—that was that Professor Ch'ien Wei-ch'ang was a Rightist. The 4s called him a "big Rightist" while the Regiment called him an "old Rightist." Between these two designations there was no difference in principle. Since both sides repudiated him, Ch'ien could not take part in the mass movement even if he had wanted to, so he spent the years from 1966 through 1968 under the supervision of whatever group came forward to claim him. At first he was shut in a room by himself and told to write self-critical material, but this became so boring that he asked for some work. He was then sent to join a construction crew which busied itself putting up the reed matting on which posters were displayed. After working at this for a while, he took charge of this team's warehouse, but when violent fighting broke out nine months later, he couldn't control the members of either faction when they came to seize materials from under his nose. He was asked to leave. Thereafter he reported to the construction team head office every day to do a few hours of paper work, or simply to sit around. The balance of his time he spent at home The air here was never still, for the residential quarter was flanked on one side by the First Classroom Building and on the other by the Agricultural Engeneering Building and both buildings, as factional centers, generated an endless stream of loudspeaker polemics. Night and day the shrill voices of the opposing propagandists flooded the whole area with amplified sound until it came to be as much a part of life's background as wind, rain, or sunlight—and, in the end, as little noticed.

Ch'ien did not fear for his personal safety even during the fiercest battles, but he did worry from time to time about where he would be sent by whichever faction came out on top. Since neither side had any use for him he could hardly look to the future with optimism.

Throughout most of this period Professor Ch'ien drew his salary, but in 1968 the amount was cut. Then, when the fighting began, Kuai needed all the cash he could get and no salaries were paid at all to "set-aside" professors. This created difficulties at home, especially since Ch'ien had to support two school-aged daughters, but his wife, who taught in a local middle school, always drew her salary, so the family survived.

Did all the polemics and upheavals have much effect upon his outlook? Not really. It wasn't until later, after the Workers Propaganda Team came, that Ch'ien faced the question of his own ideology.

The years from 1966 to 1968 passed in much the same manner for the other "bourgeois academic authorities," such as T'ung Shih-pai, the electronics specialist, and Shih Kuo-heng, the Harvard-trained sociologist. "Capitalist-roaders" on the other hand, found the going considerably tougher. To get an idea of this we talked again to Liu Ping, the University Party Committee member who had returned to the campus on June 20, 1966, confident of his "left" stand, only to be seized by student

rebels and dragged off to a struggle meeting with a tall dunce
cap on his head.

"They took me completely by surprise that day," said Liu
Ping, his face expressing some of the amazement he had then
felt. "They removed me bodily from the car and carried me
away before I even had a chance to speak. Here I was, a high
cadre of this University and the students were leading me around
with a dunce cap on my head! I couldn't accept it at all, not
at all!"

Three times the students hauled Liu Ping before large public meetings where posters attacking his administration hung
everywhere. Even when they released him and sent him home
he could not get away from the attacks because posters were
hung in front of his house and even on his house, and day and
night small groups of students came to rouse him and ask questions about past acts and statements.

"I couldn't think it through. I didn't know what mistakes
I had made. I had worked so hard and shared the hard life of the
students right out in the countryside. How come I had suddenly
fallen into this mess? From then on it was nothing but eat, go
to repudiation meetings, and read big-character posters about
myself and my colleagues."

What did the posters say? Each attacked a different facet
of Liu Ping's past work. One quoted him as having written a
few years before, "The old system is damaging young people.
I am opposed to it." "But," his critics went on to ask, "what reform did he ever carry out?"

"Why is Tsinghua's curriculum so protracted?" asked another.

"Why are worker and peasant students dropped?"

"Is your last name *Ma* or *Hsiu* [Marx or Revision]?"

Liu Ping had once given a report entitled *Break with Bourgeois Thought.* "But," said one poster, "you never mentioned
who was in power here or what line was being carried out.
You only handled a few selfish ideas in the students' heads!"

When in 1961 the administration decided that too much
time was being wasted on labor and political study, Liu had led
in cutting back on both. "Repudiate bourgeois thought, but don't

go to extremes," he had said. Now posters questioned his extremes. Had not "vocational study" and "the pure technical
viewpoint" been extremes? Liu's problem was not one of bureau-
cracy or commandism. He had been even tempered. He had
never scolded people or cursed them out. His attitudes and style
of work had always been good, perhaps because he had never
done detailed work among the people but had sat in the head
office writing big reports and drawing up key regulations. No,
Liu Ping's problem concerned political line. He had carried
out a wrong line, but at first this was not at all easy to understand.

Reading posters, hearing criticism from the masses, and
writing endless self-criticisms generated a sharp struggle in
Liu Ping's mind. There seemed to be no way out. The Work
Team would not accept any criticism that did not admit to
counter-revolutionary thinking. Since Liu Ping refused to admit
any such thing, all his statements were rejected. Furthermore, he
was not at all convinced he had made any serious mistakes.
What then should he do?

"Should I just be pessimistic and give up, or should I go on
working for the revolution, confront myself, and change myself? I found myself full of complaints. I had worked so hard,
only to end up with a dunce cap! Why not say to hell with it?

"But after all, I was brought up by the Communist Party
and Chairman Mao. I had spent my life in the revolution. Why
should I give up now? Every time that I decided 'to hell with it'
another thought always followed. If I quit, how can I face Chairman Mao? I decided to undergo this test and continue making
revolution."

When the Work Team left, the Preparatory Committee
under Liu Tao and Ho Peng-fei took responsibility for the 146
"set-aside" cadres. When the Committee was overthrown in
December 1966, and the United Regiment took over, the demands on Liu Ping remained the same: he must listen to criticism, read the posters that repudiated him, and examine himself.

"After a time I began to ask myself, 'Why is it that an old
cadre, one who joined the revolution and the Communist Party
while still so young, should have so many opinions raised against

him?' Night after night I could not sleep. I thought and thought. I studied books, I read the history of the Communist Party of the Soviet Union. I read and reread the writings of Chairman Mao. Mao said, 'We Communists aim to wage revolution, not to be big officials, our cadres are ordinary working people, not bourgeois gentlemen sitting on the necks of the people.' Stalin told an old Greek tale about the man Anteus who was strong as long as his feet stayed planted on the earth, but who immediately became weak when his feet left the earth. He was referring to the Communist Party and the masses. So I thought about Stalin's words and Mao Tse-tung's words and I began to see that I had been divorced from the masses. If that was not so, why were so many people angry at me? Why did so many criticize me? I must have divorced myself from the masses.

"Once I saw this my thinking began to change. I began to think that perhaps I really had made some mistakes. Before this, when they put the hat on my head and asked me if I had made mistakes I said, 'Yes.' But really, in my heart, I didn't agree. Now I began to see the truth and my anger began to cool. When the students wrote posters I wrote posters too. When meetings were held I joined in and actively criticized myself. Gradually, as we studied Mao Tse-tung Thought together, I realized that I had made mistakes in line and policy and then I realized that if they hadn't attacked me hard I would never have been shaken, I would never have realized my mistakes at all!

"By that time it was the spring of 1967. Before that, when I was called to meetings I didn't feel like going. But after that, when I knew there would be a meeting I went early. When they announced over the loudspeaker that at a certain time and place Liu Ping would face criticism and repudiation I went there ahead of them. I was on hand, ready to criticize myself.

"I realized that if a Communist makes a mistake it doesn't matter as long as he is willing to change. Mao Tse-tung says that mistakes are not serious if one corrects them. So my spirits revived. Under criticism, repeated attacks, and repudiation from the masses, I studied Mao Tse-tung's writings and I felt much closer to Mao.

"Once again I studied Mao's speech to the Second Plenary Session of the Seventh Central Committee. This I had not only read before, I had actually lectured to others about it. In this speech Mao talks about those who can withstand the lead bullets of the enemy, but who go down before sugar-coated bullets. Now as I read these words over and over again, I felt that I was exactly one of those who had been defeated by sugar-coated bullets. Always before, when I read those passages, I really didn't understand them. Only after I had made serious mistakes and learned both positive and negative lessons did I learn how deep this teaching was.

"When I say I was defeated by sugar-coated bullets, I don't mean that I was corrupted by soft living. No. It wasn't that. It was that I couldn't tell bourgeois ideology from proletarian ideology. I couldn't tell revisionism from Marxism-Leninism, Liu Shao-ch'i's revisionist line from Mao Tse-tung's revolutionary line. Those were the bullets that defeated me. So I read Mao's speech over and over again and each time I had a deeper understanding of it. With tears in my eyes I asked myself, 'Why couldn't I understand this before? How come I have made such serious mistakes?'

"I remembered all those who had lost their lives. Mao Tse-tung once said, 'Thousands of martyrs have died serving the people. Let us raise our banner high and follow in their bloodstained footsteps.' I thought of so many comrades, people who had been so close to me, people who had slept on the same kang with me and studied in the same classes in Yenan—those martyrs' faces swept through my head like scenes from a film and I felt terrible that after victory I had gone so far astray. But then I thought that as long as I change it doesn't matter and I decided to stand on the side of the masses."

One reason why the "set-aside" cadres only slowly understood what their mistakes had been, and only slowly came to understand that there was a serious question of a two-line struggle on the campus, was because from the moment they were "set aside" their isolation from the mass movement and from the political struggle was almost total. Under the Work Team they lived under house arrest, confined four to a room.

They were ordered to study Liu Shao-chi's *On the Self-Cultiva-tion of Communists* and asked to write endless material about themselves. Only once in a while were they allowed to go out and look at the vivid array of posters that covered the campus and reflected the debates that were raging, not only locally but throughout the country. And this privilege was granted only to let them learn about the repudiation of Kuai Ta-fu, then under attack by the Work Team. They were then asked if they did not have material which would link Kuai to the old University Party Committee. Since they saw only posters critical of Kuai and no posters put up by Kuai or his supporters, they mostly refused to make any comment.

Chiang Nan-hsiang was also isolated from the mass move-ment. But this most important "Party person in authority taking the capitalist road" was not held like the others. He was allowed to stay in the city where he had freedom of movement. He rarely confronted either posters or critics. This amounted to a special form of protection for him; all the other cadres were forced to pass the *gate** set up by the Work Team.

This *gate* was not one of mass criticism or testing by the people, but was an appraisal, by the cadres of the Work Team itself, of the self-critical material written by their victims. Since the Tsinghua students demanded confrontations, these were reluctantly arranged, but only under strict control with all the speeches approved beforehand, and no one allowed to jump up from the floor for unscheduled pronouncements. When the students demanded a face-to-face meeting with Chiang Nan-hsiang, they were told that his case had not been decided, there-fore he could not be subject to mass criticism.

Liu Ping did not question all this at the time. He thought this policy was coming down from the Central Committee. To oppose it meant to oppose the Communist Party. "I thought I'd better do whatever I was asked to do. Otherwise I would be called anti-Party."

---

*To pass the *gate* means to come before a group of one's peers to make a self-criticism and to hear criticisms and suggestions from others. In this case, the Work Team cadres instead of rank-and-file colleagues sat in judgment.

During this period the mass of the students wanted to criticize the higher cadres and liberate the lower cadres, but the Work Team did just the opposite. It focused the struggle on the lower cadres and on the rank and file of the students themselves and in this way protected important people.

As soon as the Work Team was withdrawn, the lower cadres broke away from supervision and most of them found a place with one student faction or another; but the middle and higher cadre did not dare rebel and were put under the control of the Preparatory Committee. This Committee concentrated all the remaining cadres in the Biology Building, where they ate, slept, and studied together. They went out each morning for physical work. This work was light maintenance—weeding crops, repairing roads, sweeping courtyards, and tidying pathways. While at work each cadre wore a sign on his or her back: "Capitalist-roader," "Revisionist," "Mess of Poison," "Cow-Devil," or "Snake-God."

On October 6, 1966, after the huge Peking rally of revolutionary rebels from all over the country where Kuai Ta-fu finally won national recognition as a student leader, the power of the Preparatory Committee was shaken. All the cadres were suddenly released and allowed to go home. Liu Ping and two of the three other vice-secretaries of the University Party Committee (the third was sick) returned to their own houses to live, but met each day in a little room near the old Party Committee office and there continued to study and write or meet with students who came for information. The three reported for work from time to time but nobody saw to it that they worked every day.

"At this time," Liu recalled, "students, teachers, and staff had differences of opinion about the important cadres. People kept coming to us to ask about our work and our views about the old Party Committee. Had we, in the past seventeen years, carried out Mao Tse-tung's line or a revisionist line? Since at that time none of us really understood this question of line, we all insisted that we had carried out Mao Tse-tung's line. 'We may have made some mistakes and had some shortcomings,' we said, 'but what we carried out was Chairman Mao's line.' My thinking was, 'We have turned out so many graduates and the majority have done well in their jobs, doesn't this prove that achievements are central in our work? After all, we were only working hard all those years for the revolution. We didn't know anything about a revisionist line carried out by Liu Shao-ch'i.'"

In April 1967, after the United Regiment broke into two factions, Liu Ping's life became more complicated. The 4s decided that he was a good cadre and should "stand up." The Regiment decided that he was a bad cadre and should be repudiated and isolated. Both sides came to him for material to prove their case with regard to his own role and with regard to other cadres whose potential for "standing up" was being debated. Liu wrote and wrote. Altogether he produced several million characters of comment, which each side tried to use as ammunition against the other. Since he refused to play a partisan role that would give either side the advantage, and since he refused to write out any state secrets, many people, particularly in the Regiment camp, called him a "die-hard bastard." But in such matters Liu stuck to principle.

When the fighting began in the spring of 1968 the 4s invited Liu Ping to come and live with them.

Happy to break out of his longstanding isolation, he accepted the invitation. He moved to Dormitory #3 and stayed there for about a week. This proved to be a mistake. It so angered the Regiment that they sent a squad to kidnap him. They took him to the old Party Committee office under guard. Day and night three people kept watch on him. He was locked in a small room. Three meals a day were provided but he had to ask special permission even to go out to the toilet. Under these conditions he was asked to write material proving that he was a false Communist and a counter-revolutionary. When he refused, Regiment "rods" beat him.

"I said, 'No matter how much you beat me I'll never say I have betrayed the Communist Party.' How strange! It was just as if we were back under the Work Team. Then too we had had to admit we had betrayed the Party. Now Kuai was demanding the same thing!"

Why? Why was Kuai playing the role of the Work Team? Apparently to vindicate the Regiment's effort to take over the campus by armed force. If the Regiment could prove that the 4s had harbored counter-revolutionaries, then Kuai's new program, the "violent salvation of the Tsinghua situation," could be explained as a necessary step. The Central Committee had already issued an order on July 3 against violent fighting in Kweichow. Great pressure for a peaceful settlement was coming from the leaders of the Peking Revolutionary Committee. Hsieh Fu-chih, the head, had called on Kuai both publicly and privately to take the lead in a cease-fire. Liu Feng, head of the PLA's Three Support Work Team* under the Peking Garrison Command, had visited the campus, had investigated the fighting, had looked up Kuai in person, and had asked him to call off the siege of the Science Building.

Kuai's answer was yes, he would stop, if the Security Police would arrest Lo, Wen, Li, and Jao, and hold them as counter-revolutionaries. When Liu Feng refused to consider this, Kuai made efforts to enlarge his "counter-revolutionary conspiracy" by putting more pressure on such cadre as Liu Ping and Hu Chien. He never considered ending the fighting. In part this was because he was sure he was winning. The main forces of the 4s were surrounded in the Science Building. If flames couldn't drive them out then cannons would. Kuai set his technicians to work on homemade artillery that he hoped would blast right through the brick walls and concrete floors of the 4s' fortress. They would soon have to surrender or die.

Such was the situation at the end of July 1968. Of the thousands of students, teachers, and staff who had at one time or another taken part in the movement, only a few hundred still remained on the campus, and only a fraction of these still believed that the future of the revolution hinged on a military victory for their side. The rest fought on mainly because they could find no way to stop, because the slightest weakness gave

---

*Early in 1967 the army was directed by Mao to support the Cultural Revolution. This support was called "triple" or "three" support because it included support for the political left, support for agriculture, and support for industry. In other words, the army joined in and gave support to production while giving political support to antirevisionist forces.

an advantage to the other side which might easily be parlayed into lethal action. In the meantime, more outsiders had entered the fray, outsiders whose safety was assured only so long as the fighting continued and chaos reigned supreme in this small corner of North China. Under conditions of peace, their records, their histories, could hardly stand the light of day. They were the most enthusiastic about fighting it out to the end. As the days went by they played an increasingly important role.

And so the war dragged on with shots and explosions punctuating the angry rhetoric of the loudspeakers, with interrogations and beatings fouling the atmosphere of isolated rooms, with corpses rotting in the cellar of the Science Building because the 4s could find no place to bury their dead.

It was a nightmare situation that could not possibly continue, yet continue it did while its surrealistic quality engulfed the surrounding area and tainted the whole nation.

Part III

The Working Class Intervenes

The proletariat must exercise all-round dictatorship over the bourgeoisie in the field of the superstructure, including the various spheres of culture. . . . In carrying out the proletarian revolution in education, it is essential to have working-class leadership; it is essential for the masses of the workers to take part and, in cooperation with the Liberation Army fighters, bring out a revolutionary "three-in-one" combination, together wtih the activists among the students, teachers, and workers in the schools who are determined to carry the proletarian revolution in education through to the end. The workers' propaganda teams should stay permanently in the schools and take part in fulfilling all the tasks of struggle—criticism—transformation in the schools, and they will always lead the schools . . .

Mao Tse-tung, as quoted in Yao Wen-yuan,
The Working Class Must Exercise
Leadership in Everything
August 1968

17
Use Reason, Not Violence

Suddenly at 10 A.M. on the morning of July 27, 1968, huge crowds of workers, a scattering of PLA men and peasants among them, appeared before the campus gates. Each carried a little red book of Chairman Mao's quotations and copies of the July 3 and July 24 Central Committee orders, demanding that all violent confrontations cease.*

"We warmly welcome the workers who have come to propagate the July 3 Order," blared the loudspeakers manned by the Regiment. "We warmly welcome you, but please stay outside the gates. To come onto our campus is to court danger!"

Peering past the iron bars of the closed and locked West Gate, workers could see barricades of rubble blocking the tree-lined main road. In front of the first of these a sign hanging on barbed wire read, "Warning! High voltage!" In the weeds by the side of the road another sign stated succinctly, "Watch out!

---

*The July 3rd Order demanded that all fighting cease in Kwangsi. The July 24th Order demanded that all fighting cease in Shansi.

This land is mined!" In the distance the blackened and gutted roof of the Science Building was just visible through the treetops.

"You are out of step," shouted the workers. "If you don't obey the July 3 Order and stop all fighting, we are going to come in."

"Go back to your workshops. Grasp production and make revolution! We can liberate ourselves," responded the students on guard at the gate. They all carried spears. Several flouted hand grenades hanging like bunched ears of corn from military belts. Their commander brandished a hand gun.

"Why should we go back! You're wrecking everything with your senseless fighting. We have to stop you first. Stopping you is promoting production!" retorted the workers.

The debate went on for about an hour. Then the Regiment gatekeepers, realizing that they were vastly outnumbered and hearing that other workers had already entered the campus from the south, opened the West Gate and faded back into the recesses of the University grounds.

The workers, many of them clad in T-shirts and shorts, just as they had come off the night shift, surged forward. They took up positions around selected campus buildings, especially those that were important to the respective factions. With shirts clinging to perspiring backs and sweat dripping on the open pages of their red books, they began to read aloud and punctuate their reading with slogans shouted in unison.

"Use reason, not violence. Turn in your weapons. Form a big alliance!"

The hard-pressed 4s in the Science Building, though by no means ready to give up any weapons, invited the workers inside and even offered them steamed bread hot off their fire with its bicycle-powered blower. But the Regiment "rods," resentful at the slightest interference with their impending "victory," met the workers with curses and threats.

"Little climbing worms of Yang-Yu-Fu! Go back where you came from. We don't need a nursemaid!"

At three o'clock a signal shot unleashed a hail of rocks, bolts, nuts, and bottles of black ink from all the strongholds of the Regiment. Before the workers could even assess the injuries inflicted on numerous stunned and wounded comrades, detachments of spearmen charged their ranks. In the ensuing melee, the center of which shifted with lightning speed and chaotic illogic from one section of the campus to another, spears found their mark, hand grenades exploded, pistol and rifle shots rang out, and workers' blood began to flow. "Black above and red below" was the way veterans of the incident described their appearance in the eerie hours that followed—black from the ink bottles that broke on their heads and red from the blood that flowed from their wounds. At the height of the violence the sky let loose a torrent of rain that temporarily slowed the attackers and allowed the workers to regroup and restate their extraordinary slogan, "Use reason, not violence, use reason, not violence, lay down your weapons and form a big alliance." But after the rain armed assaults continued in such disparate sections of the campus as Dormitory #10 and the handsome new building known as #9003.

When peace finally returned to Tsinghua in the early morning hours of July 28, five workers lay dead, 731 nursed serious wounds, 143 had been taken prisoner, and many of the prisoners had been beaten. Yet no group of workers had counterattacked, no students had been harmed. The only student casualties occurred when a group of Regiment "rods" fled the campus in a truck at dawn and hit a tree.

The extraordinary discipline shown by thousands of ordinary workers in the course of twenty-four hours of extreme provocation had little if any historical precedent. Who were these men and women and how did they come to be on the Tsinghua campus that fateful day?

Among those with whom we talked no one seemed to know just where or with whom the idea of a massive but peaceful invasion of the University campus first arose. It seems to have come initially from the workers of the Hsinhua Printing Plant. They themselves had experienced serious factional splits, but with the aid of a team of soldiers from the 8341 Army (the guard detachment of the Central Committee, Mao Tse-tung's own headquarters unit), they had earlier formed a big alliance. They knew of the protracted fighting on the Tsinghua campus, they knew of the injuries and loss of life, and they knew of the accelerating destruction of state property. They also knew from their own experience how hard it was to break out of factional feuding without outside help, without determined intervention. They felt that this was particularly true of intellectuals divorced from production and entangled in fine distinctions of theory. If workers, on their own, had been unable to get together to carry through the "struggle-criticism-transformation" stage of the Cultural Revolution, how much more difficult it must be for teachers and students, who, after all, were not dealing with lathes and motors, presses and paper stocks, but principally and primarily with ideas.*

With the July 3 and July 24 orders in hand, small detachments of workers had paraded through the university sections of Haitien on July 25 and 26. They had been refused admission to Peking University and had been met with armed pickets at Tsinghua's gates. While primary school students and local residents had welcomed them and their slogans, student factionalists from the higher schools they met on the streets were almost universally hostile. As the workers paraded, students on bicycles taunted them.

"Why not go in?"

"Don't worry, some day we will," answered the workers.

They planned a large rally for July 26 at Chungkuantsun, a crossroads in the Haitien district, but Peking University students under the direction of Nich Yuan-tzu blocked the streets with stalled buses and trucks. This blockade not only prevented the workers from coming to their projected rally, but also prevented many nonparticipants from getting to and from work.

---

*The first stage of the Cultural Revolution was the seize-power stage, when the people seized power back from "capitalist-roaders" or revisionists who had usurped it. The second stage was supposed to be "struggle-criticism-transformation," when the new people in power led struggles against the old system, criticizing old policies and unreconstructed cadres and transforming all aspects of life and work that were not proletarian. As long as rival factions contended for power, this second phase could not begin.

The Hsinhua Printing Plant workers decided that things had gone far enough. When someone suggested a massive intervention by the factory workers of Peking they applauded the idea. The suggestion may have come from the commanders of the 8341 Army, who were deeply involved in trying to make a breakthrough politically in six important Peking factories under Mao Tse-tung's personal direction. It may even have come in the first instance from Mao Tse-tung himself. The exact origin of the idea is less important than the fact that it was widely accepted by all who heard it as an effective plan of action, and that once it was proposed at workers' meetings in the Hsinhua Printing Plant it was immediately taken up by the plant's revolutionary committee, by the 8341 Army Work Team, by the Peking Municipal Revolutionary Committee and Party Committee, and by the Central Committee.

On the morning of July 26 the Hsinhua Printing Plant revolutionary committee decided to intervene. By nightfall it had convened a meeting of delegates from more than sixty factories where big alliances of mass organizations had already been formed—telephone calls, and messengers on foot, by bicycles, by bus, and by car alerted people to come to the meeting. It was enthusiastically attended by hundreds of delegates who debated far into the night and unanimously agreed to go ahead as soon as possible the next morning. When the meeting broke up at 3:30 A.M. a headquarters committee, chaired by Chang Wan of the 8341 Army Work Team and Lu Fang-ch'ien of the Peking Garrison Command, had been set up. Delegates had been authorized to return to their plants and bring contingents from both shifts to Tsinghua before 11 A.M.

Transportation was left up to each participating unit, but in case not enough could be provided locally the Municipal Committee agreed to help out. Worker detachments were organized according to industry and in the end there were seven columns and one "Direct Regiment" (to be directly under the headquarters group). The first column was composed of workers from the metallurgical industry, the second of instrument workers, the third of machinists, the fourth of textile workers, the fifth of construction workers, the sixth of chemical and other light industry workers, while the seventh was mixed. It included workers from plants directly under the central government ministries, such as the Generator Works, some woodworking plants, etc. The Direct Regiment was made up of workers from the Hsinhua Printing, First Printing, and Chueshanfan Printing in the western suburbs.

Because commune members who lived near the campus were suffering the most from the noise, disruption, and chaos of the fighting, people from the Haitien Peasants Representative Congress also joined.*

Column Three was by far the largest, with 6,000 in its ranks; the Direct Regiment was the smallest with only 2,000. On the average the columns were from 4,000-5,000 strong; sixty-two factories sent over 30,000 people altogether. But these figures include only those who were officially counted in the organized columns. Many other workers showed up on their own. Some say that 100,000 surrounded Tsinghua that day, and although this figure is probably exaggerated, no one knows the true count. It could easily have been twice as large as the official one. All roads leading north out of Peking were jammed with cars, trucks, and buses. So great was the exodus that ordinary citizens in Peking's streets wondered what all the commotion was about—and this in a period when mass actions and demonstrations made commotion commonplace in and around Peking.

In the small hours of the morning after the big planning meeting at Hsinhua Printing adjourned the Headquarters Committee remained in session to decide on the deployment of the eight columns, the material to be taken along, and the policies to be followed. Column One was assigned to the general area of the I-Beam House, Column Three was assigned to the area north of the campus stream up to and including the Tsinghua Middle School, Column Four was asked to surround the Meeting Hall, and Column Five was assigned to the big new electronics building. Column Six was to deploy at the Machinery

---

*Haitien is a district of Peking Municipality. Since it is primarily a rural district, there is a Representative Congress of peasants elected from the various communes in Haitien.

Building #9003. Column Seven was placed around the dormitory area, and Column Two occupied the site of the Mao statue and the Agricultural Engineering Building. Part of the Direct Regiment was ordered to stay near headquarters, which would be established wherever a convenient location with functioning communications could be found. The rest of it was to surround the Quiet House (Kuai Ta-fu's headquarters), and the First Classroom Building (the Regiment's main bastion), both positions of the greatest danger and difficulty.

Each worker brought along a copy of the red book, plus one or two large Mao quotations and copies of the two July orders. Their instructions were to: (1) Propagate the July 3 and July 24 orders. (2) Demand that all violent fighting stop, that all weapons be turned in, and that all obstructions—barricades, trenches, booby traps, mines, etc.—be demolished. (3) Talk with both factions, support neither, and demand a big alliance between the two.

No one, including the headquarters personnel, thought that this intervention on the campus would last more than two or three days. People wore their summer clothes, the clothes they had gone to work in or the clothes they came off shift in, and they marched or rode off to the northwest suburbs as if to an outing in the hills, expectation broad, morale high, yet with a feeling of power and deep purpose. They were going to carry out Mao Tse-tung's line. They were going to save the students from themselves and set the Cultural Revolution in the superstructure back on the track. Incredible as it may seem, all the contingents arrived at the campus on time. By 11 A.M. on July 27 Tsinghua's grounds were completely surrounded.

Before describing the events of the next twenty-four hours, it is perhaps important to ask why Mao Tse-tung and the central leaders had waited so long before intervening in Tsinghua's affairs. Surely the seriousness of the situation was well known to them. How could they let it continue month after month?

I can only speculate on the answer, but what seems to me most probable is that Mao could not intervene until the situation had matured to a certain point. He could not intervene until the students proved that they could not settle their affairs themselves, until the situation was clearly hopeless, and until this was apparent not only to outsiders, but also to most of the students themselves. And he could not intervene until working-class forces in Peking developed the unity and strength to do the job as it should be done through a concerted mass effort and without violence.

Prior to July the situation in the country and in Peking was chaotic. If Tsinghua temporarily remained out of the control, this could hardly be helped—there were bigger maelstroms elsewhere. In January and February, for instance, there was such heavy fighting in southeast Shansi that the People's Liberation Army could not enter Changchih and bad to drop cease-fire leaflets by helicopter. Later, conflicts in Kweichow and Kiangsi became serious.

With such problems erupting all around, Mao and his headquarters had to tackle the most crucial first, build up strength, develop forces, and then move when they could on such places as the Tsinghua campus. In the meantime they tried again and again to bring the student factions together through joint talks and interfactional negotiations.

When all these efforts failed and when the 8341 Army had developed sufficient unity in key Peking factories to demonstrate the correctness of Mao's line and generate the required political forces, then the move was made.

To the 4s in the Science Building the workers' units appeared as saviors. They were only afraid that the new Propaganda Team would come and go without breaking the siege they were under. As soon as they heard from 4s units on the east side of the campus that the workers had arrived, they formed into "break-out" teams, removed the steel plates they had welded to the doors of their fortress, defused the booby traps that surrounded the whole area, and prepared to dash out whenever the workers marched past. Instead of merely marching past, a huge crowd of workers surrounded the whole building. The 4s were overjoyed. They poured forth, hand grenades and guns in hand, to welcome them.

"Leave your weapons behind," the workers called.

"But without our weapons we are helpless," responded the 4s. "We'll be attacked and killed."

"No. The fighting must come to an end," said the workers. "We won't stand for any more of it."

They persuaded the students to stack their weapons and then went into the building to search out whatever might have been left behind. They found storerooms full of hand grenades and defused booby traps behind every door. They also found hot food ready to eat, sick people unable to walk, and two rotting corpses, the bodies of the two students shot by Regiment snipers.

Refusing all offers of food, the workers and PLA men at the Science Building quickly formed the disarmed 4s into marching columns. The sick and wounded on stretchers or broad workers' backs brought up the rear. By passing due east by the Old Generator Building they could avoid Regiment strongholds like the First Classroom Building, but then their way was blocked by the stream that divided the campus. Without hesitation a dozen workers jumped into the chest-deep black water and shouldered planks to form a bridge. A hundred students walked or were carried to safety over it. Within a few minutes a siege that had lasted over a month was brought to an end by the evacuation of the whole beleaguered force. The 4s were reunited with their comrades on the east side of the campus.

Dealing with the Regiment was a different matter entirely. A few isolated groups, finding themselves outnumbered, invited the workers in for discussions. But wherever dependable "rods" held sway over main force units, the buildings were barricaded with steel plates, barbed-wire fences were charged with high voltage current, and the militants inside shouted defiance at the masses that surrounded them.

"You are trying to dig under the wall! You want to destroy our base and seize power from us. Crawling worms of Yang-Yu-Fu! Go back to your jobs!" they screamed.

Right at the start violence flared. As the workers of the Direct Regiment approached the First Classroom Building they came face to face with "Bear," a formidable and daring fighter famous far beyond Peking whose real name was Wu Wei-ch'i and whose father was an officer in the PLA. Bear stood stripped to the waist behind a barricade of electrified barbed wire. Brandishing a knife in one hand and an axe in the other, he shouted, "Chairman Mao says anyone who suppresses the student movement will come to a bad end! Whoever enters our building will be cut in half!"

"Use reason, not violence," retorted the workers in unison as they moved slowly forward to surround the building.

Frustrated by the ineffectiveness of his threats, Bear ducked through the wire, ran across the road, and climbed up into a slit trench on the opposite hill. From this vantage point he threw a hammer and a shovel at the advancing column, but the workers kept coming. Finally, beside himself with rage, Bear took a hand grenade from his belt, pulled the pin, and started to throw it at the "enemy." Just at that moment another student who was hiding in the trench reached up and grabbed his arm. The grenade flew far to one side, exploding harmlessly in some bushes. Bear leaped on his hapless companion, dragged him from the trench, and threw him bodily down the hill, where he fell semiconscious at the workers' feet.

This one-man assault did not spark any general fighting. Most of the Regiment's crack "troops" remained behind closed doors content to shout curses at the increasingly massive encirclement. A few hotheads satisfied their urge to strike back by making guerrilla-type raids on the food trucks that had brought hot lunches for the workers' forces. The seized food was added to the Regiment's stores as cocky propagandists taunted the hungry workers for not having anything to eat.

One small but tense girl student, known as "Little Bear" because of her ferocity in battle, leaned from a second-story window, safe in the knowledge that the workers would never rush her stronghold, and slowly ate a bowl of noodles. Each time she dipped her chopsticks into her bowl she pulled a few noodles out full length, dangled them enticingly before the eyes of thousands who had lost their own lunches, then slowly lowered them into her pretty mouth.

Her companions not only seized food, they seized the trucks and cars that brought it. Vehicles useful to their cause they drove away and parked in odd corners of the campus. Those which they could not use they disabled by slashing the tires. On the following day more than a dozen cars and trucks were found with slashed tires behind Machinery Building #9003.

18
"If They Do Not Leave, Drive Them Out!"

From his headquarters in the Quiet House, Kuai Ta-fu could reach all his subordinate units by phone. When he looked out the second-story window, saw that his building was surrounded, and learned that some of his troops had already surrendered, he became very angry. He grabbed a hand gun and ran downstairs shouting, "How dare they come like this! Now they'll have to deal with *lao-tzu!* I'll settle this matter right now!"

But before he could rush out the door his own lieutenants grabbed him. "I want to fight," he yelled. But they pushed him gently, firmly, back up the stairs. When he had calmed down enough to reconsider, he wrote out an order to all units to hold fast. "If the workers try to break in, you may defend yourselves. If anyone is killed, headquarters will be responsible." This message was relayed by telephone to all buildings that the Regiment still held. Then Kuai slipped off the campus along a little used road and went by car to Peking to protest to the Municipal Revolutionary Committee.

Face to face with Liu Feng, the PLA man in charge of "three support" work, Kuai asked, "What the hell is going on? Why did you send so many workers out there without notifying us?" Liu Feng reminded him that he had called the day before to give ample warning. "We of the Municipal Committee support the workers' team at Tsinghua, and you should too," he said to Kuai. "How can I?" asked Kuai. "We are being suppressed like the workers at the Shanghai Diesel Engine Plant!"*

---

*At the Shanghai Diesel Engine Plant armed PLA forces intervened with guns to put down what was regarded as a "mutiny."

When Kuai called his campus headquarters, instead of re-laying Liu Feng's words, he reported that the opinion of the Central Committee was that the workers should return to their factories and the students should settle their own affairs.

Delighted with this news, Regiment activists rushed out of their buildings to inform the workers, who surrounded them twenty to thirty deep, that they were to leave. But the workers said, "We have no such message. Our orders from the top are not to leave until the fighting stops!" And once again they re-peated their slogan, "Use reason, not violence. Turn in your weapons. Form a big alliance!"

In this impasse Regiment headquarters, obeying orders from Kuai, sent leading members out to each unit to repeat their commander's original instructions: "The workers are ordered to go back. If they don't leave they must be driven away!"

When the workers still showed no signs of moving away, the Regiment launched a general offensive. A single shot fired from the Quiet House at 3 P.M. was the signal. Suddenly, ink bottles, bolts, nuts, and other hard objects rained down upon the workers from hidden vantage points all over the campus. Some objects were thrown from the rooftops, others were propelled by inner-tube slingshots from upper-story windows. Though taken by surprise, with many badly hurt, the Propaganda Team members still refused to retreat. Instead, workers and soldiers vied with one another to see who would stand in the front ranks and take the hail of missiles head-on. It was clear almost from the first that soldiers were a prime target, so workers, anxious to protect their soldier-comrades, insisted that they retire to the rear. The soldiers, on their part, insisted on remaining up front. After all, they had been trained for battle. They could hardly be expected to take a back seat when danger threatened.

When heavy bombardment from above failed to make any impression on the workers' ranks, Regiment units armed with spears and hand grenades sallied forth for hand-to-hand com-bat. The first such attack took place outside the Meeting Hall, where a sizeable Regiment force had already surrendered some arms and invited the workers in. Just as a team of workers led by their PLA representative entered the building to see if more weapons might be found inside, forty or fifty people came across the bridge from the north. Those in front held spears in charge position while those behind hurled rocks. In the lead strode Bear, brandishing another hand grenade. The workers at the Meeting Hall outnumbered their attackers by about 500 to 1, but because they flatly refused to raise even a finger in their own defense they were forced to retreat or be run through in cold blood. In the course of this charge the students stabbed several workers and injured ten with flying rocks.

Having captured the entrance to the Meeting Hall, Bear ordered everyone out of the building except the PLA representatives. But the workers refused to leave anyone behind. They formed a column, with the soldiers in the middle for protection, and tried to break out. As this group emerged from the doorway, Bear ordered his men to break it up and capture the soldiers—especially the officer from the 8341 Army who led Column Four. In the ensuing melee someone threw a homemade grenade. It rolled to a stop in front of a soldier. Everyone immediately fell to the ground except Ch'ang Ch'un, a worker from the knitwear factory, who stepped between the soldier and the grenade to take the force of the blast. He was badly wounded on his back and rump. Stunned and bleeding, he still protested as he was led away for medical treatment. He wanted to stay and see the struggle through.

In a second charge that followed the explosion the PLA commander was wounded by a spear thrust. He and several other soldiers were captured and hustled inside the Meeting Hall. There they were questioned most of the night. The red tabs were torn from their collars and the stars from their caps. They were beaten repeatedly and several were stabbed as their Regiment captors tried to extract from them confessions that they had been sent by Yang-Yu-Fu.*

As the fighting around the Meeting Hall died down, it began to rain. Rain fell hard for almost an hour wetting attackers and victims alike. While the workers, with the exception of

---

*Since Yang, Yu and Fu had already been removed from command, what the students wanted was a confession that supporters of this clique had sent the workers' columns.

those routed in the charge, stood their ground and shouted slogans in a downpour that soaked their red books and their clothes, the hail of missiles and rocks continued unabated.

When the rain slacked off, another frontal assault began. By that time Bear's spearmen had reached the First Classroom Building, where they joined with other Regiment "rods" from inside the building to mount an offensive against the workers of the Direct Regiment. Bear leaped from a first-story window, gun in hand. A young woman with a spear twenty feet long leaped after him. Five or six young men followed with shorter spears and hand grenades. They coordinated their charge with that of a second group of spearmen who came at the workers from positions on the ground outside the building. Both groups concentrated on a section of the workers' line manned by women textile workers, most of whom had just retreated from the confrontation at the Meeting Hall. Male workers tried to get the women to move to the rear, but they refused to retreat and bore the brunt of this new assault.

A worker who faced Bear's forces in this incident said: "The girl with the twenty-foot spear rushed at us and ran her weapon right through Shih Wen-shing's leg. To this day the muscle is damaged so that two of his toes cannot be straightened out. They broke into our ranks and drove us in all directions. Then they threw three hand grenades. Hsu Kang-jung lost a piece of his heel in one explosion. Several others were badly wounded. If these had been industrial grenades with fine shrapnel many more would have fallen, but the students' homemade grenades broke into big pieces and were not so dangerous.

"I've no idea how the Regiment leaders knew that Hsinhua Printing workers had started the intervention on the campus, but they seemed to be well aware of it and when they threw rocks, or charged with spears, or lobbed grenades they always aimed at the 8341 Army men from Hsinhua Printing. So, of course, these soldiers suffered the most. Near us was a truck from the printing works and behind that another that had brought the headquarters personnel. They went after the latter with three grenades, but none of them exploded. All in all they made it so hot for us printing workers that we had to get out of there. We had to retreat. Then as we retreated four students rushed in, seized the army man who was the political director of our column, and hauled him inside the First Classroom Building. There they blindfolded him, tore the star off his cap and the tabs off his collar, bound him, beat him, and questioned him. All night they beat him and questioned him in turn.

"As we retreated we discovered that they were trying to drive us in a set direction. So we quickly pulled away and gathered at House A [Wang Kuang-mei's old headquarters] and tried to send messengers out to command headquarters. Two workers and a soldier started out. The soldier, because his clothes were darker, got through, but the workers in white T-shirts stood out in the gathering dusk. They were seen and seized by the students. They were badly beaten. Between them they lost several teeth and their eyes were blackened. Their clothes were searched. When the students found that they were from the printing works they beat them even harder. One of them, Wang Chen-jung, was a member of our plant security force. They said, 'There are no good security men,' and beat him an extra time for good measure.

"Afterward they took these two to the West Gate and tied them there in the dark. We found them only the next day, bound and unconscious.

"Altogether more than forty prisoners were hauled to the Quiet House. Some were held in rooms under guard. Others, after interrogation, were tied—either singly or in pairs—to posts or pillars, or they were thrown into the toilet room. Just before dawn, when Kuai and his lieutenants ran off, those who were not tied released the others and they all ran out together."

If the students arrested workers and PLA men wholesale, the workers and soldiers temporarily held and questioned quite a few students. Just before the rout at the Meeting Hall, when the members of Column Four were trying to persuade the students to come out and turn over their weapons, a single student did emerge from the back door. He tried to pass quietly through the workers' lines. Thinking that he must be a messenger, they surrounded him.

"Why do you still put up resistance?" they asked.

"Because the reactionaries have not been defeated," he answered.

"But the July orders call for a ceasefire!"

"The July orders are meant for Kweichow and Shansi, not for Tsinghua. Here we confront the Kuomintang!"

"But these two orders come right from the Central Committee. They apply to the whole nation, to any place where fighting is still going on. You have been deceived by class enemies. What class are you in, by the way?" the workers asked the student.

"The eighth class."

"And your family background?"

"Poor peasant."

"We work hard so you can go to school," said the workers. "Peasants planted all the grain that you eat. We weave the cloth that you wear. Now look at that Science Building. Look at the burned-out roof! What sort of people wreck state property?"

"Surely you can't say that I oppose Mao Tse-tung and the Communist Party," said the student. "No one in my village ever went to a university before Liberation. Without the Communist Party I'd never have had a chance to study. Without the Communist Party I might not even be alive. I'm for Mao and the Party with my whole heart and soul."

"Then how do you explain people like Pao Ch'eng-keng?" asked the workers. "Isn't he the Regiment vice-commander? He helped seize one of our PLA men. Several people took him inside and removed his jacket. Then Pao put it on and came out to wander freely among us. He used his disguise to spy out the situation and to maintain liaison between the different buildings. When we finally stopped him he said he was from the 8341 Army. But army men don't wear blue pants and besides, we know all our army representatives. So the question is, can people like Pao be revolutionary?"

The student ducked this question.

"The other side started the fighting," he said. "We are only defending ourselves. We are defending Mao Tse-tung Thought. Why don't you talk to the others?"

"We are trying to," said the workers. "We want both sides to stop!"

These arguments moved the young militant. With tears in his eyes, he began to recall the bitter life of his family before Liberation. Then he warned the workers to be careful, showed them where two mines were buried in front of the Meeting Hall, and pointed out which wires carried charges.

Quiet talks like this, not beatings and counterattacks, helped disintegrate the students' ranks.

Another Regiment "rod" who was won over in the course of the battle was the student who raised his arm to deflect the hand grenade that Bear threw from the trench in front of the First Classroom Building. As he rolled to the bottom of the hill, his face badly cut, the workers of the Direct Regiment sent a group to pick him up and carry him to safety. Later he helped them find their way around the campus and identified key Regiment leaders for them.

A third fierce battle occurred after the rain at about 5:30 P.M. By that time most of the workers were shivering. Their wet clothes were drying only slowly in the cold wind that had arisen, and the evaporation from the rain-soaked cotton chilled them to the bone.

Perhaps it was for that reason that members of Column Seven began to enter the dormitories. One group easily occupied the first and second floor of Dormitory #10, then suddenly found itself under attack both from above and from below. Regiment occupants on the fourth and fifth floors tried to drive the workers downstairs, while other Regiment forces on the ground outside blocked the doors and windows to prevent anyone from escaping. This dormitory was a stronghold of drifting elements from off campus and they fought with a viciousness the students had not shown.

Threatened by hand grenades and charged by spear handlers who did not hesitate to puncture defenseless flesh, quite a few workers jumped from second-story windows and were hurt. Others rushed down the stairways, only to pile up in the blockaded ground floor. As the narrow space filled with people, a hand grenade came bouncing down one of the stairwells. Wang Sung-lin, a worker from Machine Tool Factory No. 2, threw himself on it. The grenade exploded under his stomach, rupturing him badly. As he raised himself with both arms to see if anyone else had been hit, a spearman rushed at him down the same stairwell and ran him through the chest. He collapsed on top of the blown grenade.

Wang Sung-lin was thirty-six years old, a Communist Party member and vice-head of his department's Party Committee. Because his wife was due to give birth that day, his workmates had asked him not to go with them to Tsinghua. He had insisted on joining the movement anyway. He died only a few hours after his wife bore him a new child.

As the angry, weeping, but still disciplined workers broke out of Dormitory #10, the attackers from upstairs rushed out behind them with spears and wounded several more. One of them bled to death before he could be taken to the hospital. This was Chang Hsu-tao, a thirty-year-old worker. His eighty-one-year-old widowed mother, who had worked many years as a servant to feed her children, listened dry-eyed to the report of his death. "He died to propagate Mao Tse-tung Thought," she said. "His death is as heavy as Mount Tai."*

A third worker was killed outside the dormitory when he picked up a hand grenade hurled by the attacking forces. His aim was to throw it to some harmless place. The grenade went off in his hand, driving a fragment of shrapnel through his eye. This man's name was P'an Chih-ling. He was thirty years old, a worker in the Peking Electric Bureau, a veteran cadre and a Communist. His youngest daughter was born on August 18, twenty-two days after he died.

---

*In *Serve the People*, a short essay about the death of a soldier who helped make charcoal, Mao Tse-tung says that the death of a person who selflessly serves others is as heavy as Mount Tai (a sacred mountain in Shantung important to Confucians), while the death of one who only serves himself is as light as a feather.

19
Headquarters Story

By six o'clock in the evening the Workers Propaganda Team command post was in pandemonium. It had been set up in a photography shop near the Family Quarters. News of the clashes and the casualties flowed in by messenger. Distraught people came running from all parts of the campus, out of breath, weeping, covered with mud, ink, and blood. Showing their wounds and their bruises, they demanded help, more forces, ambulances. And they demanded retaliation. "There are so many workers out there bleeding and dying! Can we just let them stab us and blast us, and blast us and stab us again?"

Lu Fang-ch'ien, who together with Chang Wan had manned the heaquarters on that fateful day, told us what it was like to face the aroused workers in this unprecedented crisis. Lu Fang-ch'ien was tall and lean like a northerner, but had the dark olive skin of a southerner and more stubble on his clean-shaven face than is usual in China. He seemed the very model of an army commander. Even in the hottest part of the day, when the sweat ran down one's body in rivulets, he never removed his army jacket or his red-starred cap, for this was a part of army discipline. At first glance his severe countenance seemed to match this unshakeably correct behavior. I remember wondering how such a formal, impressive military man could ever unbend enough to tell us the kind of details we wanted to know. But I was quite wrong about Comrade Lu. After very little of the rhetorical introduction with which so many revolutionary Chinese begin their story, he launched into the most vivid description of the confrontation between the students and the Workers Propaganda Team, including many details—such as the fact that Little Bear dangled her noodles and Bear wore no shirt—that made the whole ghastly night come alive. Lu Fang-ch'ien turned out to be a most sympathetic and observant informant.

"You can imagine the situation," said Lu, warming to the

tale. "Some hotheads wanted to strike back. I got very angry myself. As the reports flowed in of more wounded and more killed, I cursed and pounded my fist on the table, but in the end I still had to calm down, because we had come for propaganda work not for fighting and if we leaders lost our heads the whole situation could have gotten out of hand. We had to remain cool. One wrong word could have cost many lives, one wrong word could have led to disaster. Bloody incidents were swirling all around us but we had to stick to one idea and one idea only: 'Use reason, not violence, use reason, not violence.'

"Some of us had directed battles in wartime, but never had we seen anything like this, never. Never anything to inflame the emotions like this. Chang Wan was magnificent. I remember him so clearly. Fat, soaked with sweat, ravenous for food, but calm—sitting there quietly repeating over and over, 'Use reason, not violence.'

"We had had nothing to eat since 3 A.M. and we hadn't slept for two days. It was hot, stifling, in our crowded headquarters. No order anywhere. Originally the messengers stood in line to take turns, but now they just came crowding in, each with worse news than the last—more wounded, more killed. It was enough to confuse anyone's mind.

"I was so tired I just leaned against the wall with my eyes half closed and even before people finished what they had to say, I interrupted, 'No violence. Use reason. Do your propaganda work well.'

"What we depended on really was the workers' loyalty to Mao Tse-tung. They had a deep understanding of Mao's strategic plan. With 30,000 people one can't rely on the consciousness of a few for there are always those who have lost contact with headquarters. They still have to stick to their orders no matter what the provocation. And they stuck, in the main, throughout that terrible day and night. They didn't strike back. They didn't counterattack. And that's because we had done a lot of educational work. Together we had studied the PLA's 'Five-Won't Policy' over and over again.*

---

*When hit, don't hit back; when cursed, don't curse back— these are the first two of the "five won'ts."

"And throughout that whole day and night the educational work continued. Our throats were parched and our mouths were dry, but this was Mao Tse-tung Thought and we stuck to it. At one point we called an emergency meeting of the leaders from each column, reaffirmed our policy, and sent them back to remind everyone else. We repeated over and over that the students had been deceived, that they had been misled, and that they had to be awakened. And the workers, who had themselves been through factional struggle, understood and didn't blame the students, even when they came at them with spears.

"There was only one serious break in our ranks. When the fighting first began one group of men got angry. They went home to make some spears out of pipe. They found helmets and sticks and returned in their trucks in the early morning hours of July 28—truckloads full of men ready to strike back. But as they approached the West Gate other workers saw them and reported to us. We understood what was in their minds. They were very, very angry. They had some ultra-left thinking too and lots of pride and daring. They were aching to go on the offensive.

"So we took emergency measures. We called their leaders in to headquarters and sent cadres out to speak to the rank-and-file. At first they wouldn't listen to reason. They kept saying, 'Our comrades have been wounded, our comrades have been killed.' But we talked to them for several hours and finally they went back to reorganize themselves. They returned later without weapons and helped resolve the problem our way.

"Of course, I can't say that none of the workers broke discipline. A few individuals did grab a few students here and there and even struck a few blows. But these incidents were few and far between because everyone in the vicinity raised an outcry and said it was not right.

"There was also one worker from one of the factories where the big alliance was not really solid who sent information to Kuai that was of great help to him. This worker belonged to one of the factions that had strong ties to the Regiment—one of the Heaven factions. He supported Kuai politi-

cally. After he ran to Kuai with his message, his workmates
criticized him severely. But his anti-working-class act later
helped them expose and solve the factionalism in their plant.
So a bad thing turned into a good one!"

Lu Fang-ch'ien went on to tell how his headquarters was
first established right out in the open at the northern edge of
the Family Quarters on a stone platform that had traditionally
been used by chess players. Two red flags were planted beside
it to let everyone know where the commanders could be found.
The trouble was that the Regiment "rods" in the First Classroom Building could also see the spot and recognized it as
command headquarters by all the commotion—the arrivals and
departures, the vehicles and the messengers. When messengers
went out they were trailed and kidnaped. After that messages
had to be sent in code. The code proved to the various column
leaders that the messenger was indeed from the Propaganda
Team and not some student in disguise. Every messenger, of
course, ran some risk. None of them knew the campus too
well. If they wandered about too long they were apt to be
seized, but there was no way to contact the column except by
messenger. Kuai had ordered all telephone lines cut. That ended
communication both inside the campus and between the campus and the city, except, of course, for the concealed lines
that Kuai kept open for his own use.

Command headquarters arrived with telephone equipment
but couldn't find anything to hook into. Finally someone discovered a live line that Kuai's men had overlooked in the
photography shop. So headquarters was immediately moved
from the outdoor chess block to the vacant shop. There behind
the counter where film had once been sold Lu and Chang
stood and listened to the reports as they poured in—first the
rout in front of the Meeting Hall, then the confrontation at
the First Classroom Building, and finally the macabre clashes
at Dormitory #10.

When Lu and Chang learned that three people had been
killed, they contacted Kuai and asked for talks. By that time
Kuai had returned from the city and his conference with Liu

Feng. He also wanted to talk. A meeting was arranged at the Tsinghua Middle School on the far northern edge of the grounds. Chang Shih-chung of the 8341 Army, Chih Chin-ch'ing of Hsinhua Printing, a comrade from the Peking Gear Factory, and a comrade from the Peking Garrison Command met with Kuai there. A five-point ceasefire agreement was soon worked out—cease fire, turn in all weapons, remove all obstruction, form a big alliance, and cooperate with the Workers Propaganda Team. But for more than an hour Kuai refused to sign. He insisted on a stipulation that his Headquarters Committee concur before the agreement could be broadcast. The Propaganda Team negotiators finally accepted this stipulation. Then Kuai, the two officers, and the Gear Factory worker went to the Bright House to convince the Headquarters Committee. There, in the building that housed the Regiment's broadcasting station, Kuai tricked them. The three team members were held in a second-story room under guard while Kuai pretended to act as a go-between, holding discussions in the broadcasting room, then returning to the captive negotiators to report stumbling blocks and unavoidable delays. Even if the negotiators had evaded their guards, they could not have gone far. The Bright House was equipped with electronically controlled steel doors that only insiders knew how to operate. Actually Kuai was playing for time. He had decided on a general withdrawal and was busy making the arrangements while pretending that his Headquarters Committee had not agreed to stop the fighting. On the one hand, Kuai planned to have most of his fighting units off the campus before dawn, thus presenting the Workers Propaganda Team with an "empty city." On the other hand, Kuai sent a special fighting team to surround Building #9003 in the dark. At an appropriate time, one last counterattack would be launched.

Since the Propaganda Team had come to stop the fighting and bring the factions together, the "empty city" could be called a victory of sorts for the Regiment. Kuai's forces, though geographically dispersed, could be said to be politically alive. "As long as the mountain is green, fear not for lack of fuel!"

was the slogan taken from an ancient text. This meant: As long as there are forces in being one can make a comeback, however long it may take.

Launching one last counterattack while his main force retreated was a desperate attempt to provoke the kind of violent retaliation from the workers and soldiers that previous incidents had failed to generate. If only Kuai and his "rods" could trick or force the Propaganda Team into a bloody assault on the students, they could go before the country as innocent victims of violent repression and perhaps salvage something politically from an increasingly disastrous situation. As things stood at midnight on July 27—three workers dead and hundreds of workers and soldiers wounded while the students maneuvered unscathed—it was quite clear to all observers that the campus invaders had carried out Mao Tse-tung Thought while the defenders had wildly violated it. Unless something could be done to redress this balance the Regiment would find it hard to maintain any semblance of a reputation as fighters for Mao Tse-tung's line. As a means of redress Kuai gambled on one final provocation, which, if it failed, could only make the situation that much worse.

Once he had made this reckless decision, Kuai developed both sides of his strategy with precision. While he personally stalled the Propaganda Team negotiators, orders went out to all the main units to evacuate their fortresses and retreat with their arms, either to the Aeronautical Institute to the south, or to the Nankou campus of Tsinghua near the Great Wall to the north. Once this stealthy evacuation was well underway, Kuai suddenly agreed to all the terms of the ceasefire and it was announced to the whole campus from the broadcast room of the Bright House at 2 A.M. In the meantime, Kuai's special fighting team, the Red Spears, had secretly surrounded Machinery Building #9003. When concerned aides pointed out to Kuai that this team could no longer be called back in case of agreement, he said, "Never mind, let them go." The actual attack on Machinery Building #9003 was launched at 1:30 A.M., just half an hour before the whole campus was told that all fighting must cease. When the broadcast came it was too late.

With his armed column already in motion, Kuai laid the groundwork for a simultaneous political offensive by drafting an urgent telegram to Chairman Mao and the Central Committee which read as follows:

Extremely Urgent! Chairman Mao Tse-tung, Vice-chairman Lin Piao, the Central Committee of the Chinese Communist Party, the Central Cultural Revolution Group, the Military Commission of the Central Committee, Premier Chou En-lai, Comrades Ch'en Po-ta, Kang Sheng, Chiang Ch'ing:

On July 27 in the name of propagating the July 3 Order, 110,000 hoodwinked workers under the careful manipulation of a sinister hand suddenly surrounded and overwhelmed the Tsinghua campus with arms. Dozens of Chingkangshan fighters have been captured and held. Several hundred have been wounded or brutally beaten. In order to avoid further clashes our Chingkangshan fighters have all withdrawn from the campus. We have no food or clothes and no guarantee of our lives. Tsinghua Chingkangshan is threatened by extreme danger. The situation is ten thousand times perilous. I appeal for help to the Central Committee. I appeal for help to Chairman Mao Tse-tung. I beg the Central Committee to receive Kuai immediately.

Machinery Building #9003 had been surrounded the previous morning by Column Six, the chemical workers. During the day their propaganda efforts had been crowned with success. After prying welded steel plates off the doors of the building, they had persuaded most of the occupants to come out and talk. They had also searched the building and removed large quantities of arms. Then the afternoon rain had driven the Propaganda Team members and the students back into the building. Study classes had been set up and discussions begun; some students listened sympathetically to the workers while others talked back sharply.

At 9 P.M. all electricity was cut off, ending both the water supply and the lights. At 10 P.M. a worker came to report that ceasefire negotiations had been successful, but no announcement came through the air. Suddenly at 1:30 the building was lit up from the outside by the lights of dozens of trucks. They had been turned on by members of the Red Spear fighting team and were the signal for attack. As the lights went on the main forces of the Red Spear fighting team charged out of the corn field where they had been lying low. The male Red Spears had all stripped to the waist, but each had a white towel wrapped around his arm so that he could be distinguished by his comrades in the dark. They ran into the building yelling incoherent battle cries that were supposed to frighten their victims but seemed to those who heard them to indicate that they themselves were frightened. The Propaganda Team members retreated to the fourth floor, only to be followed there. The truck lights made the outside of the building bright, but inside it was still too dark for fighting. Red Spears poured machine oil on the floor of the west end and lit it. Then they twisted paper into rolls, soaked them in oil and lit them. Under the light of these flaming, smoking torches, they pushed tables ahead of them down the hall hoping to corner all the workers in one spot. Their goal was to seize the soldiers in the ranks of the workers' forces. After they had grabbed about forty soldiers and locked them in a separate room, they said they wanted to negotiate.

The workers, cornered at the end of the floor, sent delegates over to talk. But as soon as they came face to face with the students, the students said, "Who will talk with you?" and arrested them too.

One man, Hou Po-chih, a Communist, stepped forward to try once more.

"Who sent you here?" the students asked. "Was it Yang-Yu-Fu?"

"No. Chairman Mao sent me," said Hou. "You should listen to Chairman Mao."

"We only listen to Kuai Ta-fu," retorted the students.

A strong man grabbed Hou, hit him over the head with a flashlight and then, having knocked him down and opened a bad cut over one eye, dragged him by the feet the whole length of the corridor and down the stairs from the fourth floor to the first. Hou's head bumped on every step all the way down. When he reached the bottom he was unconscious. When he came to, he called out, "Long Live Chairman Mao." When his captor heard this he tried to choke him. Hou still managed to gasp, "Use reason, not violence, use reason, not violence." His captor then stuffed a towel into his mouth. When the towel also failed to silence him, his tormentor, who turned out to be not a student, but one of the lumpen brawlers from Dormitory #10, moved to gouge out his eyes. This stirred to action several student rebels who up to this point had looked on but dared not intervene.

"Why should you be so cruel?" they shouted. "What crime has he committed?"

They pulled the would-be torturer away and scuffled with him long enough to allow Hou to escape from the building.

Han Chung-hsien was not so lucky. The Red Spears surprised him in a second-floor room talking with a shopmate. A girl student held a burning torch high as several of her comrades rushed in to seize the pair. One of the attackers ran a spear right through Han's chest, severing an artery. The wounded man made it to the door before he collapsed. His companion took him on his back but before he could reach the stairway Han was dead. His clothes and the clothes of his would-be rescuer were soaked in blood. The July 3 Order which he carried was also soaked. Han was thirty-six, a Communist, and a member of the Revolutionary Committee of Food Factory No. 1.

Li Wen-yuan, the fifth worker to die that day, was killed by a bullet. He was standing guard not more than a few yards from the edge of the corn field where the Red Spears had hidden themselves before the attack. A pistol shot caught him in the stomach and severed an artery. He was taken to the hospital at Haitien too late to be saved. Li was also thirty-six, a Communist, a militia man, and a model worker in the Rubber Factory.

Firing guns into the air, waving spears, and swinging hand grenades around their fingers by the trigger strings, the militants of the Red Spears fighting team drove the workers from the fourth floor to the first, then retreated upstairs and barricaded the stairwell with bricks, stones, and bottles of sulfuric acid. While the workers down below continued to carry on their propaganda work, the students up above sat in sullen silence and waited for dawn.

Dawn brought more rain. The campus, with tens of thousands of people milling about, dissolved in mud. One hundred soldiers came to Building #9003 to tell the students about the ceasefire agreement. The students released the soldiers, who had been stripped and beaten, but did not dare come out themselves. They knew that the chemical workers were angry about the casualties of the night before and they feared retaliation. It was only after the soldiers persuaded the workers to withdraw at least three yards from the door, brought trucks for the students to ride away in, and promised to guard the roads all the way out that the students finally agreed to tear down their barricades, surrender their weapons, and come out. Even then they did not dare stand up in the trucks. They lay flat so that the workers along the road could not see them. After the unprovoked assault they had mounted, they could not believe there would be no revenge.

Furthermore, Kuai had diligently spread rumors that the workers were arming for a counterattack and would soon return to the campus with weapons. His followers, having never experienced anything like this peaceful encirclement, were prepared to believe that violent assaults would in the end be met with violence.

As the Red Spears abandoned Building #9003 at 10 A.M., the last off-campus militants quietly left Dormitory #10 in groups of two or three. They slipped away through the ruins of the Yuan Ming Yuan. With the last pockets of resistance liquidated, more than one hundred days of fighting at Tsinghua came to an end.

Kuai Ta-fu, the man more responsible than any other for the violence, left the campus soon after the 2 A.M. broadcast and went by car to the telegraph office. There he drafted and sent off the message already quoted and proceeded to the Aeronautical Institute where Propaganda Team members who had been looking for him all over the city finally found him. They were looking for him in order to transmit Mao's personal request that he and the four other well-known Peking student leaders appear for a discussion. In the small hours of July 28, Mao Tse-tung met with Kuai Ta-fu, Tan Hou-lan, Wang Ta-ping, Han Ai-ch'ing, and Nieh Yuan-tzu, and spoke to them bluntly.

He told Kuai that he was swollen in the head—in fact, he was swollen all over. He was turning into his opposite. University and Institute people had said they wanted to begin the "struggle-criticism-transformation" stage but had pushed on to armed fighting instead. They had divorced themselves from the workers, the peasants, from the local populace, and from the majority of their own peers. If they persisted in fighting, they would turn into bandits. They would have to be surrounded and wiped out.

Mao outlined four possible consequences of continued fighting: (1) The campus could be placed under military control; (2) the fighting could continue until one side won; (3) the school could be divided into two parts; (4) the whole school could be dissolved.

The last choice he said would be "struggle-criticize-dissolve!" If it came to division, one part of the school would be sent north, the other part would be sent south. Did that make any sense? To continue fighting after the July 3 Order could not be allowed. Therefore, if they refused to listen to the Propaganda Team they would be faced with military occupation.

Taking up the charge made by Kuai that the Workers Propaganda Team was manipulated by a sinister hand, Mao said, "If you are looking for a sinister hand, I am that sinister hand. I sent the Team. You will have to blame me."

But even the face-to-face meeting with Chairman Mao did not win Kuai over. He returned to the campus saying that Mao's words had been, "One hundred thousand workers invade Tsinghua. The 4s are happy. The Regiment is unhappy and I too am unhappy."

Thus when the workers and soldiers called to the hold-outs in Building #9003, "Mao Tse-tung criticized you when he met Kuai," they answered, "No, Mao supported us."

And when the workers said that Mao had summoned Kuai, the hold-outs replied, "Not at all. Mao received Kuai."

It was exchanges such as this that postponed the evacuation of the building until 10 A.M.

When the Regiment "rods" fled the campus in the middle of the night they finally suffered some of the casualties which the Workers Propaganda Team, in spite of all provocation, had refused to inflict. Twenty hard-core rebels fled toward Changping County at a breakneck pace in a small truck. Afraid that squads of workers would follow and attack them, those in the rear of the truck sat with grenade strings in hand, ready to let fly at the slightest provocation. The truck went out of control, hit a tree, and turned over. One of the grenades went off, killing two and wounding several, including Little Bear, the girl who had so tantalized the hungry workers with her full bowl of noodles. Her leg was broken and her skull was crushed: to this day she has a plastic plate in her head. But she has made her peace with the workers and now operates a lathe at Machine Tool Factory No. 1.

Those who did not flee but surrendered to the Propaganda Team turned over considerable quantities of weapons. The complete list of the arms collected from both factions follows. It includes not only those arms found on July 27 and 28, but everything found thereafter.

5 semi-automatic rifles
57 rifles
31 pistols
12 homemade rifles
5 small-bore rifles
5 air guns
1,038 bullets
688 hand grenades
52 homemade cannon
9 explosive satchels (for antitank use)
168 homemade mines

16 packages of dynamite
2 homemade tanks (tractors with armored plate)
50 bottles of poisonous gas
185 bottles of acid and other corrosive chemicals
15 big knives and bayonets
1,435 spears
380 short knives
9 steel whips (made of fine chain)
25 cannon shells
2 type-59 semi-automatic rifles
1 type-56 assault-gun (tommy-gun)

Many of these arms had been made on the campus. Others had been seized outside Peking and sent to Tsinghua by liaison personnel or by factional supporters in other places.

To sum up the statistics once again, altogether 5 workers were killed, 143 were seized and beaten, and 731 were seriously hurt. Three years later (1971) a wounded worker still remained in the hospital and many still suffered from bullets in their bodies or permanent crippling.

20
End Factionalism

Ending the fighting was not the same thing as ending factionalism. It took the Propaganda Team less than twenty-four hours to suppress the violence but more than three weeks to persuade the students to form a big alliance—and even then the alliance was more formal than real. A whole year of careful political work was required before the militants of both sides came together in their thinking and two years after that the Propaganda Team was still at Tsinghua supervising the transformation of its education. Of course, not all of the 30,000 workers who arrived on July 27 stayed on to complete this political task. Most of them withdrew on July 28, leaving behind a team of several hundred that included delegates from each participating plant. They continued the work under the leadership of Wang Ch'en and Lu Fang-ch'ien, then rotated back to their original jobs as others came out to take their places for six or twelve month stints.

The first problem that the Propaganda Team faced was to prove its nonpartisanship. The 4s, who had welcomed intervention, tried very hard to win support by declaring their undying love for the workers and denouncing the Regiment "rods" for their violent resistance. They invited Propaganda Team members to a series of meetings where the Regiment was exposed and repudiated. But the Team members, once they learned the content of the meetings, refused to attend. Their position was that the rank-and-file of both organizations were honest revolutionaries, that the leaders of both had made serious mistakes, and that each side must first make self-criticisms before criticizing the other. When asked for their opinion and their position vis-à-vis the two sides, they responded only with support for Mao Tse-tung Thought: "Whoever does things that are in accord with Mao Tse-tung Thought we support, whoever does things that are not in accord with Mao Tse-tung Thought we criticize and help to change, whoever does things that violate Mao Tse-tung .Thought we oppose and resolutely fight against. If you support the correct direction today we will support you. If you oppose the correct direction we will oppose you. If on one question you support Mao Tse-tung Thought we will support you on that question. If at the same time you oppose Mao Tse-tung Thought on another question we will oppose you on that."

This position stunned the 4s, for they assumed that they had survived the fighting as heroes. It gave the Regiment a new lease on life. "After all," they reasoned, "perhaps we do have some political capital." In neither case did it quickly lead to self-critical examination, for each side was still primarily interested in justifying its own record and in exposing the record of the other.

Before any review of the past could begin, several pressing problems of social order had to be solved. The students who had fled the campus had to be persuaded to return, the prisoners held by each side had to be released, the arms each side still concealed had to be turned in, and the equipment, most of it electronic sound equipment seized by the opposing sides from public stocks, had to be returned. All of these problems seemed insuperable to the students who had been involved in the fighting, but the Propaganda Team attacked them with energy and optimism.

A large number of the Regiment fighters had fled to the Aeronautical Institute in the early morning hours of July 28. That very evening a high-level team of cadres that included Hsieh Fu-chih, head of the Peking Revolutionary Committee, went to the Institute to persuade these Tsinghua "refugees" to return. More than three hundred of them listened respectfully to Comrade Hsieh and responded to his appeal with slogans of support for Chairman Mao that indicated how little the events of the past twenty-four hours had educated them. One young woman, red band on her arm, military belt around her waist, bookbag over her shoulder, and two short braids protruding almost at right angles from under a military-style cap, led the cheering with, "Chingkangshan Regiment people will be loyal to Mao Tse-tung forever! Chingkangshan Regiment people have acted correctly from beginning to end!" Before the meeting closed this firebrand and her comrades had at least agreed to return to the campus so that negotiations could begin. In the course of the next day and evening they dribbled back in two's and three's to repopulate Dormitory #10.

But until arms had been surrendered and prisoners exchanged there was not much hope that the many thousands of students, staff, and workers would return. They had to be convinced that the peace was stable before they would move back to the scene of such protracted and bitter conflict. Even if one no longer ran the danger of being hit by some random hard object, there was still the possibility that one might be seized and held hostage by one side or the other. Hence an effective prisoner exchange became the key to any return to normal.

Even to set up talks on the subject was difficult, however. Neither side trusted the other.

Lu Fang-ch'ien told us how he managed to arrange the first meeting.

"I personally went to notify the 4s that they should come to talk about prisoners. I didn't know my way around. How would I find any of their leaders? I started walking in the direction of the New Main Building. Suddenly a girl appeared in the bushes outside.

" 'Where are you going, PLA?' she asked.

" 'Who are you?' I asked in turn, somewhat startled.

" 'I am the 4s,' she replied.

"It turned out that she was Chang Hsueh-mei, a member of their Headquarters Committee, who was taking her turn on sentry duty. As soon as she heard that I was from the Propaganda Team headquarters she began to praise the PLA to the skies. When I said I wanted to talk to the 4s' leaders, she quickly arranged it and they all began to talk at once about how the Regiment had wrecked the big alliance of 1967.

" 'Never mind the past,' I said. 'Let's try to get together again now. I want you to meet with some Regiment leaders in the Agricultural Engineering Building.'

"But they didn't dare venture that far across the campus. They were afraid that the Regiment would capture them. I had to guarantee their safety and take them over and back in military cars. Regiment leaders, on their part, were also afraid to meet. They were afraid that once they showed their faces the masses would rise up and seize them for repudiation. So I had to guarantee a PLA guard all around the meeting place as well. After much hard work and persuasive talk I finally got the meeting underway on August 7."

At this preliminary get-together both sides agreed to exchange the captives they already held, and not to seize any more captives no matter what the provocation. They also agreed to give good care to all captives before the final exchange and not to allow any to escape. All this was settled after long debate, but the time and place of the exchange was not agreed upon. Comrade Lu wanted action then and there, but the factional leaders held out for consultations with their membership. The meeting broke up without final agreement and soon afterward both sides violated clauses they had just agreed to honor. The Regiment seized two more of the 4s, while the 4s allowed two members of the Regiment to escape.

As a result, the second meeting opened with a serious quarrel, each side denouncing the other for the flagrant violations of the night before. When the 4s accused the Regiment of seizing two 4s, the Regiment charged the 4s with holding two Regiment people while pretending that they had escaped.

"But they ran back to your headquarters," said the 4s, amazed.

"We haven't seen them. How do we know you aren't still holding them?" retorted the Regiment.

This problem was resolved by the members of the Propaganda Team, who knew very well that the two Regiment prisoners had returned to their faction. They exposed the Regiment lie, causing its spokesmen to lose face. Thereafter the talks went a little more smoothly. The Propaganda Team immediately demanded full lists of the prisoners held by each side. Both the 4s and the Regiment balked. "Why don't we just search the campus and release everyone we find," suggested Kuai Ta-fu, who had long since shifted his prisoners to far-off Nankou. "But don't you have prisoners off the campus?" asked the workers. Kuai had to admit that he did. "We demand the release of Lo Chung-chi," said the 4s, knowing full well that he had already escaped to Canton. On the list they presented his name came first. "Is this accurate? Dare you sign your name to this?" asked the workers, fully aware of Lo's whereabouts.

"Well, we're not 100 percent sure," said the 4s.

On August 9, late in the evening, agreement was finally reached on the prisoner question. Early the next morning, before sunrise, cadres of the Propaganda Team got the leaders of both sides out of bed. Any delay in effecting the exchange, they reasoned, would give both the 4s and the Regiment time to move some prisoners to new hiding places and thus abort the whole deal. The entire Regiment Headquarters Committee was loaded onto trucks bound for Nankou, where the Regiment prisoners were held, while the 4s leaders led the way across the campus to the building that served as their prison.

One clever member of the Regiment Headquarters Committee fooled Lu Fang-ch'ien, however. He lingered beside the truck talking until it pulled away without him. Lu Fang-ch'ien talked to him awhile, then let him go back to his dorm, thinking that "this one fellow would not matter." But as soon as this "rod" got away from Comrade Lu he found a telephone and called Nankou, alerting the Regiment there to what was happening. By the time the prisoner exchange group arrived, two of the seven people held had already disappeared.

"I wasn't vigilant enough," said Lu. "But in the main we had planned well. We knew they had over one hundred people there, so we went in force. We sent about three hundred along. Feeling that they might resist with arms, as they had done only a few days before on the campus, we were organizationally prepared. In case any one of us got killed, someone else was designated to take his place.

"The Regiment people at Nankou were real 'rods.' They wanted no part of any study classes. They were capable of anything. Sure enough, when we arrived at the·compound there was wire all around and the inner wire was charged. We had to negotiate even to get inside. Kuai Ta-fu, Ch'en Yu-yen and Ch'en Chi-fang, three top leaders of the Regiment had come with us. What the people at the gate wanted to do was to let Kuai in to negotiate, then stall us outside. We didn't buy it. We insisted on entering all together. So after hours of arguing they had to let us in. By that time it was already afternoon.

"What we found inside was shocking. The place was worse than any jail. Steel sheets had been welded to the doors on each floor of the building, and the doors were banked with sandbag fortifications. All the rooms had iron bars on the windows. All five of the prisoners that we released were pale from malnutrition. One was very sick and had to be carried to the truck. The prisoners had been sleeping on the bare floor. Even in the hot July weather they had to keep their jackets on. Food—one mantou [a bun of steamed bread] a day and a bowl of cold water—had been passed in through a small hole in the door. When they saw us they shook with fright. They thought we were some new jailers who would take them somewhere else to be tortured. When they learned we were Propaganda Team members sent by Mao Tse-tung they were overjoyed. They shouted 'Long live Chairman Mao! Down with Fascist torturers!'

"We confronted Kuai with these crimes, but he said he knew nothing about them. 'The masses did it,' he said.

"When we learned that two of the Lo-Wen-Li-Jao 'clique' had been removed to another place, we were very angry. What Kuai had done was to order Li Kang and Wen Hsueh-min sent to the Peking Garrison Command to be arrested and held as counter-revolutionaries. Lo Chung-chi had already escaped— we brought him back later from Canton. So the only one of the 'clique' liberated that day was Jao Wei-tsu. She was in terrible shape with such a bad wound on her rump that she could neither sit down nor stand up for long. Her bodily functions were damaged. She couldn't control her bladder and her back had been hurt. All this had affected her mind. She remembered the past with difficulty.

"When the Peking Garrison Command returned Wen Hsueh-min to the campus he was all but deaf and his teeth were gone—pulled out by his Regiment captors at Nankou. They demanded confessions from him and each time he didn't comply out would come another tooth.

"The entire case against these four was a frame-up. The Regiment used torture to extract confessions and then used Li's words against Lo and Lo's words against Li, backed up with twenty different methods of punishment. Confessions were manufactured one sentence at a time on tape recorders and then patched together to make damning admissions which the sentences on their own did not imply.

"This whole frame-up was a counter-revolutionary act. The Regiment leaders assured everyone that if the four were not counter-revolutionary then they themselves were, and if they themselves were revolutionary then the four were counter-revolutionary. It must be one or the other, they claimed. Apparently it was the former, for behind all this ugly business lay a concerted attempt to bombard the proletarian headquarters, to bombard Mao Tse-tung.

"Actually the person in charge in Nankou was not a Tsinghua student but one of the outsiders—a specialist in torture who turned out to have a counter-revolutionary record. Factionalism made it easy for people like that. They used the blind hatred of the factional leaders to take class revenge.

"Most of the rank-and-file, after they listened to our explanations, welcomed our coming, even clapped and gave us a send-off when we left.

"It was after 8 P.M. when we got back to the campus, but right then and there all the prisoners in our hands were exchanged in front of the Generator Building, with each side checking to make sure the exchange was fair.

" 'This,' said one of the 4s, 'shook everyone up. Here was a problem that could not possibly be solved. We had been deadlocked over the prisoner question for more than a year. Yet by the evening of August 9 it was solved!' "

After this many people, both students and staff, returned to the University from all over the country. Some had received letters from the Propaganda Team; others heard of the new situation through the grapevine. They came dribbling back, a few today, more tomorrow, and gradually re-established a more normal campus life.

On the heels of the prisoner exchange a major search for arms was organized, and every building, every corner, every foot of ground was checked. Everyone on the campus was mobilized for this. Twice as many arms were found as had been turned over on the evening of July 27. Even so, when the campus stream was later excavated for its rich lode of fertilizer still more arms were found lying deep in the mud. It is probable that some arms still remain in secret hiding places.

As for the sound equipment seized by the two factions, the Propaganda Team didn't make an issue of this until it became obvious that loudspeakers in factional hands made mass meetings difficult if not impossible to run. From the beginning the Team had used the broadcast facilities manned by the

Regiment in the Bright House. This comprehensive system made it easy to relay speeches live to the whole campus. But somehow it always worked out that when Regiment people spoke the system worked beautifully, but when anyone else spoke static drowned out their words. Regiment technicians made frequent apologies as they busied themselves looking for technical difficulties, but the Team leaders soon decided that the difficulties, far from being technical, were political. They demanded and got the surrender of the whole system. After that everyone could be heard.

21
Big Alliance (2)

As people came back to the pacified compus they were assigned to political study groups in their respective departments, each department in turn having been assigned to one or another column of the Workers Propaganda Team. Column 1 (metal workers) took over the basic courses and the clinic. Column 2 (instrument workers) supervised the department of automation. Column 3 (machinists) took over mechanical engineering, and Column 4 (textile workers) assumed responsibility for mathematics, physics, radio engineering, and water conservation. Column 5 (construction workers) took over civil engineering, power, and agricultural engineering. Column 6 (chemical workers) took over chemical engineering, industrial chemistry, and industrial physics. Column 7 (state-owned, mixed) took over electrical engineering, while the Direct Regiment (printers) took over the administrative offices of the whole University and the old Communist Party Committee.

Everyone—students, members of the teaching staff, workers in the maintenance department—was expected to take part in one class or another, but some were reluctant to do so. This was especially true of the members of the Regiment who had fought so hard. They were afraid that the Propaganda Team would take revenge.

One engineering student reported to his class the first morning only to find that it was led by a lathe worker whom he had personally stabbed with a spear. He turned and ran. The worker ran after him shouting, "Come back. We must settle accounts." Hearing this, the student ran even faster. When he was finally cornered he was amazed to hear the worker say, "I don't mean to settle accounts with you personally. What we must do is study Mao Tse-tung Thought together and settle accounts with Liu Shao-ch'i. The only reason that you are swollen all over, as Chairman Mao said, is that you have been poisoned by Liu Shao-ch'i's line. That's why you used your spear on July 27. You were misled by bad people."

This student came from a working-class family. The lathe worker's magnanimity touched his heart. He returned to the class and in time became one of the staunchest advocates of a big alliance.

It soon became apparent that with the factional leaders involved in the classes little progress could be made. Whatever arguments the workers put forth during the day were refuted at night by the "rods" of each side. So special classes were organized for factional leaders, the members of the respective headquarters committees. They were all thrown together for study, but were isolated from the rank-and-file who quickly accepted the idea of a big alliance and pushed for it from below.

The leaders of both factions, sensing that this isolation could only lead to disaster for their ambitions, tried hard to leave certain less well-known "rods" down among the ranks to carry on factional agitation. But the members of the Propaganda Team were well informed as to who had played what role and when they found a "rod" trying to slip into the rank-and-file classes they sent him of her back to the leadership class. Rank-and-filers on both sides who wanted unity helped with this. When they saw a factional leader in a regular class they called out, "What are you doing here? Go back to your own class."

The campus workers, who met in separate classes of their own, very quickly formed an alliance between those among themselves who had supported the Regiment and those who had supported the 4s. They said that in the future they would never follow student partisans again, and they pushed hard for their leaders to form an alliance at the top. These leaders, who had all along manned factional workers headquarters that paralleled the students' two opposite headquarters, were also singled out for separate study. When they found that their followers really wanted an alliance, they gave up factional positions much more quickly than did the students.

The Propaganda Team purposely threw the leaders of both factions together for study and for daily living. At first, particularly with the students, this didn't work at all. People from opposite sides refused to sit near each other in class and refused to speak to each other in the dormitories or at meals. If there were two from each side in a room, these two spoke to each other, or gathered with others of their faction in the hall for whispered conferences, but they would have nothing to do with their roommates from the other faction. At night, when formal classes were over, the "rods" held factional meetings behind the campus hill or out in the Yuan Ming Yuan. Thus they reinforced one another in resisting the unity the Team was promoting.

As far as the Regiment was concerned, the 4s were counter-revolutionaries, Kuomintang reactionaries. As far as the 4s were concerned, the Regiment people were nothing but Kuai bandits, another form of Kuomintang reactionary. Neither side saw any basis for unity. If the Propaganda Team insisted on unity, then it could only happen after the rights and wrongs of the whole struggle had been argued out—in other words, only after the 4s granted and agreed that the Regiment had been right all along or, vice versa, only after the Regiment granted and agreed that the 4s had been right all along. The 4s kept repeating that the Regiment had shot down peaceful workers. The Regiment kept repeating that the 4s were led by a counter-revolutionary conspiracy, as was proved by the confessions of Lo-Wen-Li-Jao. These confessions were copied ad nauseum and even posted in front of the Propaganda Team headquarters in order to force the Team to take a stand.

But the Team refused to choose between the two factions and instead "carried the water-bowl level," insisting that in the main both sides were revolutionary and should get together.

The Regiment leaders then said that unity was possible if everyone recognized that the Regiment's mountain top was higher — that is, that the Regiment had more members, more power, better politics, and more prestige. Since the Regiment was *"hsiang tang-tang"* (bright and hard—really groovy) it must be the core. With the Regiment as core, a big alliance would be possible. Give the 4s, those old conservatives, a few posts to make them happy. Then everything would work out.

But the 4s were in no mood to recognize the Regiment as the core of anything. The 4s insisted that in fact they had more support than the Regiment, whose reputation, if the truth were known, came only from doing extreme things, most of which were harmful. The 4s insisted that they had a solid base among the students and much broader support among the lower cadres (this last was true) and so in any alliance they must carry greater weight—that is, *they* must be the core.

The Workers Propaganda Team responded with arguments for unity. Don't the masses of both factions love Mao-Tse-tung? Don't the masses of both factions support socialism? Since Chairman Mao started the Cultural Revolution, hasn't the goal of both sides been to overthrow the Liu Shao-ch'i clique? Aren't the masses of both sides committed to carrying the Cultural Revolution through to the end? Wasn't it actually bad people, suspicious characters, who led both sides into violent fighting and aren't there suspicious, reactionary persons in each faction? Since to all these questions the leaders and the rank-and-file of each side had to answer yes, the Propaganda Team said the theory of "no common goal" could not stand.

While these issues were being debated in the study classes, events in the outside world stepped up the pressure for unity. Very important was the gift of mangoes which Mao Tse-tung made to the Workers Propaganda Team. Foreign Minister Arshad Hussain of Pakistan, who had arrived in Peking on August 3, had given the Chairman several dozen mangoes. Mao Tse-tung, in turn, sent the fruit to the Team as a symbol of his support. At the same time he issued a statement that in China the working class was the leading class, that it should directly supervise the superstructure, and that the teams that had gone into selected universities should stay there permanently to run higher education.*

The gift of mangoes and this statement of support had a profound effect. Few people slept at all that night. Everyone wanted to see and touch the mangoes that came directly from Chairman Mao, and everyone wanted to discuss this extraordinary idea that the propaganda teams, far from being a temporary, emergency expedient, were a form of permanent supervision over higher education. If the workers could not contain their joy, most students and staff members were also carried along in the great wave of enthusiasm that Mao's act generated. The original mangoes were preserved, put in glass cases, and displayed in the reception rooms of key factories. Later numerous models of these mangoes were made and displayed by all the other factories that had taken part in the pacification of Tsinghua. A veritable cult arose around these mangoes, as if they were some religious relic—a hair of the Buddha, a nail from Christ's cross. It was hard for us as outsiders to understand the emotions which this gift aroused, but when we learned of the horror and the heroism of those twenty-four hours between July 27 and July 28, when workers stood with their red books in hand, saw five of their comrades killed and more than 700 wounded, and never broke their nonviolent discipline, this response began to come into focus.

The result, of course, as far as the Tsinghua students were concerned was greatly to increase the pressure from below for an alliance to be agreed upon by the factional leaders.

----

*Mao intervened dramatically in order to make it clear that the Workers Propaganda Team, unlike the work teams sent by Liu Shoa-ch'i, had his support. Intervention by the Work Team after the fifty days of "white terror" in June and July 1966 had been so made to "stink" and the slogan "we don't need a nursemaid" had been so glorified, that only a major effort by Mao Tse-tung himself could have reversed the trend and convinced people that teams were once again necessary.

On August 15 Chairman Mao moved again by holding a reception for the Workers Propaganda Team. Mass meetings were held at Tsinghua to celebrate and the students shouted until they were hoarse, "Long Live Chairman Mao. Chairman Mao's reception for the Workers Propaganda Team gives us infinite encouragement," and similar sentiments. "If you really mean that, then show it through action," the Team members told the students. "Show it by forming a big alliance." The students responded with demands on their leaders for a big alliance right away. Bowing to pressure, the factional leaders met in all-night session while the rank-and-file watched. "If you don't agree we'll never leave," shouted the masses. Under these conditions there was no way out short of an organizational merger.

Nevertheless, the negotiations lasted until dawn. The leaders of the 4s and the Regiment couldn't agree on representation, they couldn't agree on a name, they couldn't agree on a quote from Chairman Mao to introduce their proclamation, and they couldn't agree on who should head their new, united organization.

Just to settle the name question took hours. The 4s wanted to call the new group the Tsinghua University Big Alliance Committee. They had originally borne the name Chingkangshan April 14 Regiment, but the Chingkangshan designation had more and more come to be associated with the Regiment and not with the 4s, so now they wanted to drop both words altogether. The Regiment "rods" would not hear of this. They were known as Chingkangshaners and were proud of it. In the end they agreed to drop the word Regiment from the title but to retain Chingkangshan. The new organization would be called the Tsinghua University Chingkangshan Big Alliance Committee.

Having settled the name at last, they began to quarrel over representation. At that time the most important thing in the world to the factional leaders seemed to be to have a controlling seat on the leading body of the Big Alliance Committee. The Regiment at first demanded a nine to four advantage. The 4s held out for fifty-fifty. Then the Regiment, knowing that the Propaganda Team would not agree, suddenly said that four to nine would also be all right, what does representation matter? The 4s still held out for fifty-fifty. The Propaganda Team finally suggested sixteen for the Regiment, fifteen for the 4s. This broke the deadlock and this is what was agreed.

Then they had to settle who should be the chairman. Kuai said, "Let Shen Ju-huai be the chairman."

Shen Ju-huai said, "Let Kuai Ta-fu be the chairman."

This of course was only a method of saving face. Each knew that his followers would push his own candidacy to the end. Finally, since Kuai Ta-fu's reputation was truly much greater than Shen's, they decided that Kuai should be chairman and Shen vice-chairman.

With the question of top leadership settled, the make-up of the committee down below was not too difficult to resolve. Then the negotiators finally fell to quarreling over what quotation to use from Chairman Mao's works.

The 4s wanted to use this statement: "The revolutionary Red Guards and revolutionary students' organizations should realize the revolutionary great alliance. So long as both sides are revolutionary mass organizations, they should realize the revolutionary great alliance in accordance with revolutionary principles."

But the Regiment wouldn't hear of this. Regiment leaders said that any quote would do, but not that one. In their view the unity being forged that night was purely one of expediency. They were not really willing to grant that the 4s were revolutionary or that they had united with them on the basis of revolutionary principle. They proposed instead to use, "You should pay attention to state affairs and carry the Great Proletarian Cultural Revolution through to the end," and "We should encourage comrades to take the interests of the whole into account. Every Party member, every branch of work, every statement, and every action must proceed from the interests of the whole Party; it is absolutely impermissible to violate this principle."

The implication of this choice of quotations was that even a temporary unity with counter-revolutionaries could be justified in the interests of the Party as a whole, and so the Regiment agreed to go along. The 4s also agreed, and at last, as the hot August sun rose over Tsinghua on the morning of August 17, Bulletin #1 of the Tsinghua University Chingkangshan Big Alliance Committee was issued. The full text follows.

HIGHEST DIRECTIVE

"You should pay attention to state affairs and carry the Great Proletarian Cultural Revolution through to the end."
—Mao Tse-tung

"We should encourage comrades to take the interests of the whole into account. Every Party member, every branch of work, every statement, and every action must proceed from the interests of the whole Party; it is absolutely impermissible to violate this principle."
—Mao Tse-tung

The Tsinghua University Chingkangshan Revolutionary Big Alliance Committee of the Red Guards Representative Congress.

Bulletin #1

The news of our Great Leader Chairman Mao receiving the Peking working-class representatives and the publishing of Chairman Mao's new directives is like a strong east wind. It became the motive force pushing forward the Great Proletarian Cultural Revolution. The former two organizations at Tsinghua University, along with this sweeping east wind, closely following Chairman Mao's great strategic plan, under the guidance of the invincible Thought of Mao Tse-tung, with the help of the Peking Workers and Peasants Mao Tse-tung Thought Propaganda Team, realized a revolutionary big alliance based on revolutionary principles on August 16, 1968. This is another great victory for the invincible Thought of Mao Tse-tung on the Tsinghua compus.

The Tsinghua Univesity Chingkangshan Revolutionary Big Alliance Committee now issues a Bulletin #1, as follows:

1. Representatives of the two former factions of Tsinghua University, under the care of the great leader Chairman Mao, with the help of the Peking Workers and Peasants

Mao Tse-tung Thought Propaganda Team, fighting self and repudiating revisionism, after consulting decided that the Tsinghua University Chingkangshan Revolutionary Alliance Committee is made up of representatives from former Chingkangshan Regiment headquarters: Kuai Ta-fu, Pao Ch'eng-keng, Jen Ch-uan-chung, Ch'en Yu-yen, Wang Liang-sheng, Hsieh Te-ming, Liu Ts'ai-t'ang, Ma Hsiao-chung, Ch'en Chi-fang, Chang Hsueh-shen, Weng Wen-ping, Ts'ui Chao-shih, Fu Yu-an, Sun Ping-hua, Kao Chi-hung, Kung Kuo-shang; and of representatives from former Tsinghua Chingkangshan April 14 Regiment Headquarters, Shen Ju-huai, Hsu Ch'ang-chung, Liu Wan-chang, Chi P'eng, Wang Yung-hsien, T'an Hao-cheng, Ch'en Pang-fu, Kao Chi-chang, Fu Cheng-t'ai, Yim Tsun-sheng, Chou Jen-lao, Li Yuan-tsung, Ch'en Ch'u-san, Kuo Jen-k'uan, Chang Hsueh-mei.

1. A daily work group is set up under the Tsinghua University Chingkangshan Revolutionary Big Alliance Committee made up of representatives from former Tsinghua Chingkangshan Regiment headquarters, Kuai Ta-fu, Pao Ch'eng-keng, Jen Ch'uan-chung, Ch'en Yu'yen, Wang Liang-sheng, Hsieh Te-ming; and from Tsinghua April 14 Regiment Headquarters, Shen Ju-huai, Hsu Ch'ang-chung, Liu Wan-chang, Chi P'eng, Wang Yung-hsien. Chairman of the group Kuai Ta-fu. Vice-chairman Shen Ju-huai.

3. The Tsinghua Chingkangshan Revolutionary Big Alliance Committee is going to continue to put into effect Chairman Mao's series of new directives and the July 3 and July 24 orders, and also the various agreements that the former two factions have arrived at with the help of the Peking Workers and Peasants Mao Tse-tung Thought Propaganda Team.

4. The daily work of the Tsinghua University Chingkangshan Big Alliance Committee . . . will be carried out by the daily work group.

5. All members of the Tsinghua University Chingkangshan Revolutionary Big Alliance Committee . . . must carry out Chairman Mao's great teaching: "We should let every comrade be clear that all speech and actions of Communists must stick to the principle of the greatest interest of the broadest masses of the people and be supported by the broadest masses of the people."

6. The Tsinghua University Chingkangshan Revolutionary Big Alliance Committee . . . must raise high the big red banner of Mao Tse-tung Thought; put proletarian politics in command; closely follow Chairman Mao's great strategic plan; firmly control the main orientation of the struggle; thoroughly repudiate the reactionary theory of many centers, which is the bourgeois theory of no center; recognize in time and resolutely smash the obstruction and wrecking of the class enemy from the right and the ultra-left; further repudiate *shan tou chu yi* [mountaintop-ism], individualism, sectarianism, and all other manifestations of bourgeois world outlook; put up a thorough and uncompromising struggle against right splitism; closely link with the masses, consolidate and develop the revolutionary big alliance; promote the revolutionary three-in-one combination; make great efforts to set up the three-in-one combination of red power of Tsinghua University—a revolutionary committee; strive to win all-round victory in the Great Proletarian Cultural Revolution; swear to transform Tsinghua University into a big red school of Mao Tse-tung Thought.

Tsinghua University Chingkangshan Revolutionary Big Alliance Committee of Red Guards Representative Congress and representatives of Peking Workers and Peasants Mao Tse-tung Thought Propaganda Team: Liu Yi-an, Chin Man-yin, Chang Te-ch'un, Jan Shih-min, Wang Chih-yao, Wei Hsiu-ju, Liu Feng, Tsou Shang-shan, T'ang Hui-p'ing, Ma Yu-chu, Representatives of Revolutionary Big Alliance Committee . . . Kuai Ta-fu, Pao Ch'eng-keng, Ch'en Chi-fang, Ch'en Yu-yen, Wang Wen-ping, Shen Ju-huai, Liu Wan-cheng, Wang Yung-hsien, Ch'en Pang-fu, Chou Jen-lao.
—August 17, 1968

Once this agreement was reached, Lu Fang-ch'ien, of the Peking Garrison Command, tried to get Kuai Ta-fu and Shen Ju-huai to shake hands. They had not talked with one another, except in official negotiations, for over a year and a half. Even though they were now jointly in command of a united organization they found it hard, very hard, to extend a hand in greeting. Finally, after much urging, they clasped palms weakly. This sealed an alliance which all knew in their hearts was nothing more than a marriage of convenience, a form of shot-gun wedding.

Before this organizational unity could develop into ideological unity and provide the basis for a functioning revolutionary committee at Tsinghua, a lot more work had to be done. The Workers Propaganda Team, encouraged by the progress thus far, set out to consolidate the victory with a more vigorous program of study. A small beating incident that occurred on August 19 provided a good starting point from which to draw important lessons against factionalism.

22
Clearing Class Ranks

Shortly after the big alliance agreement was signed, a student in the Power Engineering Department, a former 4, returned to the University. He was shocked by the condition of his old room in the dormitory. Students were not rolling up their quilts, hanging up their clothes, sweeping their quarters, or cleaning up after meals. On returning from study class they shed their clothes like snakes shed their skins, climbed into rumpled quilts to sleep, then rose to cook makeshift meals over coal stoves in the hall, throwing their garbage and ashes into any convenient corner.

"Look what a mess you've made of the dorms!" said the new arrival.

When another former 4 supported him, Hu Chia-chu of the Regiment got very angry. He slapped his two former opponents in the face and bloodied the nose of one of them. The newly returned student, blood on his jacket, ran to find Wang Yung-hsien, now a member of the Big Alliance Standing Committee.

"Fights have been a-dime-a-dozen at Tsinghua. We had been killing each other with spears and guns. What did a little nosebleed amount to?" said Wang Yung-hsien, who told us the story. "It was hardly worth making a fuss over, but I reported it to the PLA man assigned to our department and went back to sleep.

"All of a sudden, at 3 A.M., the Standing Committee members were called to an emergency meeting in the Water Conservation building. It was all about this bloody nose. The cadres of the Propaganda Team headquarters considered it a serious violation of the July 3 Order. They said it amounted to a counter-revolutionary incident aimed at the Team.

"We on the Standing Committee said, 'It really doesn't amount to much, it's run of the mill.' But the Team leaders disagreed. 'We have a big alliance now,' they said. 'We have to get rid of factionalism and we have to get rid of violence.' They felt that an incident like this could have a very bad effect, that it might undermine the whole alliance if it was not dealt with properly. They considered it an unhealthy wind that must be stifled before it gathered momentum.

"So the issue was taken up by the Standing Committee with a request that a mass meeting be convened. There Hu Chia-chu would criticize himself and the alliance leaders would criticize themselves for not having properly educated the rank-and-file, regardless of faction. All of the 4s delegates on the Standing Committee voted to hold the meeting. But Kuai couldn't agree. A Regiment member had bloodied the nose of a 4. The whole thing made the Regiment look bad. Why make a big public issue of it? Regiment people were afraid they would lose too much face, perhaps even collapse as an organization.

"The Propaganda Team argued patiently that factions were not on trial. What was on trial was a dastardly act. If it was not repudiated people would not dare to return to the campus, for they could expect nothing but endless violent incidents.

"The meeting went on for two days. The people on campus waited and so did many in the city of Peking. Everyone was waiting to see if the Workers Propaganda Team could control the situation. If this issue could be resolved well, it might mark a turning point. Not only did the Team members debate with Kuai, but so did a lot of rank-and-file people. The meeting was held on the ground floor and hundreds of people listened in through the open windows and even joined in the debate. The pressure for a public meeting was so great that in the end Kuai had to agree.

"The first attempt to hold the mass meeting failed, however. Some Regiment 'rods' cut the loudspeaker wires so that none of the speeches could be heard. The event had to be postponed until the following day. For some reason the sound system worked this time and everything went off as planned. Shen Ju-huai sat in the chair. Hu Chia-chu made a detailed self-criticism, weeping all the while, and Kuai Ta-fu spoke for the Big Alliance Committee.

"In the three years since that afternoon there has not been a single violent incident on the campus. It truly was a turning point; after that all the remaining stay-aways returned one by one. Of course, we still had factional feelings and we often quarreled bitterly, but whenever a quarrel became tense we reminded one another of Hu Chia-chu and cooled off. Violent fighting had been made to stink on the Tsinghua campus. From that day forth it was against the law in fact as well as in name."

In order to win agreement on the terms of the big alliance, each faction had met separately several times prior to August 16. On the last of these occasions, when it was clear that an alliance was inevitable and that factional activity would become increasingly difficult, Kuai made a long speech to the Regiment "rods," urging them to persevere. He quoted from an old classic: "Sleep on a wooden plank, eat bile, gather forces for ten years, review the bitter lessons for another ten years." It was a plea for organizational continuity, albeit underground, until conditions were more favorable. It was a plea for a comeback twenty years later. It proved that for Kuai the big alliance was pure expediency. When the time was ripe he intended to make another bid for power.

Sometime earlier a few of the leaders of the 4s had written a long article entitled, "The Trend of Thought of April 14 Will Surely Win Out." This made clear that the 4s also looked on the big alliance as only an expedient. Since the main enemy was still considered to be Liu Shao-ch'i and the capitalist-roaders allied with him, it was important to unite with the Regiment rebels in order to beat down Liu; but later the contradiction with the Regiment must surely come to the fore again and their organization must be smashed.

In late August and September these two documents—Kuai's August 16 speech and the 4s article—became the heart of the curricula for all the study groups. Both violated Mao Tse-tung Thought. Both took "I am the core" as their central theme and advocated onesided victory rather than unity based on revolutionary principles.

The Propaganda Team encouraged the 4s to examine their article critically while the Regiment discussed Kuai's speech. As both groups began to see serious mistakes in their own policies, the two sides were brought together for further discussion. They discovered, much to their amazement, that they could sit down together and talk things over. But this was possible only because each was willing to admit mistakes and because the Propaganda Team, rather than seizing on these mistakes to beat them down, used the admissions to encourage unity. Unity was also promoted by meetings to remember past bitterness—the life in pre-Liberation times—by careful study of Mao Tse-tung's writings and recent directives, and by reading important editorials and newspaper articles. There was, for instance, a statement Mao made summing up his southern trip of 1967 in which he stated categorically that there was no material basis for antagonistic contradictions within the working class and that consequently workers could and should unite. There was also an editorial about the "theory of many centers," which amounted to a theory of no center, which amounted to anarchy; and there were articles such as the one in the *New Anhui* which pointed out that factionalism provides a shield for class enemies and that class enemies promote and use factionalism for counter-revolutionary purposes.

The Workers Propaganda Team supplemented this reading and discussion with endless heart-to-heart talks and with reports from typical workers and typical commune members in plants and on farm brigades where factionalism had been effectively dissolved. All this brought results. More and more rank-and-file people were won over. A few leaders even began to soften their attitudes. One of these was Ch'en Yu-yen, the most militant young woman on the Regiment Headquarters Committee. Once she began to understand the true character of factionalism, she helped expose the mistakes of the Regiment, especially the fighting of July 27, and mobilized the rank-and-file to repudiate them.

It was a slow process. At first even self-criticism really took the form of veiled attack on the other side. Wang Yung-hsien of the 4s explained how this worked. "At the start," he said, "I had the idea that these classes were pretty good. We could clarify our differences and prove who had been right (us) and who wrong (them). Whenever we made a self-criticism we always managed to attack the other side indirectly to show that we were right.

"I was in the same class with Ch'en Yu-yen. Hsueh, from the Propaganda Team, urged us to 'fight self, repudiate revisionism' with some genuine self-criticism. So Ch'en said, 'We made a mistake. We didn't treat the 4s correctly. When they split away we didn't try to unite with them or educate them. No matter how numerous our own shortcomings were, we should have tried to help the 4s.

"To this I responded, 'Even though Ch'en was manipulated by Ch'i Pen-yu, she was deceived and we should not put her in the same category as the conscious wreckers.'

"To which Ch'en came back with, 'Of course, there were a lot of bad people in the 4s, but we should have made a distinction between these bad people and the masses.'"

Both of these statements implied that the other side was riddled with truly bad people, the likes of which were not to be found on one's own side. In order to correct such misunderstandings and simultaneously clear the ranks of undesirables, the Propaganda Team urged each side to look into its own forces and expose the counter-revolutionaries and manipulators hidden there. The Regiment had based its whole case on supposed counter-revolutionaries embedded in the 4s; now they were forced to ask if they did not perhaps harbor some counter-revolutionaries of their own. Facts proved that they did.

The most notorious of these was Sung Ch'ing-ying, a leader of the Red Teachers Union who built up his reputation as a spokesman for the faculty radicals to the point where he was not only proposed by the Regiment as a member of the revolutionary committee which they tried to set up in May 1967, but he was elected to the Regiment Headquarters Committee and its operating committee.

It was Sung, a gentleman of landlord origin, who had first propounded the theory that the revolutionaries of the late 1960s must be sought among the people under attack and out of favor in the early 1960s. Sung had also publicized the idea that he, a professor of engineering with a salary of 200 yuan a month, was more revolutionary than a Communist Party cadre with a salary of 40 yuan a month because his political status was lower, he wielded no political power—he was, in his own view, oppressed. Therefore he was a revolutionary.

In 1966, after Wang Kuang-mei's work team left the campus and as the Chingkangshan Regiment began to win power, he announced that he too wished to rebel. "I'm going to sell my piano and do what I can to support the rebels, if that means only sweeping the floor and carrying water." His willingness to perform such menial tasks made a deep impression on everyone. Visitors from the outside, seeing him at work, asked, "Who is that?"

"An old professor," replied the Regiment members, shaking their heads with amazement at an intellectual who was not afraid to soil his hands.

Wherever there was action Sung tended to take the lead. He helped raid the arms stores at the University and led the attack on the Peking Security Bureau when "the madman of the modern age," Ch'en Li-ming, was held there.

In May 1967, not long after the 4s split from the Regiment in the dispute over which cadres deserved support, they learned from Sung's son that Sung had been a member of the

Kuomintang. They publicized this information on a big-character poster and blasted the Regiment for harboring such a man. Regiment leaders then went to Sung to ask about his past.

"I was a Kuomintang member," Sung said, "but that was a mere formality, a move to protect my rice bowl. I never lived through one day of party life."

The Regiment leaders believed him and eventually published an article in their factional paper about "the good non-party cadre Sung Ch'ing-ying." This article put the 4s temporarily off the track. In time Sung's activism and good behavior allayed any lingering suspicion that remained. Later, when people asked Sung's defenders in the Regiment how they knew he was all right they said, "We got our material from him."

Actually, the attempted exposure by the 4s helped Sung. The Regiment, unwilling even to consider the idea that it sheltered bad people, rallied to his defense as soon as he was attacked. As former Regiment member Wu Wei-yu said, "Some people were obviously no good, but if the other side attacked them it was taken as an attack on the whole faction, so everyone rallied to their support. If, on the contrary, we had struggled against them and exposed them it would have been like struggling against ourselves. It reflected on us that we had such people in our ranks, so we defended them to the end 'as good, not bad'!"

As factional feelings simmered down after the big alliance, everyone began to look with more objectivity at people with historical problems and Sung's case came up once more. Even though Sung refused to talk himself, his son now exposed the fact that his father had joined the Kuomintang not once but twice. Student investigators were sent to the county outside Peking where Sung had lived at the time. There they found people who had acted as his sponsors in joining the organization and people who had been members of the same Kuomintang unit.

With this material in hand, the investigators returned to question Sung. They also urged his family to persuade him to make a clean breast of the whole story. Finally, aware that

a frank confession could lead to lenient treatment, Sung re-
counted his former reactionary activities, including many facts
still unknown to his listeners. It turned out that he had not
only been a member of the Kuomintang but had risen to the
position of district head. Furthermore, he had been in charge
of the maintenance work for a Kuomintang army unit that
was engaged in war against the People's Liberation Army.

All this would ordinarily have been enough to put him
in the category of a historical counter-revolutionary, but because he had not committed serious crimes as a Kuomintang
district secretary, because he had frankly exposed his past, and
because he had worked well afterward, he was treated not as
an enemy but as one of the people. His own view was that
the Workers Propaganda Team had saved him. "I was afraid
every day that I would be found out, and I thought that once
I was found out, I would be done for, for I did not really believe there was such a thing as good treatment."

When they asked him why he stepped forward as an active
rebel during the Cultural Revolution, he said, "To protect myself. I pretended to be a rebel so that I wouldn't be discovered
and exposed as a reactionary."

But this explanation did not satisfy the students or the
Propaganda Team. "To say that he only wanted to protect himself did not fully explain his acts," Lu Fang-ch'ien said. "He not
only covered up his past, he posed as a revolutionary, deceived
a section of the masses, and led the masses to fight one another.
He spread the reactionary theory that the revolutionaries of
today are those who were suppressed yesterday, and he seized
arms and attacked police headquarters. In other words, he
voluntarily stepped out on the stage of history and tried to
play a role. Didn't this make him a conscious counter-revolutionary? If he had stayed home he might have slipped through.
He chose an active role and thereby exposed himself. Which
only goes to show that counter-revolutionaries do not voluntarily step aside. 'People struggle before they die' [an old
classical quotation]."

In 1971 Sung Ch'ing-ying was once again on the teaching
staff of Tsinghua. He had been assigned to an automobile fac-

tory and had organized a research project with other staff members. His group had already come up with some valuable innovations. His future seemed fairly bright.

Counter-revolutionaries and people with questionable historical records were also found among the 4s. One of these was Li Fang, the man the Regiment seized and tortured and the 4s defended to the end. It seemed he had a suspect past, but in July 1971 his case had still not been settled. As part of his contribution to the manipulation of the masses he had helped develop the thesis embodied in "The Trend of Thought of April 14 Will Surely Win," which had deepened factionalism and prolonged the fighting.

Another of the 4s who turned out to be a class enemy had fought bravely throughout the hundred-day war, apparently without a thought for personal safety. It turned out that he had an ulterior motive, however. He wanted to train himself in military affairs, then retreat to the mountains for guerrilla war. If the fighting went on long enough not many people would be left; then he and his small clique could dominate the 4s and turn them into a counter-revolutionary instrument. He tried all kinds of tricks to win people to his side. He studied small personal habits. If someone liked to smoke he'd light the brand they preferred and smoke alongside them. If someone expressed conservative thoughts, he'd sympathize and fan them.

This student was among those who had repeatedly urged Wang Yung-hsien, the commander of the 4s in the Science Building, to break out of the Regiment siege regardless of consequences. "If I had listened to him we would all be dead," said Wang. "After he was exposed we realized how deeply factionalism had blinded us to the political character of some of our allies."

Exposing and weeding out class enemies from the ranks on both sides was indeed a potent education for everyone. Up to that point few had realized how easily a reactionary could maneuver under the cover of a false red flag, and how provocative his or her words and acts could be. They were also shocked to find how careless they all had been, accepting support simply because it was offered, defending people simply because they were attacked, without making any thoroughgoing investigation of the background or political position of such "allies."

23
Kuai's Last Stand

The intensive study in September widened the support given the Propaganda Team, led many people to re-examine their factional commitments, and mobilized them to expose rather than to defend past mistakes. But the hard-core leaders remained untouched. On Friday evenings word went around among the "rods" of each side about where to meet that Saturday or Sunday—the Western Hills, the Summer Palace, or Tien An-men square. Then those who were still loyal would gather to complain about the shambles their organization had fallen into and discuss what to do in order to recoup their losses. If the meeting place was the Summer Palace the Regiment die-hards would rent a rowboat, go way out on the lake, sing factional songs, and recall the glorious deeds of the past when Kuai Ta-fu held power on the campus and distant masses waited breathless for his telegrams.

"We felt," said Wu Wei-yu, "that it wouldn't do to go on as we were. If we continued in this direction we were finished. People were dropping away every day. We had to do something to recoup our prestige. We thought that we still had some prestige. We thought that we still had some capital with the masses so we ought to make use of it before it was too late. We thought we could still attack the Lo-Wen-Li-Jao clique, expose and crush the leading core of the 4s, and create a situation where only the Regiment held power."

Prior to October 1 everyone was too busy studying to act. But the celebrations commemorating National Day brought a hiatus in the program of the Propaganda Team, key factional leaders like Shen Ju-huai were released from class to help organize Tsinghua's National Day program, and Kuai found time one Saturday night to call together a meeting of the "rods."

"I have brought you together to discuss how we can take the initiative at Tsinghua," said Kuai. "Once we bring the problem of Lo-Wen-Li-Jao into the open the Propaganda Team can hardly answer us. The people will be mobilized and the Team will lose control of the movement."

Kuai was too smart, however, to begin with his full program. Instead he drafted a letter to the Central Committee reviewing the merits of the Chingkangshan Regiment and complaining about the fact that all its power had now been taken away by a Propaganda Team that was riding roughshod over the campus. At the same time, he found four people in his Headquarters Committee who had not taken part in the violent fighting of July 27 and therefore still had some grounds to make complaints. They wrote a poster which made a small "point of order" critical of the Team.

The issue they chose was Shen Ju-huai's absence from classes. This had been thoroughly debated in the Big Alliance Committee and voted on by all. Now Kuai's lieutenants protested that the Workers Propaganda Team was not fair. They allowed the leader of one faction to miss study. Furthermore, the poster said, Shen Ju-huai was a counter-revolutionary who didn't even deserve equal treatment, such as inclusion in regular classes—not to mention special treatment, such as the right to organize for the October 1 celebration. "The enemy," said the poster, "is in front of our faces. To fight self-interest means to fight the enemy here on the campus." This was only another way of saying that Shen should be the target of attack and not the leaders of the Regiment.

Regiment "rods" hoped and expected that this poster would once again mobilize the rank-and-file to take the offensive against the 4s and the Propaganda Team. They thought it would stimulate a rash of posters in support and produce a new "rebel" groundswell. They were grievously disappointed. By evening plenty of posters had gone up on the campus, but instead of supporting the initial thrust, they were opposed to it, taking it apart sentence by sentence and attacking those who wrote it. The opposition posters were signed "so-and-so—a proletarian revolutionary from the united masses."

Regiment "rods" watched closely to see if most of these posters came from former 4s. If so they would have an issue. To their dismay they found that they came from former activists on both sides and, as the posters piled up, they more and more concentrated their attack on Kuai's order to shoot workers and on his August 16 speech advocating a comeback in twenty years. "If you can't fight self," several posters warned Kuai, "we'll remove you from office."

These posters were concentrated around the Quiet House, where the study classes were held. Few posters had ever been posted there. Now suddenly they appeared by the thousands to refute the Regiment's position. More mats had to be put up to make room for them all, and the call from the masses to settle accounts with Kuai's crimes became louder and louder. "We haven't even begun to settle accounts with you for the death of five workers. You say you have no self-interest to fight. If you don't change that attitude we'll settle accounts with you! Since you have brought up the issue we'll take you up on it!"

Little maneuvers such as the factional meetings at the Summer Palace and the gathering of material about the Propaganda Team were also publicly exposed, and questions were raised concerning all those strange happenings of July 27, which at the time had seemed spontaneous but which now looked as if they might have had some pattern—a pattern linked to Kuai Ta-fu.

Up to this point Kuai had maintained that the shooting began down below on the spur of the moment. But posters written by the masses said that Kuai had given an order and had even signed his name to it. The more the Regiment "rods" denied this, the more evidence the people and the Workers Propaganda Team brought forth. The ideological struggle became very sharp and the longer it went on the more clear it became that the Regiment, far from having any capital with which to appeal to the masses, had actually committed some very bad crimes which required answers and explanations.

Ch'en Chi-fang, one of the key Regiment leaders who had up to this point loyally supported Kuai, now decided that things had gone too far. He mobilized an inside group that collectively exposed the whole Lo-Wen-Li-Jao frameup. He produced evidence that the counter-revolutionary statement made by the four had been extracted under torture. Ch'en knew about the torture, which Kuai claimed to be unaware of, because he had organized an internal investigation during the period of violent fighting and had seen the treatment meted out to the "counter-revolutionary clique" with his own eyes.

A few days after the first poster aroused such a wave of opposition, Kuai himself, together with twelve others, put up an opinion in support of the original position. He said that important problems concerning the Team's methods and fairness had been raised. Therefore there should be a debate.

The Propaganda Team took up the challenge and organized a mass debate to which all headquarters and branch headquarters members of both factions were invited. At this meeting all the material gathered for the posters was presented verbally and Lu Fa-hsien, Propaganda Team leader in the Peking Garrison, read aloud Kuai's July 27 order to the Regiment fighting-teams to shoot. Unable to counter this offensive directly, Kuai charged that the Team had spread false rumors about the events of that day, but Team cadres refuted this with evidence that it was Kuai, not the Team, who had spread false rumors. Kuai had told all who would listen that workers had arrested and beaten up students. He could say things like that because most of his listeners were not eyewitnesses, but had been absent from the campus. Asked for facts at the meeting, he was unable to come up with any, and so his position collapsed.

After this meeting Kuai and some comrades wrote a "clarifying point," saying that they had made mistakes but that their position had been misunderstood. When this "clarifying point" was also repudiated, Kuai finally wrote a poster saying, "I surrender to the working class." But even this was only a maneuver. Privately he still worked hard to hold the Regiment together. He led a group to the Summer Palace to be photographed

with their Chingkangshan armbands on, and when Bear
left for a year of work at a PLA farm Kuai saw to it that dozens
of Mao badges were pinned to his chest. Regiment "rods" all
hugged Bear and cried. Bear's crimes were great enough to
warrant repudiation and punishment, but his comrades gave
him a hero's send-off.

Obviously Kuai was still working night and day to hold
the Regiment together. This was still possible because there
were people like Tsu, who felt that all the study had become
nothing but an attack on the Regiment. Tsu had left the campus
before the Propaganda Team came and was fired on. He had
returned only in mid-September. The fact that his side had
killed and wounded workers sent by Chairman Mao seemed
to him to be decisive. It was like falling and breaking one's
backbone. How could any member of the Regiment ever stand
up again? How could any member of the Regiment ever again
boast of past merits? This one incident was enough for the
opposition to lay hold of and permanently beat all Regiment
supporters down. Yet Tsu was still loyal to the Regiment and to
its glorious rebel past. Since there was no way out, he would
go down with the rest. After all, as far as he was concerned
the 4s were hopeless conservatives. What had they ever done
but curse the Regiment? That was, it seemed, their whole program. They had built a movement cursing the Regiment and
now they were still at it.

The Team members nevertheless maintained a friendly attitude toward Tsu. They blamed the violent fighting not on
the faction as a whole but on a few bad or hoodwinked members. They consistently maintained that the Regiment "rods"
were good revolutionaries and that they had played an important, even a crucial, role during the work team period and
for many months afterward. As for the 4s, were they not also
good revolutionaries? Surely they must be seen as comrades
who opposed the capitalist road, and not as enemies. If they
had criticisms of the Regiment, shouldn't one examine them
on their merits and accept those that were true?

In the end Tsu, too, was won over. When he examined
the criticisms made of the Regiment he decided that in the

main they were true, that the 4s had uncovered precisely the Regiment's weak points, and that the weakest point of all was the Regiment "rods" conviction that they and they alone were revolutionaries. This made it impossible for them to follow Mao's advice and unite 95 percent of the people and 95 percent of the cadres in opposition to Liu Shao-ch'i and for the socialist transformation of Tsinghua.

Lu Fa-hsien, who played a leading role on the Propaganda Team throughout, summed up this period by saying: "We learned from this struggle that bourgeois factionalism and mountaintop-ism is very stubborn. We learned that one has to struggle against it continuously. If we don't struggle against them, they will struggle against us. If we don't fight back we cannot maintain our position on the campus, Mao Tse-tung's policies can't be carried out, and the movement for struggle-criticism-transformation can't advance one step. Even though factionalism is so stubborn we must hold fast to the main orientation of our work and educate and unite the student masses. We must use reason to convince them. Most members of the masses can accept working-class education, support working class leadership, and follow Mao Tse-tung's policies. Facts prove this."

The overall results were good. As winter approached most of the leaders of both factions got together. They even put joint plays on stage under the slogan, "Welcome to the Big Alliance Study Class!" And in the classes they behaved well. Only a few, like Kuai, and for a long time Bear, remained die-hards. In the end even Bear was moved to make a serious self-criticism.

The big alliance, the study classes, the patience, and the protracted work of the members of the Propaganda Team so changed the climate of opinion on the Tsinghua campus that in January 1969 it was possible to form a revolutionary committee along the lines originally proposed by Mao Tse-tung—that is, a committee of mass representatives, cadres, and People's Liberation Army personnel. This revolutionary committee then led the whole university in a review of the politics and class background of everyone on campus, exposing the reactionaries, the Kuomintang agents, and the criminal characters who had crept into the ranks of the mass movement on both sides. Having "cleared the class ranks," the committee went on to lead a Party rectification movement which had as its goal the weeding out of unqualified people, the reinstatement as Party members in good standing of all "healthy elements," and the recruitment into the Party of outstanding new people who had played a role in the Cultural Revolution. This movement took the better part of a year, and it wasn't until January 1970 that the new Party Committee of Tsinghua University was established. Only then did the movement to transform the educational system really get under way.

24
Carrying Poles for Parker "51's"

This account has concentrated on the students and staff members who made up the mass movement. Almost nothing has been said about the "set-aside" cadres. But in the fall of 1968 the Workers Propaganda Team also did a great deal of work among the higher cadres who had been removed from office in 1966 and now needed rehabilitation. The first task was to find them and win their release.

Early in the morning hours of July 28, 1968, when Kuai decided that the Regiment must retreat from the campus, he sent Liu Ping, the former vice-secretary of the University Party Committee, and other capitalist-roaders held by the Regiment to Changp'ing County, where they were held along with the ordinary prisoners seized from the ranks of the 4s. The August 7 release of prisoners from both sides did not include "set-aside" cadres and before the 300 members of the Propaganda Team arrived at Nankou to set free the Regiment's captives, Liu and his colleagues were transferred to hidden lock-ups on the grounds of the Aeronautical Institute. They were moved several times thereafter, but were released on August 29 when all prisoners were finally freed by both sides.

Liu Ping was immediately put into a study class led by members of the Propaganda Team. In November he was sent back to his original unit—the University Party Committee—to study jointly with them. Finally, the Party rectification movement in 1969 helped Liu to think through and understand all that had happened to him since 1966 and to recognize his mistakes prior to that time.

"In July 1967, I began to realize that I had made some mistakes," said Liu Ping. "But I didn't have any deep understanding of them. In October, when both factions began to study and discuss the old educational line, I began to understand more. But it wasn't until the Workers Propaganda Team came that I arrived at any deep understanding and began to have an overall analysis. This was because we studied Mao Tsetung Thought together with the Team cadres, not as targets of attack, but as students seeking knowledge. Together we were able to repudiate Liu Shao-ch'i's line and review our own line. By early 1969 I began to see things quite clearly. Then the Party rectification movement began and this cleared up all the remaining problems. Each of us used Chairman Mao's fifty-character slogan to examine himself,* to see if he was up to standard. Non-Party members also took part and organized mutual-aid groups. Each of us made a self-criticism and listened to criticism from the masses—sometimes in front of the whole University.

"In April I passed. We were all liberated. Then I joined another study class and went to work in the campus Truck Manufacturing Shop where I helped set up the shop revolutionary committee and took part in its meetings. In the meantime, in January 1969, the Tsinghua revolutionary committee

---

*Mao's fifty-character slogan reads as follows: "The Party organization should be composed of the advanced elements of the proletariat; it should be a vigorous and vital organization of vanguards which can lead the proletariat and the revolutionary masses in struggle against the class enemy."

was set up. It had none of the old leading cadres on it. But in January 1970, when the new Party Committee was established, I was elected vice-secretary, the same position I had held before."

Liu Ping was returned to power as vice-secretary of the Party Committee because the Propaganda Team and large numbers of staff and students' thought that he had really learned the lessons of the whole movement. For us he summed up these lessons in three points:

"1. The revolution divides into stages but the revolution continues. I feel that a Communist must see not only the current stage but the stage that is coming, the tasks of the future. We made a serious mistake after our victory in the whole country in 1949. Our thinking stopped with the democratic revolution. We were victorious, the working class was in power. The socialist revolution had to be carried forward but our thinking stopped. And this was even more true after socialist ownership was established throughout the economy and the struggle went into the superstructure. We weren't prepared for such a shift. Our subjective understanding fell way behind objective developments. Serious and complicated class struggle was the order of the day but we were blind and didn't see what was going on. We made bad mistakes. So one has to grasp the idea of stages on the one hand, and of the revolution continuing on the other. One can't go beyond the stage one is in, nor can one stop once that stage is completed. To sum up: the revolution develops by stages and the revolution continues!

"2. Every individual is a motive force and also a target of the revolution. From both positive and negative experience we have learned that each one of us must transform his own outlook. If you don't transform yourself you can't lead the masses to fight the enemy. For example, when we carried out the bourgeois reactionary line, the revisionist line, it was because we had the wrong thinking in our heads. We couldn't tell what was what. We couldn't distinguish the class nature of our policies, what was 'regular' and what was not. Why was Yenan called only a 'training class' and why were they now calling for a 'regular' school. What was meant by 'regular'? Whose 'regular' did we want?

"The difference between 'regular' and 'not regular' is a question of class stand. We were educated under the old system. From our youth we were influenced by the bourgeois educational system. I used to read stories about Edison, Fulton, and Watt. I thought, even if they didn't go to college, colleges are to train people like them. So after they said that Yenan was not a 'regular' school, I thought it probably wasn't. Why did I accept the idea of the professors' Communist Party? Because I had wrong ideas in my head. I thought everyone must have some expertise, so I accepted the idea of experts in charge of education.

"Everyone carries out the line that reflects his world outlook. A Communist who makes a mistake in line but doesn't see it as a question of world outlook is not a true revolutionary! If you don't aim at revolution with determination you can't succeed. For a Communist the question of correcting mistakes is a question of whether or not one can carry on the revolution. For this lesson we paid a heavy price. We only learned it through mistakes. A good revolutionary must revolutionize his own mind first before he can lead the masses. Only this way can we break with traditional ideas. We must make a big effort to do this.

"3. One must correctly handle the relation between being a cadre and being an ordinary worker. As rank-and-file people, youths who knew next to nothing, we joined the revolution and grew up under Chairman Mao's guidance. Gradually we became cadres and took on more and more responsibility. This was not because of any great merit of our own, but because the Communist Party and Chairman Mao cultivated and developed us. The credit belongs to the Party, to Chairman Mao, and to the people. But after long years as cadres we began to think that we were quite able. We thought we were above the masses. Like Anteus in the fable, our feet left the ground. So we couldn't reflect the feelings of the people and we couldn't carry out a revolutionary line. Chairman Mao's line reflects the common will of millions. A real revolutionary fighter must always understand that. And he must realize that he is an ordinary worker who must wholeheartedly serve the people. If we don't put ourselves in a correct relationship to the masses we can't serve them or the revolution. Then we have lost the road as Communists."

To make these points more vividly, Liu Ping told us about the three gifts which his colleague Hu Chien had received on being elected to the revolutionary committee of the May 7 Cadre School which Tsinghua University set up on wasteland in Kiangsi. These three gifts were:

1. A book of Mao Tse-tung's quotations.

2. A notebook inscribed with, "Let everyone speak"—a book, that is, for recording the criticisms and ideas of others.

3. A carrying pole with four sentences burnt into it:

Put this pole on your shoulder.

Remember Mao Tse-tung's teachings in your heart.

Never forget the lessons of history.

Continue making revolution and go forward always.

Liu Ping contrasted these gifts to the three gifts that Liu Shao-ch'i and Po Yi-p'o had arranged to give to every cadre at the provincial level or above after victory in 1949. Each of them received a woolen suit, an American-made Parker "51" pen, and a Swiss watch. These gifts pleased the cadres enormously. As they put on their woolen suits, strapped on their Swiss watches, and clipped their fountain pens into their pockets, they threw away their old Liberation Army fighting style and took up the life and outlook of officials. They became "regular" in dress and manner and they made the desired impression on the urban bourgeoisie.

Looking back with post-Cultural Revolution consciousness, it was easy to see that the suits, pens, and watches were not revolutionary gifts at all but sugar-coated bullets—small bribes with big implications. Mao's quotations, a book for criticism, and a carrying pole said to the cadres, "Study Mao Tse-tung Thought, stay close to the people, and work hard." A woolen suit, a wristwatch, and a fountain pen said to the cadres, "Now you are somebody special." Here in the realm of cadre policy was the two-line struggle—to line up with the laboring people or to line up with the bourgeoisie, that was the question. In 1971 Liu Ping saw it clearly. There was two-line struggle in everything, that was the big lesson that three years in the "wilderness" had taught him. It seemed unlikely that he would soon forget it.

25
Intellectuals Remolded

"Before, when I was not yet sixty, I used to want to be sixty as soon as possible so that the masses wouldn't be after me so much, so they would excuse me on account of my age. But now, since we have begun the transformation of education here and have recognized our past mistakes, I consider myself a young person and I compete with youth on the road of revolution."

These words were spoken by Ch'ien Wei-ch'ang, the professor of mechanics, and reflected great change in an erstwhile avowed Rightist. They could be attributed in part to the hard work of those cadres of the Workers Propaganda Team who made the remolding and rehabilitation of the reactionary professors and the "bourgeois academic authorities" their main task. While a majority of the Team had concentrated on the student movement and a special group had worked with the "set-aside" cadres, this group had made the old professors their primary concern and they had done a remarkable job with them.

Among other things, to transform the education at Tsinghua meant to transform these older professors whose knowledge was vital to the socialist transformation of China. This was a crucial test for Mao Tse-tung's policies. Mao's basic program for the Cultural Revolution, the "Sixteen-Point Decision," had called on the people to struggle against and overthrow those "persons in authority who are taking the capitalist road," and to "criticize and repudiate the reactionary bourgeois academic authorities."

The aim of this criticism and repudiation was not to get rid of them, to dispense with their services altogether, but to transform them and bring them into the mainstream of working-class politics. Liu Shao-ch'i had a policy of unity with the academic authorities which in practice mean unity on their terms. The ultra-left students wanted only to attack them and were quite willing to do without academic authorities altogether. Mao's policy was to unite with them but to unite for socialist goals, which meant that they had to be remolded, something that could only occur if the Cultural Revolution touched their "souls."

Mao summed up his views on this question as follows:

> The majority or the vast majority of the students trained in the old schools and colleges can integrate themselves with the workers, peasants, and soldiers, and some have made inventions or innovations; they must, however, be re-educated by the workers, peasants, and soldiers under the guidance of the correct line, and thoroughly change their old ideology. Such intellectuals will be welcomed by the workers, peasants, and soldiers.

As soon as the Workers Propaganda Team brought the fighting to an end—that is, on July 28, 1968—study classes were set up for the old professors. "They had me read Mao Tse-tung's works," said Ch'ien, "especially his 'Speech at the Conference on Propaganda Work.' After each paragraph they asked me where I stood in the struggle. I recalled my whole history and examined each stage of it. This took two months. I didn't know how to study, so they held long individual talks with me. In September 1968, we had seventeen long talks, each of three hours duration or more. Once we began at 7 P.M. and ended at 5 A.M. because of a problem that I didn't understand. All this study made me realize that my past road was wrong. I was encouraged to do what I had never done before, even in the anti-rightist movement of 1957—to make a self-criticism."

Intense study convinced Ch'ien Wei-ch'ang, T'ung Shih-pai, and many others that there was something basically wrong about their attitude and work in the past, but it took more than study and discussion to inspire them with a new set of ideals and goals. The next step was to involve them in productive work where they could get to know and share the life of ordinary people. Two forms of work experience were organized by the Team. The first was to go into a Peking factory for an extended period; the second was to go down to the Tsinghua University May 7 Cadre School established on the shores of Poyang Lake in Kiangsi Province. There intellectuals joined in reclaiming lake bottom land and planting it to crops.

T'ung and Ch'ien were among those who went into factories. Both thought that since they were targets of the Cultural Revolution, their main function would be to serve as negative examples. They would labor hard, take part in study classes, and listen to criticism from others. They were surprised when they were asked to set up technical courses for the plant workers and lecture in their special fields. Both learned as much from direct attempts to teach workers as they did from taking part in productive labor.

"My first class went pretty well," said T'ung. "Everyone sat still and listened. But my second class fell apart. The workers, all of whom had a lot of practical experience with electricity, said, 'Your lecture is too empty. We can't take it. You set up too many rules and too many complicated formulas. When we listen to you we lose all confidence in our ability to control electric power.' This shook me. I always thought I had a useful ability as a teacher. I never expected failure in this field. I had not only lost face but perhaps even my rice bowl as well. But the Propaganda Team members worked with me and we met in groups to discuss the class character of education, what people were trying to cultivate, and what a teacher should do to ensure revolutionary successors with working-class consciousness. Gradually we found the way."

Ch'ien Wei-ch'ang, for his part, went to the Capital Steel Mill to work and teach. A series of incidents forced him to rethink his personal, elitist philosophy. He laughed heartily as he told us about watching the furnace workers mark the ingots they had produced. His first thought was that they were writing their names on the steel. As the writer of a whole series of technical books, he took for granted that attaching one's name to one's product was most important. In fact, there was nothing in life that had given him more pleasure than affixing his name to a completed work. If he had not been able to look forward to this he doubted that he would have had the stamina to finish some of his more difficult books. The name, fame, and income that came with authorship made up for all the anguish of creation. Consequently he assumed that producers just naturally required personal recognition.

When he looked more closely at the steel ingots he found that the workers were simply marking batch numbers for purposes of quality control and to keep the output from consecutive and perhaps very unlike heats apart. He was embarrassed by his original thought. When he told the workers about it later they all had a good laugh together.

On another day he went to fetch a piece of high-carbon steel. In the laboratory at Tsinghua where he had modern testing equipment he had lectured on the differences between high carbon and ordinary steel and had demonstrated again and again how to tell them apart through hardness tests, tests of tensile strength, etc. But he had never had to pick out the original samples; an assistant had always done this work. Now he approached the steel rack in confusion. All the steel looked exactly alike. The rods and bars were all a uniform blue-black with no apparent differences in weight or quality.

Professor Ch'ien lingered in a dark corner for many minutes wondering what to do. A young worker guessed his dilemma, came over quietly, and showed him how by hitting each piece with another piece of steel one could tell from the sound which was hard and which was soft. Ch'ien was embarrassed but grateful. This young worker was not calling him a fool, or ridiculing him before the whole shop, but was patiently helping him. He thanked the young man profusely. The response was, "Never mind, Professor Ch'ien, we always knew that your theory was divorced from practice and now you know it too! Here on the production site you can bring the two together." That was the end of the incident, but it made a profound impression on Ch'ien. He realized that he had much more to learn from the workers than he had ever imagined.

A third incident drove this lesson home. The furnace workers discovered that the crystallized steel in the pouring channel at the base of the ingot always broke off at one particular spot. They wanted to know why. They brought Ch'ien one of the broken pieces and asked for an explanation. Ch'ien used a technique he had often used with students in the past—he thought of a highly technical term which really said nothing at all. "It's stress concentration," he said. This temporarily stumped the workers. They fell silent and walked off, but Ch'ien had a feeling they would be back the next day. All night long he tumbled the problem about his mind. It was no use. He had no better explanation in the morning than he had had the day before.

Sure enough, the workers returned for an explanation of "stress concentration" and Ch'ien had to admit that he had been bluffing. "Let's study the question together," he suggested. Later, after some protracted collective research, they solved this problem.

"This was the first time I had ever admitted in public that there was something I didn't understand," said Ch'ien. "When dealing with theory you can muddle through, but when you are up against practice it's no use pretending. When the workers pressed me I had to say I didn't understand. For me this was progress."

The closer he came to ordinary people, the more Ch'ien's attitudes changed. He knew something had really happened inside when he chose a research problem that was divorced from mathematics and in a field about which he knew very little. He chose this problem (the details were never spelled out, probably due to security) because of its critical nature and tackled it collectively with other scientists, technicians, and workers, without giving too much thought to his personal name and fame. This was a new departure. Formerly when choosing a topic for study he had always picked something at which he could personally shine, checked in the library to make sure no one else had ever solved it, and then proceeded with the idea of enhancing his reputation.

"To choose something out of my field, to tackle it collectively, to meet defeat and return to tackle it again—such a thing I had never imagined before," said Ch'ien. "At the height of the Cultural Revolution I vowed never to undertake scientific work again, yet here I was up to my ears in work and already half transformed! Without this revolution intellectuals like me would be a waste product. Now we have been saved."

The experience of labor at the May 7 Cadre School in Kiangsi was equally effective in transforming the outlook of intellectuals.* We talked with Hsia Ming-yi, a young electrical engineer who had graduated from Shanghai University's School of Transportation when the educational line there was dominated by capitalist-roaders. He had been told that if he loved China, served socialism, and worked where he was asked to work, he was politically advanced. But these standards only opened the road for vocational expertise: mastering technology

---

*The May 7th Cadre schools were so named for the date—May 7, 1966—when Mao Tse-tung wrote Lin Piao a letter outlining his proposals for the revolution in education. The key paragraphs are as follows:

"While the main activity of the workers is in industry, they should at the same time also study military affairs, politics, and culture. They too should take part in the Socialist Education Movement and in criticizing the bourgeoisie. When conditions permit, they should also engage in agricultural production and side occupations, as is done at the Taching oilfield.

"While the main activity of the peasants in the communes is agriculture (including forestry, animal husbandry, side occupations, and fishery), they too should at the same time study military affairs, politics, and culture. Where conditions permit, they should also collectively run some small factories. They should also criticize the bourgeoisie.

"This holds good for students too. While their main task is to study, they should, in addition to their studies, learn other things, that is, industrial work, farming, and military affairs. They should also criticize the bourgeoisie. The period of schooling should be shortened, education should be revolutionized, and the domination of our schools by bourgeois intellectuals should by no means be allowed to continue.

"Where conditions permit, those working in commerce, in the service trades, and in Party and government organizations should also do the same."

was equated with serving socialism; individual interest was equated with public interest; and Hsia buried himself in the technical studies he loved, happily unaware of two-line struggle, of the class nature of his Shanghai education, of his own bourgeois outlook.

Down at the May 7 Cadre School he joined productive labor for the first time in his life. While a student he had eaten "remember bitterness" meals of husks and bran that served to remind everyone of the rural past. But it wasn't until he ate such a meal after hard labor in the fields that it moved him and made him really think.

"We planted rice and cut wheat," said Hsia. "After the wheat was cut we had to carry it on poles to the threshing floor. The weather was so hot we drank a jug of water each trip and sweated it all out on the way. Never had my metabolism functioned so rapidly.

"Planting rice gave me such a backache that I could not stand up. Pulling weeds with the sun overhead and the water evaporating down below made me feel faint. After that, eating the 'remember bitterness' meal was different. After a whole year of labor, struggling with the sky and the earth and with my own thoughts, realizing that the peasants had often had nothing so good as the bran and the chaff, I understood the crime of class oppression and exploitation. I began to feel like a peasant and wanted to make sure that the old days would never come back!"

Shih Kuo-heng, the Harvard-trained sociologist who heads the Tsinghua library, had been with Hsia in Kiangsi. This lean, bespectacled wisp of a man had made studies of Yunnan peasants and tinworkers in the past but had never entered the people's lives. His investigations had not been aimed at transforming society but at making a name for himself in the academic field. He found life at the May 7 Cadre School very hard at first. There were no vegetables until the summer crops ripened, so they all ate bean curd day after day. Shih was used to his own private room, clean and neat: sharing a hut with others was a shock. But when he figured out that it took the labor of fifteen peasants to create his salary he was ashamed.

All his traditional feelings of superiority crumbled and he began to ask himself, "What contribution have I made?"

His favorite possession at home had always been a brush painting of peasants planting rice on a rainy day. In the picture the peasants in their bamboo hats and their straw raincoats moved forward in a line as the rain came slanting down. Sitting comfortably on his sofa, Shih appreciated the beauty and balance of the scene. "Now suddenly I was *in* the picture, not looking at it. And it was raining too. I began to understand that labor is not easy, the grain doesn't just roll from the land. I was all shaken up. For decades people had been supporting me, yet I despised them. This was a question of class feelings.

"When we carried grain to the threshing floor I didn't carry much, but it got heavier and heavier as I walked along. The peasants saw that I was swaying with my load and they taught me how to keep my balance. I was moved by their concern. Before Liberation I had ridden in sedan chairs with my weight pressed on the shoulders of laboring peasants, but I had felt no pain at all. I had ridden all the way to my destination without a thought for the men beneath. But now when I met problems they came to help me. Thus they showed their class feelings, and I realized that 'whom to serve' was indeed the key question for intellectuals.

"I learned countless lessons from the farm laborers and peasants. During the early rice harvest we left the threshed rice overnight in a pile on the threshing floor. The radio predicted rain. At three in the morning the peasants called us to get up and cover the rice. I thought, 'Why such a crisis? There will be time enough in the morning to save the grain.' But no sooner did we have it covered than the rain fell hard. If it had been up to me the crop would have been damaged.

"Later we all worked in water up to our chests to save a dike that had sprung a leak. I couldn't help but admire the spirit of the peasants and the PLA men who jumped in without a moment's hesitation, linked arms, and formed a human chain. It was a profound education."

A woman architect who helped save that dike told how

she had turned a corner in her inner life that day. Her group
had walked two hours under the hot sun to get to the work
site. When she got there she found she could not carry baskets
of soil without getting dizzy. Since she could not work, her
comrades urged her to go back to her lodgings on a motorcycle
owned by the farm. "I climbed on behind the young driver.
The faster the motorcycle went the sharper my mental struggle
became. As long as my comrades remained the dike would
hold, but here I was running away. I had heard many stories
about heroic people fighting floods but just when I had a
chance to contribute I left. Halfway home I asked the driver
to stop. I got off, walked back, and worked the rest of the day.
The trouble was that I had not fully decided to transform my
world outlook. Once I made up my mind I found I could move
ahead."

On our last day at Tsinghua we saw some very lively
skits put on by faculty and students. Among them were several
that dealt with the May 7 School in Kiangsi and the liveliest
and most humorous by far told the story of two intellectuals assigned to raising ducks. The first, a confirmed pessimist, knew
that "in the duckyard the stink rises to the sky. A whole pen
full of shit with no place left to stand . . . Anyway, I'll try
to temper myself." The second, a confirmed optimist, saw himself standing by a little river, "peace all around. The little
ducklings play in the water until the sky grows dark, then in
response to my shouts, wobble, wobble, wobble—all come to
my side, I, commander-in-chief of Ducks, lead them home . . .
How can raising ducks present any difficulties?"

But on the first day the ducks leave their stinking pen
only to go completely out of control. "When I tell them to go
left they insist on going right and when I tell them to go back
they insist on going forward. When they reach the water
things really get in a mess."

"Ya ya ya, ya ya ya," call the duckherds in unison as
they plunge into the river. But the ducks do not understand
their dialect. They scatter hither and yon.

"Old Wang, do you still feel so poetic?" asks the pessimist.

"Poetic, hell," says the optimist. "I'm wet all over."

By the time the ducks are at last herded home it is midnight.

But with revolutionary commitment the two intellectuals persist. An old peasant, Grandfather Wang, gives them lessons in the use of the duck whip, they learn to sweep maggots from the privy, wash them, and feed this "delicacy" to their charges. Finally, the optimist says, "I have changed and so have the ducks. When I stop walking forward the ducks stand still, wherever I point the duck whip, there they go. When they feel like eating they quack to me and I understand their dialect. Truly I am commander-in-chief of Ducks. Thus does the political flower, brilliant and bright, turn into economic fruit shining and full."

Experiences like these in factory and farm prepared Tsinghua's professors and teachers for the transformation of the University itself. If they were to replace the bourgeois orientation of their institution with a proletarian one, they had first to change their class stand, to reach out toward working people, whether shop workers or peasants, and realize the importance of serving them as the goal of education at whatever level. Though no one could argue that a few months, a year, or even several years in factory or cadre school could completely transform an intellectual, still the experience of hard labor, the experience of working and studying alongside workers and peasants, had a profound effect. Coming as it did on the heels of a mass repudiation of past practice at the University and a mass repudiation of the teaching methods and outlook of each staff member individually, coming as it did in the midst of an immense political struggle that wracked the whole nation and involved everyone, whether they liked it or not, in politics, this grassroots labor certainly helped to turn people around, to set them on a new path, to open their eyes to the possibilities of a socialist future which they had formerly either never imagined or never taken seriously.

26
Revolutionizing Education

As the staff members returned to their posts they plunged into the educational revolution that the Propaganda Team, now a permanent feature of University life, was leading, and found their lives taking on new meaning. To give structure to the movement, the Propaganda Team helped organize an educational transformation group in each department, and since liaison with local factories was a key element in the transformation envisaged, education transformation groups were also organized in each factory that had established a permanent relationship with Tsinghua. These education transformation groups began systematically to evaluate and reconstruct everything, from the admissions system to the curriculum to the textbooks.

Admissions policy was perhaps the most important single issue in the field of education. Now that Mao Tse-tung's directives were at last to be taken seriously and applied universally, it was taken for granted that workers, peasants, and soldiers should be the core of every student body. But how in practice should those few actually brought into the universities be chosen from among the many tens of thousands of qualified young people who wanted to study? Since the old examination system had proven in practice to favor the urban bourgeoisie and professional groups, this was scrapped without too much argument. But what other method would prove viable in the long run? Should students be chosen from middle schools or from workshops and communes? And if from the latter, what would be the basis for making the choice?

It was decided, on a national level, that middle school graduates would not immediately go on to higher study but would all, without exception, go to work—in factories, in rural brigades, or in the army. Young people would then be chosen to enter the universities on the basis of five criteria:

1. How well they studied and applied Mao Tse-tung Thought on the job and in daily life.

2. The quality of their links with the masses.

3. Their record in middle school.

4. Their work record during at least three years of practical assignments.

5. Their age level, which was to be around twenty. (To be much younger was impossible if one was to work three years; to be much older was a handicap in study.)

The last point was not rigidly adhered to. Special groups of older workers and peasants were to be periodically selected for special courses. In the first class chosen to attend Tsinghua in 1970, there were 400 workers with over ten years practical experience, many of whom had not attended middle school at all, but all of whom had mastered their own trade. Their course was to concentrate, in the main, on the newest developments in their technical fields and was to last from a year to a year and a half, not longer.

The actual mechanics of choosing people now went through the following steps: (1) Those interested in going to university applied. (2) The masses—their peers—discussed all applicants and chose the best. (3) The leaders of the production or army units approved the list, rejecting or adding names in consultation with the masses. (4) The school authorities, in this case Tsinghua University cadres, checked over the list with the power to accept or reject within reasonable limits.

"This system," said Liu Hsueh-chiao, a young woman student of peasant background from Kiangsi, "selects young people who are politically good and have a clear aim in mind. They are not the same as students in the past who came for personal reasons. Even so, they have to put revolutionary ideology, self-transformation, first, or they can change their character on coming here."

When the students arrive on the campus they are assigned to organizational units structured like units in the army. The students in any special field are organized into a company, each company is further divided into platoons, and the platoons into *pans* or classes of about forty-five people each. These

classes are in turn split into squads, or study groups, of ten
or twelve. These are mutual-aid study groups where each student helps the other so that nobody falls behind and all master
the subject matter if it is humanly possible. "We are carrying
the weight of the hopes of the people back home. We have
the same goal so we can't let one brother fall behind," said Liu
Hsueh-chiao. "To struggle hard for revolution is different from
individual struggle."

The entering companies, platoons, and classes do not begin
with classroom work but instead go for several months to the
factory most related to their field of study. Liu Hsueh-chiao,
a student of foundry work, had spent her first four and a half
months at Tsinghua in a foundry. There she spent time at every
basic operation and joined classes attended by, and often given
by, workers in front of the furnaces and machines. Only after
the students become familiar with the whole process in the
plant do they return to the campus for more intensive theoretical study. And even then they work two and a half days each
week in the University foundry and attend classes in between.

This method of linking up course work with practical experience in plants has necessitated a very complicated system
of liaison between the University and industry. "Before there
was a wall around Tsinghua, but now this wall does not exist."
In fact, the peasants of a nearby commune were constructing
a wall of rock and mortar around the newest section of the
campus in the south and east when we were there. It linked
up with the old wall that enclosed the northern and western
sectors so that the whole campus was encircled by a material
wall of some height. But the cultural wall that ensured the
isolation of the old University had been pierced in a thousand
ways. The new University could by no means be said to stop
at the eight feet of solid masonry that protected its grounds.

The University now has permanent links with dozens of
factories. Not only do students go out to work and study:
workers come in to teach and study. Problems that arise in the
plants are brought to the campus for solution and problems
that arise on the campus are taken to the plants for solution.
Research is undertaken at both ends.

Whole departments of the University have actually gone into the field more or less permanently. In the summer of 1971 the Water Conservation Department had moved, lock, stock and barrel, to the site of the San Men Dam on the Yellow River in Honan, while the Civil Engineering Department had moved out to three factories in Peking—the East Is Red Oil Refinery, the General Machine Plant No. 1, and the Capital Steel Mill.

Even this moving was a two-way street. If some departments left the campus to locate at suitable factories and construction sites, workers from key plants left the shops to come to the campus to establish industrial units where serial production was also undertaken whenever possible along with research in new products.

Linking up study with actual production made set classroom hours and rigid course content difficult if not impossible. Lecture and lab time expanded and contracted according to the needs of the day. Real problems formed the core of the curriculum, and since some were big and others little, varying amounts of time were spent on each. This system tended to break down all the formalism of the past and to establish in its place a very lively atmosphere where theory and practice nudged each other forward and faculty and students alike became deeply involved in the production problems of greater Peking.

It seemed to me that the on-campus workshops, particularly, might limit the breadth of study because each shop, regardless of the products it turned out, could deal with only a small section of the scientific and engineering problems in the world. Furthermore, once the shops were built, later classes would have much less to do. They would need only to operate and not to construct the equipment.

I was told that the campus workshops were used only as a take-off point for practice. For instance, welding in the campus auto factory was mainly spot welding on the bodies of the trucks. Having mastered this, students went far afield to find, practice, and understand all the other major kinds of welding. As for bogging down in routine serial production, there was little danger of that because one of the main tasks of these campus-based workshops was to pioneer in the production of new products and new machines. There would always be designing, re-tooling, inventing, and testing to do that would introduce new problems and stimulate new solutions. The workshops themselves could never be said to be completed. Each class would shape them to its needs.

Obviously setting up course work in this creative, practical way called for a lot of arranging and many points of contact. The teacher dealt almost as much with people as he did with ideas and things. To do it well meant that one had to, in Mao's phrase, "play the piano"—that is, move all ten fingers at once to juggle and balance many problems simultaneously. One had to be flexible and innovative. One had to know what was going on in the sphere of production and relate it to theory in a way that could push things ahead. There was no place here for a cut-and-dried approach, for formal solutions. The professors to whom we talked seemed to like this challenge and to be responding to it with enthusiasm.

T'ung and Ch'ien, famous for the textbooks they had written in the past, were reworking their material from the ground up. "At first," said T'ung, "I thought I would only have to make some minor readjustments in my old wares. But that was absolutely wrong. When looked at from the point of view of the needs of today, those old textbooks are completely inadequate. By the time the Workers Propaganda Team came I already realized that there were class questions involved in the development of science and in the teaching of science. I knew that world outlook made a big difference, but since my own world outlook was still pretty much bourgeois I didn't want to write any more textbooks. I felt, 'If I write and spread more bourgeois poison I will only be repudiated again'!

"But the workers said, 'Under Liu Shao-ch'i's leadership you were so active and you worked so hard at writing, how come you stop when we have come to power?' This was hard to answer. I decided to go on writing even if I made mistakes. But now I write with a group. We all discuss together. Formerly, if we had discussions I always had the last word, but now my opinion is only one of many and it is often wrong.

"We observe three principles in writing now:

"1. Study Mao Tse-tung Thought and apply it.

"2. Make our work serve the workers, peasants, and soldiers. Don't start from personal ambition and don't show off.

"3. Start from the practice of the three great revolutionary movements—the class struggle, the struggle for production, and scientific experiment—and write material that reflects the level of development of our technology today.

"The main trouble with my textbooks in the past was not that they were out of date or that they dealt with foreign technology (Mao Tse-tung says we should learn whatever is useful to us), but that they lauded the wrong heroes. Judging a textbook is just like judging a play or a novel. The first question one must ask is, 'Who is the main character? Who is the hero?' In my books the main characters are definitely not the working people but the experts. I admired and worshiped the scientists with 'superior' brains who put these brains to work to create great inventions. Consciously or unconsciously, my whole book, from preface to references, stresses the role ·of geniuses —and the reader is supposed to admire me too. When very small I decided to become famous but this was only possible if I put myself in a special category along with those other 'geniuses' of science. So that is one aspect of my works which poisons young people. There is no hint anywhere that working people create the world.

"Another problem with my writings was their metaphysical basis. I never used a dialectical viewpoint to analyze things in motion, in inter-relation, and from two sides—the good and the bad, the positive and the negative. If I liked something I wrote all about how good it was without analyzing its shortcomings. I set up a lot of absolute rules, one after the other, and all this led students to think in a stagnant way.

"A third problem was my scholastic method. I just piled everything up without sifting through to find the principle facts and the laws that would enable people to analyze phenomena for themselves. When we checked up on our graduates we found that they were not much good at solving real problems of production. I thought that was because I hadn't put enough into my book. They were running into problems that I hadn't included in my text, so I wanted to make my books longer rather than shorter. But the real problem was we didn't teach our students how to think.

"Take transistors, for example. There are thousands of different circuits. If you take them up one after another you can spend two years going through them and pile up a huge mass of information. That road is hopeless. We have to abstract the key laws of these circuits so that our students can master whatever circuits they come across. If the teacher doesn't approach things dialectically but only uses scissors and paste to cut and patch and pile up information, he can't solve the problem at all."

At this point in our discussion Liu Ming-yi, the steel worker on the Standing Committee of the Tsinghua University Revolutionary Committee, broke in saying, "It makes a lot of difference what examples you use to explain things, too."

I was struck by Liu's attitude toward the distinguished professors with whom we were talking. Though he had come to the University right off the shop floor, he showed not the slightest trace of deference to age or prestige. He clearly felt himself to be the equal of these men technically and their teacher politically. He had very definite ideas concerning how the old professors could best serve the working class and he was working with them patiently to develop their new role. When T'ung deprecated his old textbook and implied that it was worthless, Liu interrupted to make clear that the book still had great value, that it could serve as the take-off point for much better books in the future. Now, when the discussion turned toward methods of teaching, Liu gave concrete suggestions for matching explanatory examples to the experience of working people.

"Take electrical resistance, for example," Liu said. "We can compare it to the loss of water in an irrigation ditch. Everyone knows that the water that actually reaches the field is less than that which flows out of the reservoir. And the same goes for electricity in a wire. Or take calculus. Every worker knows that bricks are straight, yet round chimneys can be built out of straight bricks—countless little straight lines become one even curve. When you are familiar with actual practice it is easy to use examples that have meaning for people."

"But of course," added Professor T'ung, "one has to be careful with these examples too because the analogy is never 100 percent and sometimes students take it too literally. I usually compare a capacitator to a cup, the longer it is the more electricity it will hold, just as a bigger cup holds more water. But once when I laid a capacitator on its sides, one of my students turned it upright so that the electricity wouldn't spill out!

"So finding appropriate examples which are clear, and the limitations of which are also clear, is very difficult. We never just draw diagrams on the board any more, but look at the real thing and see it in action first. Thus we start with Chairman Mao's principle that perceptual knowledge is the basis. If we don't, people are liable to get very strange ideas. We draw these huge circuits on the board and then they find that the transistor itself is so small it gets lost in the hand. It's best to start with the transistor and then go to the blackboard."

The consensus on the part of the professors, the workers, and the PLA men who took part in this discussion was that all this was in the experimental stage, and that the new teaching methods could only be proven in practice and constantly refined. The rule which they laid out was: Make a critical analysis of the old, retain what is good, and transform it in line with the needs of the present.

In line with these principles and those for applying Mao Tse-tung Thought already mentioned, T'ung had helped to write five new textbooks, one on the application of silicon-controlled rectifiers, three on transistor pulse and digital computer circuits, and one on transistor circuits and transistor amplifiers.

"The subject matter is as complicated, if not more complicated, than anything I have handled before, while the students coming in do not have the same background in mathematics, physics, and electricity that we used to demand. Yet by abstracting the basic principles, finding good examples, and simplifying the explanations, we are having greater success than before. We have no alternative. Technology is leaping ahead from ordinary transistors to integrated circuits to large-scale integrated circuits to solid-state circuits. And we have to keep up!"

We could hear groups of students going by on their way to the swimming pool—the shuffle of cloth shoes, muffled conversation, laughter. From the distance came the shouts and cries of those already in the water. Steel worker Liu poured us all some fresh hot tea. We went on to discuss the future of science.

"After all," I said, "a university not only has the function of bringing students up to the technical level of the day but of advancing scientific knowledge. How is this done under your new system?"

I asked this question because it is generally assumed in the West that research scientists, the real innovators, must be some sort of an elite which, under special conditions in a special environment, uses its brains, usually at a very early age—say from nineteen to twenty-six—to break through to important discoveries. Since the productive years are so short, it would be absurd to ask these people to engage in productive labor, to link up in practice with workers and peasants, or even to study politics. The Western way is to create a sort of hothouse environment where brilliant young people under "ideal" conditions stimulate one another to extraordinary achievement.

None of these assumptions is accepted by Tsinghua scientists or by the worker Liu, who was the first to respond to my question.

Liu said that all the students come from worker, peasant, and soldier backgrounds. After graduation they return to their farms, plants, or army units and invariably carry on research that is linked to practical problems. If they can't solve them on the site they refer them back to the University. At the same time, a few graduates are assigned to research institutes which are engaged full-time in solving problems—usually urgent problems relating to defense, such as atomic explosives, or nose-cone materials for rockets, etc. This research may well tackle the frontiers of science but it is linked to practical problems.

No matter what the problem or what the organization, research is done by three-in-one teams of workers, technicians (scientists), and cadres. These teams encompass everyone involved in the project and everyone takes part in the heavy physical labor as well as in the discussions and planning. Such methods involve the masses in research, not just a few students and advisors.

Liu cited the problem of the Peking Refinery as a typical example. If the problems of pollution could not be solved, the refinery could not continue to operate because it was too damaging to its surroundings. This stimulated very fundamental research in the transformation of waste. Organic and biological methods were developed for the treatment of polluted water and these raised very complicated scientific problems. They also involved extensive use of nightsoil as a breeding source for the necessary bacteria. Since everyone recognized the great significance of the research, everyone, including the top scientists, joined in handling the nightsoil, digging it from the privies and transporting it to the experimental sites.

What Liu stressed over and over again was the importance of involving masses of people in research and not leaving it to just a few.

T'ung, the electrical engineer, stressed the fact that research is very closely linked to the state of industrial development. In building apparatus one cannot depart too sharply from the materials and methods available in society. Thus a knowledge of the general state of industry—practical experience in shops and plants—is important in making research decisions. Furthermore, without the work of many hundreds of shop workers and ordinary technicians no complex equipment can be created or experiments carried out. A few brilliant scientists cannot do everything by themselves. Since hundreds of people are involved in the simplest of experiments it is much more productive to involve them consciously and mobilize them to help.

Ch'ien was the first to admit that research scientists, even in China, do live and work under special conditions, but he was not at all convinced that this in itself made them an elite or corrupted their ideology. After all, he argued, they all took part in manual labor and shared in the routine tasks of their institutes and they all studied revolutionary policies, two-line struggle, and the important questions, such as whom to serve and how best to serve. "You can't say that whoever deals with cash will eventually steal some, that whoever writes books will eventually hold nonwriters in contempt, or that whoever masters technique will eventually use it to further his own advancement. Not only does everyone work physically part of the time, but there is the question of the road they are taking and of the directing thought. If the ideological struggle is carried on continuously, people do not automatically deteriorate. If they do, we'll just have to have another cultural revolution," said Ch'ien cheerfully.

"I used to think as the Americans do," Ch'ien continued, "that the productive years in research are from ages nineteen to twenty-six. But now I think that young or old, if you are armed with Mao Tse-tung Thought and use dialectical materialism you can do just as well. The main thing is the basic thinking you use. Maybe it's just because I am old and I don't want to set myself aside. But look at Chairman Mao. He's old but he's still a brilliant scientist. He led us through all the twists and turns of the Cultural Revolution. Who else would dare launch such a movement? Who else could direct it? Young people dare to think and act, but they don't have experience. So Chairman Mao's three-in-one combination not only unites workers, technicians, and cadres but also young, middle-aged, and old. That's a powerful combination!"

Ch'ien went on to discuss concretely the frontiers of science which he catalogued as (1) the uses of atomic energy, (2) space science, (3) the theory of fundamental particles, (4) the life sciences (proteins), and (5) pure mathematics. With regard to atomic energy, he maintained there could not be much of an argument. China was obviously carrying on such research and development, and it was not just a few scientists either, but large numbers of workers and technicians all working together in three-in-one combinations.

In the other four fields he said that theoretical research was not the main emphasis, but nevertheless in the ten-year plan approved by the Central Committee for the development of science, such research was not neglected. Already it had borne fruit on at least two fronts, with published material to prove it. One front dealt with geology on a grand scale and had produced a geological survey of Tibet and the Himalayan mountains. This was not simply an investigation of national resources, etc., but basic research concerning the past, present, and future of the Himalayan range, why and how it continues to rise out of the sea, and what that means for Tibet and Asia.

The other front dealt with proteins and had produced the synthesis of insulin. This project had tapped and coordinated all branches of science. It had involved over 600 high-level scientists and thousands of less-advanced personnel. Starting with a rather backward base, China now led the world in this field.

Research in the field of fundamental particles and in higher mathematics was also going forward. Everywhere three-in-one combinations were formed for such work, with more rather than fewer people involved than ever before.

Summing up, Ch'ien said, "I believe that science will develop faster when it is not left to a few experts, but instead millions of people are mobilized."

It was already lunch time. People were passing House A by the score on the way to the dining hall. It even seemed to me that I could smell a faint odor of frying pork wafting to us on the warm July breeze.

Ch'ien, choosing his final words carefully, returned to the question of his own teaching. "There's just no way to compare what we are doing now with what we did before," he said, raising his hand in a gesture of helplessness. "In the past when I lectured no one dared ask any questions. In the first place I didn't welcome questions, for that implied I hadn't explained things clearly, so I lost face. In the second place to ask a question meant that the student had not understood the lecture, hence he or she lost face. Since the aim of the course was not to understand but to get a good grade, no student dared risk this double loss of face. It was better to sit silent. Furthermore, since no one had any practical experience, the subject matter was very abstract and few could grasp enough of its significance to ask an intelligent question anyway! Today all that has changed. Now our students, even if they only come from junior middle school, all have three years production experience under their belts. When they get here they work in local factories. If what I tell them doesn't fit their own life experiences, they immediately object and raise no end of questions. Sometimes everyone talks at once. Of course this puts much greater demands on me. No bluffing will do. If I can't answer we go into research together. Our education has been transformed and so have I!"

27
Once Again: Pull Out Kuai

Li Wen-yuan's sixteen-year-old daughter stood in the center of the stage facing an audience of thousands. She showed not the slightest trace of fear or self-consciousness.

"It was you, Kuai Ta-fu, who grabbed away my father's life as he stood guard at the edge of the cornfield! It was you and the evil May 16 Group! This blood debt must be repaid! When I look at my father's photograph it is as if he stood before me still, telling me the bitter history of our family before Liberation; it is as if he were sitting there at midnight studying Mao Tse-tung's writings after a long day's work; it is as if he were standing in Tien An-men square on National Day waiting for Mao Tse-tung's inspection. In my ears I hear my father's voice. Before my eyes I see his face and the tears roll down my cheeks."

From the back of the Meeting Hall came the shrill voice of a girl student: "Kuai, you owe a blood debt to the working class!"

Then from every throat in the audience came the thunderous response: "Kuai, you owe a blood debt, a blood debt to the working class!"

"But when I remember that my father fought for the revolution and died for the people, I dry my tears and grow strong," continued Little Li in a voice that strained the ears with its intensity. "The more I think the more I hate the May 16 Group that took my father's life."

Kuai, sitting on the right side of the stage, stared straight ahead through the thick lenses of his square-framed glasses. He was the only person in the hall who did not join in the shouting. Two of his former Regiment comrades, Jen Ch'uan-chung and Ts'ui Chao-shih, sat across from him on the left. As the slogans mounted in number and excitement they stood up to take a more active part, but Kuai never moved at all.

"I will be a loyal Red Guard forever. I will carry the revolution through to the end. I will never quit the battlefield until all cow-devils and snake-gods have been wiped out!"

As Little Li finished, both her arms raised high in the air, a student rushed across the stage with dead worker Li's blood-stained shorts in his hands and thrust them in front of Kuai's face.

"Look, take a look at these! Is this not proof of your crime?"

"Smash the May 16 Group!" shouted the crowd. "Smash Wang-Kuang-Ch'i!"

At this mass meeting, held on March 25, 1971, Kuai once again found himself the target of the whole Tsinghua community. It was part of the national drive launched by the Communist Party to expose and repudiate the May 16 Group, which by that time was alleged to include not only Wang Li, Kuang Feng and Ch'i Pen-yu of the Central Cultural Revolution Group, and Yang Ch'eng-wu, Yu Li-hsin, Fu Chung-p'i, and Hsaio Hua of the People's Liberation Army, but also Ch'en Po-ta of the Political Bureau of the Central Committee.

Members of this clique were said to have recruited selectively among the militant rebels of both student factions and among their worker allies in key industrial plants and now an effort was being made to find out who were the conscious conspirators, as distinct from the thousands of young people influenced by ultra-left ideas who had taken part in such extreme and anarchistic acts as the burning of the British Mission, the encirclement of Tungnanhai, and the campaign against the commanders of the People's Liberation Army.

Under sharp questioning thirty Tsinghua people, including several members of the Regiment Headquarters Committee, admitted that they had actually been members of the May 16 Group and that Kuai was one of its leaders. Together they named some 230 others who had been recruited over the years. All of these people were under investigation to determine their ideological commitment and their role in the organization. Since most rank-and-file members had been unaware of any goals beyond militant defense of Chairman Mao, and had accepted the covert nature of the organization as a necessity because of the "reactionaries" in powerful positions "encircling" Mao, it was not considered a serious mistake to have become a member. To have been a leader, conscious of the organization's "seize-power aim," conscious of its efforts to disrupt and frustrate programs coming directly from Mao Tse-tung and his proletarian headquarters, was something else again.

Here the evidence implicating Kuai Ta-fu was extensive. He had over and over again consulted Ch'i Pen-yu, Wang Li, and Kuang Feng, and had consistently followed their advice when it was in flat contradiction to that of Vice-Premier Hsieh Fu-chih, Premier Chou En-lai, and Mao Tse-tung himself. He had led the Regiment in extreme and provocative acts on many occasions. He had insisted on a "violent solution to the Tsinghua problem" at a time when all fighting was clearly proscribed, and he had never abandoned efforts to hold his faction together, even after the disaster of July 27 and the exposure of the Regiment's serious crimes.

The meeting of March 25, the complete tape of which was played back to us during our visit, concentrated on the events of July 1968 and on Kuai's role in resisting the Workers Propaganda Team. A few weeks earlier Kuai had denied that he ever issued an order to combat the workers with arms, saying, "I never thought of and never did, in fact, give an order to anyone to shoot at workers. No one can accuse me of ordering anyone to shoot because I never issued any such order."

In the intervening period, Regiment "rods" like Tsui Ta-kuang, Ts'ui Chao-shih, Liu Yao-ch'i, Fu Lien-chih and Jen Ch'uan-chung had all made public depositions contradicting Kuai's denial. After exposure and repudiation by some of his closest comrades-in-arms, Kuai could hardly maintain this innocent stance when the masses gathered once more in the Meeting Hall.

"Kuai, speak out, was it you who ordered the shooting?" demanded Hui Hsien-chun, of the People's Liberation Army, a member of the Standing Committee of the Tsinghua University Revolutionary Committee, and chairman of this mass meeting to confront Kuai.

"Yes," said Kuai in an almost inaudible voice.

"Will you take this statement back later?"

"No," said Kuai.

"Now you say it was you. Only a few weeks ago you insisted that it wasn't you. Which statement counts?" Hui then turned to the audience and spoke very loudly—shouted, in fact: "It is obvious that right up until today Kuai is using two-faced tactics to resist the people. But we intend to marshal facts that will expose who was behind the ugly slaughter on July 27, 1968."

Thereupon Tsui Ta-kuang, who had been in the Quiet House with Kuai when the decision to resist was made, stepped forward to describe what happened. "On the one hand Kuai drafted an appeal to the Central Committee, on the other he drafted an order to all units to resist." Tsui backed up his own testimony by reading a deposition from Liu Yao-ch'i, a Regiment activist who was out of town because he had been assigned to work in Shansi. "I was in the Meeting Hall talking to Kuai on the phone," wrote Liu. "I told him the situation and he said don't let them in. I said what if they insist. Then fight them, Kuai said."

Fu Lien-chih, who had stood beside Liu in the Meeting

Hall that day, then took the stage. He confirmed this order.

"Speak out, Kuai, what have you to say to this?" asked Hui.

At this point the whole audience, led by a few enthusiastic cheerleaders, shouted loudly and fervently, "Lenient treatment for those who talk frankly, harsh treatment for those who resist. It's no crime to be deceived. Turn around and fight back, you will win merit."

But Kuai stood silent, unwilling to say any more.

Yuan Ch'uan-tung, another Regiment "rod," then mounted the rostrum and spoke with great emotion.

"I am evidence that Kuai gave the order to fire on the working class. Who ordered me to shoot and pushed me down the criminal road? It was this original Kuai, Kuai who cannot be forgiven! Now I clearly see your true nature—Kuai, black general of May 16, ambitious bourgeois politician. I will never believe you again!

"At noon on July 27 he called a few of us into Room 202 of the Quiet House. At this black meeting he faced us. 'We are done for whether we fight or not. But we will go down fighting and maybe it will be better that way.'

"I asked Kuai if we should use weapons.

" 'If it is necessary to shoot,' he said, 'use hot weapons.'

"Then after giving this order he asked me, the fastest writer in the group, to write out the order with his pen. I wrote a statement which called on each building to resist resolutely. It was copied out five times. We all signed our names. Black writing on white paper! How can you deny it?

"Then Kuai sent the order out in three ways. He found three little girls whom no one would suspect. They carried the written words. I personally called the Bright House on the telephone and asked them to broadcast the order in code. We also called each group directly on the phone. And every group that got the message began charging with spears, throwing hand grenades, and firing guns point-blank.

"Kuai couldn't hide his hatred of Mao Tse-tung Thought. He took his pistol and ran down the stairs shouting, '*Lao-tzu* [your grandfather] can't take this.' When we tried to stop him he said, 'Take your hands off me. Let me go.' He meant to run out and lead the fight but I stood in front of that May 16 black general Kuai and protected him, saying 'Don't go. Too many people will recognize you!' I convinced him to stay inside and I myself went out to carry the message to House A, to the Meeting Hall and to Dormitory #3. I not only ordered others to attack the workers, I led attacks myself!

"I instigated one bloody incident after another. I stabbed workers with spears and threw three hand grenades. I carried out May 16 black general Kuai's orders and committed unforgivable crimes against the Workers Propaganda Team, the People's Liberation Army, and Mao Tse-tung.

"Kuai, you not only signed the order, you ordered me to direct the violent fight all over the campus. Today I want to expose your crimes and settle accounts with you!"

Ts'ui Chao-shih of the Regiment Headquarters Committee followed Yuan on the stage. He said that as early as July 15 Hsieh Fu-chih of the Peking Revolutionary Committee had asked Kuai to stop the fighting. But Kuai had told his companions, "The affairs of Tsinghua reach to heaven [we have backing higher up]. Hsieh can't do anything about us. We'll fight on."

Ts'ui then told how, on July 27, he received Kuai's order in the Bright House and organized the charge at the Meeting Hall that wounded one hundred workers. Later he seized a PLA member, beat him up, stripped him, and took him back to the Bright House for questioning. With great emotion he concluded his speech: "I am a fascist slaughterer with the blood of the working class on my hands. I bow my head. I owe blood to the people. I wish the Communist Party would punish me harshly. . . . I did not remold my world outlook so the devils Wang-Kuang-Ch'i, Yang-Yu-Fu, and Kuai Ta-fu dragged me down into the ditch. I hate those counter-revolutionary schemers, those ambitious politicians. . . . I resolutely cut myself off from Kuai and vow to expose all I know about his vicious schemes. I want to change completely and be a new man."

As soon as Ts'ui finished other Regiment members who had received Kuai's order described the bloody attacks they had taken part in. Then a letter from the wife of Han Chung-hsien, who bled to death from a spear wound in Building #9003, was read aloud. Finally Li Wen-yuan's daughter spoke from the center of the stage. She broke into uncontrolled weeping as her father's bloody shorts were thrust before Kuai's face.

"Smash May 16! Smash Wang-Kuang-Ch'i!" intoned the crowd.

"Can we fail to exercise proletarian dictatorship over Kuai?" Hui asked of the aroused audience.

"No, no, no," they shouted back with one voice. "No, no, no!"

Through it all, from beginning to end, with the exception of a few questions which he answered with monosyllables, Kuai stood mute. He did not admit to counter-revolutionary thoughts or counter-revolutionary actions and he did not admit to any connection with the May 16 Group.

This meeting nailed down the fact that it was Kuai who ordered the violent dispersal of the Workers Propaganda Team in conscious defiance of orders from the very top. Other evidence that Kuai had consistently defied Chairman Mao's instructions in favor of advice and exhortation from Wang Li, Kuang Feng, and Ch'i Pen-yu was marshaled by the leaders of the Team and summed up for our benefit under a score of headings. I record only a few here.

In August 1966, when Chou En-lai failed to clearly designate Kuai as a member of the "true left," Kuai consulted with Wang Li, then personally instigated a campaign of slander against the Premier which culminated in a poster by Liu Chu'an of the Regiment entitled "The Dog-Sheep Person."* When this provoked a wave of protest Kuai used his prestige to calm the campus and gave full support to Liu Chu'an and his "Grab Devils Group" as bold militants who dared to think and dared to act!

In January 1967, when T'ao Ch'u was exposed, Kuai consulted Wang Li once more and launched a campaign aimed at suspecting and overthrowing all cadres in power. He sent out teams to investigate all the Central Committee leaders. The

---

*A dog-sheep person is one who combines the viciousness of a dog with the gentleness of a sheep—hence a two-faced opportunist.

slogan was, "Only Mao Tse-tung and Lin Piao can be considered spokesmen for the proletarian headquarters; everyone else is subject to overthrow." What this amounted to, as steel worker Liu of the Propaganda Team pointed out, was putting Mao Tse-tung and Lin Piao in an empty frame. If all of Mao Tse-tung's real support could be pulled out, the Chairman would be isolated and the Cultural Revolution wrecked.

—In July 1967, after overseas Chinese had been attacked and killed in Burma. Chou En-lai issued a protest statement. Ch'i Pen-yu attacked this statement as too mild, too conservative. He said it represented a foreign policy of three surrenders and one betrayal.* Immediately Kuai Ta-fu, Han Ai-ch'ing of the Aeronautical Institute, and Nieh Yuan-tzu of Peking University, the three key leaders of the Heaven Faction, mounted a huge demonstration in front of the Imperial Palace to denounce the Burmese government and then paraded in front of the Foreign Ministry denouncing China's response.

—On September 5, 1967, when Chiang Ch'ing, speaking on Mao's behalf, openly attacked the May 16 Group and warned all militant students against ultra-left thinking and ultra-left policies—such as attacks on the army—Kuai Ta-fu asked, "What ultra-left policies?" He wrote an editorial for the Regiment newspaper questioning the whole idea that there could be an ultra-left.

—In December 1967, after the Peking Revolutionary Committee was set up, Kuai helped instigate a "left" opposition inside it. Not quite a year earlier, revisionists in several provinces had responded to the workers' power seizure in Shanghai by arranging false power seizures, a musical-chair-type reshuffling of officers which they conveniently labeled "revolutionary committees." Nanking provided an outstanding example. Wang Li, Kuang Feng, and Ch'i Pen-yu, seizing on this, took the position that all the revolutionary committees established since were nothing but capitalist restorations and repeatedly urged young people to overthrow them. Hence, when the Central Committee

---

*Surrender to imperialism, to social imperialism, to domestic reaction; betrayal of the world revolution.

proposed Vice-Premier Hsieh Fu-chih as chairman of the Peking Revolutionary Committee in December 1967, Kuai Ta-fu, Han Ai-ch'ing, and Liu Ch'ang-hsing (head of the rebels at the Athletic Institute), all of whom were named members of this same committee, set up an opposition group that supported Ch'i Pen-yu for the post. Besind the scenes they had the backing of Chou Ching-fang, secretary of the committee, and Fu Chung-p'i, commander of the Peking Garrison. Together these activists mounted a large-scale campaign against Hsieh Fu-chih which involved both Tsinghua factions at the grassroots level. The campaign, including demonstrations on the streets, lasted from December 1967 through March 1968, when the Yang-Yu-Fu clique was exposed.

The mass demonstrations against the revolutionary committee of the Normal College, which have already been described, served as prelude to this anti-Hsieh campaign and were inspired by the same sources.

—In July 1968, as armed conflict raged in Kweichow, Kiangsi, and Shansi, the Central Committee issued the famous July orders against violent fighting and called in representatives of the warring factions from several provinces for study classes and discussions aimed at bringing unity and peace. At this critical point, Kuai Ta-fu and Han Ai-ch'ing, violating specific instructions against liaison meetings, organized conferences of the "left" rebels at the Aeronautical Institute and at Tsinghua. There they mobilized their provincial counterparts not for unity and peace but for "a second seizure of power in the country." At these meetings a Rebel General Headquarters was created with Kuai and Han as co-leaders. Its first act was to issue a statement of support for the "left" rebels in Kiangsi. This was the opening salvo of a new campaign to overthrow revolutionary committees everywhere.

—On July 30, 1968, only two days after the fighting at Tsinghua was brought to an end, Kuai called a special meeting of Regiment leaders to set up an investigation group to uncover the "black hand," the sinister leader behind the workers' invasion of the campus. Since Mao Tse-tung himself had already told Kuai, "I am the black hand, I am the sinister figure," this was considered outrageously brazen. It was the sort of thing only a May 16 conspirator, with ties leading to "heaven" (i.e., connections at the highest level) would do.

When this record was added up, Kuai looked very much like a counter-revolutionary May 16 conspirator. Yet all agreed that he had been an honest rebel in 1966. Here are Lu Fang-ch'ien's words concerning Kuai:

"Our theory is that Kuai went from ultra-left to counter-revolution. He was a genuine rebel, but before the intellectuals hook up with the working class they are inclined to waver. At a certain stage his bourgeois outlook was exposed. He moved from the ultra-left to reaction, he sank deeper and deeper until he could not get out.

"As to his personal position, he was dissatisfied with the proletarian headquarters (Mao and his closest comrades). He was not just unconsciously opposed to their headquarters but consciously opposed. He openly investigated the background of the proletarian leading group, and some under his leadership openly attacked the proletarian headquarters. He never fought against these people but actually supported them. Some Regiment members criticized him for this but he didn't correct these tendencies. He developed them and helped develop dissatisfaction with proletarian headquarters.

"He himself wanted to be a Party member, and a Central Committee member at that. Actually he was only a Youth League member but he developed very severe individualism. On the surface he said he supported Mao Tse-tung, and that others opposed Mao Tse-tung, but he could never find much concrete material to prove his case. Meanwhile evidence against him piled up. For instance, his attitude to Hsieh Fu-chih. He supported Hsieh before he was himself chosen as a member of the Peking Revolutionary Committee, but he afterward decided to oppose Hsieh—openly oppose him. His ambition was to be not only a member of the Standing Committee, but to be chairman of the Revolutionary Committee.

"He had a good class background—he was a poor peasant but he was deeply influenced by the bourgeois educational system. At first he was only used and deceived by the bad people, but then he became ambitious. People with good backgrounds must constantly change—there is no such thing as 'automatic red,' but only 'transformed red.' To have a revolutionary father doesn't mean that the son is revolutionary.

"He thinks he was revolutionary at the start and only afterward he took the counter-revolutionary road. It was not because he hated the socialist system, but only because bad people misled him. Of course, this kind of thinking is only an excuse. We asked him about it. How can you be deceived on a whole series of things, a whole series of questions? If you are deceived, why such open criminal activities? Actually, it seems he has sunk so deep he cannot pull himself out. And he has opportunistic thinking. He knows he is one of the five big Red Guard leaders. Maybe the authorities can't do too much about it. Perhaps criminals down below will be treated harshly but famous Red Guards like Kuai will get lenient treatment anyway.

"We feel that for a criminal to really admit error and change his stand is a slow process. We must patiently explain policy, explain the situation, give him class education and show him a way out. If he can really talk frankly and expose the whole conspiracy according to the facts the masses will welcome him back to the Mao Tse-tung revolutionary line. We still have the policy to save him and we want him to wage revolution after this, in the future."

In the face of all this evidence and in spite of long hours of patient private discussions that filled the time between mass meetings, Kuai still refused to bow his head. Though admitting mistakes and even crimes, he steadfastly denied counter-revolutionary goals and any knowledge of the May 16 Group.

Kuai's defiance raises a number of questions. If he had indeed degenerated into a bourgeois opportunist, as all affirmed, why would he not try to salvage something from the debacle by cooperating? Why would he guarantee a harsh settlement of his case by defying the new Tsinghua revolutionary committee to the end? Either, it seems to me, he was innocent of the main charge—that of being a counter-revolutionary conspirator—or he had backing in high places which led him to believe that the

tables might once again be reversed. After all, he had defied
the concentrated fire of a work team before when convinced
that he was right and confident that his support led to "heaven."
Perhaps he would succeed in doing so again.

Lu Fang-ch'ien had a different explanation for Kuai's stubbornness. He said Kuai realized how serious his crimes were and
did not believe that anything he could now say or do would
win lenient treatment. It was better, therefore, to stand mute.
Let punishment be imposed without his cooperation. This explanation was not entirely convincing because the lenient policy
of the Communist Party had been so clearly demonstrated in
so many similar cases.

The fall of Lin Piao, in September 1971, put this whole
problem in a new framework. One had to assume that the
ultra-left line, up to that point blamed on Ch'en Po-ta, must
link through to Lin Piao himself. If that was indeed the case,
then, if Kuai had a mentor in "heaven," it must have been none
other than Lin Piao, and Kuai's stubbornness could be interpreted
as unwillingness to bow his head as long as Lin Piao stood firm.
If, on the other hand, Kuai was not part of any conspiracy, the
drive against him could be seen as something entirely different—
an attempt by Lin Piao and his fellow plotters to create a
diversion, to keep the arrow of attack off the real target, themselves. In other words, Lin Piao and his clique were guilty of
launching a new "bourgeois reactionary line," once again hitting
hard at the many to protect the few. And Kuai was once again
the target of a frame-up—a frame-up not in the sense that this
time he was being charged with crimes he had not committed,
but in the sense that his very real crimes, his ultra-left acts and
ultra-left statements, were being taken as evidence of a con-
spiratorial May 16 role that may have in fact not existed.

With the information available at this time there is no valid
way to make a choice between these alternatives. There is just
too much that is not known about the May 16 group, about
Lin Piao's role on the "left," about the circumstances of Lin
Piao's political collapse. One fact stands out from my own experience: the campaign against the May 16 Group, which was
the center of political activity throughout much of China in

the summer of 1971, did not continue with any force through the fall, if it continued at all. Almost everywhere we went prior to National Day (October 1) we were told about the May 16 Group and its influence on the local struggle, particularly in Shansi. After October 1 we heard much less about it. Other groups traveling in the fall of 1971 heard little if any mention of it. This leads me to think that, to a certain extent, the big campaign against the May 16 Group in the summer of 1971 was a smokescreen to divert attention from Lin Piao and his clique. This does not mean that this ultra-left conspiracy did not exist, but it does indicate that it was perhaps not so important or so extensive as the earlier campaign against it might lead one to believe.

With that in mind it would hardly make sense to take at face value the estimate of Kuai Ta-fu and the May 16 Group we heard at Tsinghua during our visit. Right at that time the biggest problem of "left" politics, Lin Piao himself, was still riding high, and as a result a large part of the struggle then going on was concealed. Many key questions could not even be raised not to mention answered, and contradictions in what we heard abounded.

In a sense, then, we traveled to China too early to unravel the full story of the Cultural Revolution. Like the agrarian revolution and the socialist transformation that preceded it, it swung from "right" to "left." Since we arrived in China just as the "left" formalist phase was cracking under pressure from Mao Tse-tung and Chou En-lai, we found it hard to get a true picture of the woods for the trees. For me the historical equivalent of this situation would have been to have left Long Bow Village between the First and Second County conferences in Lucheng in 1948.* Had I done so I would never have known that the land reform work team was following a "left" line, that "middle peasant status for all" was a "left" slogan, and that commandism, extreme equalitarianism, and extreme democracy

---

*See *Fanshen: A Documentary of Revolution in a Chinese Village* (New York and London: Monthly Review Press, 1966), pp. 367-416 and 489-508.

were all excesses that flowered in the hot-house of ultra-lft politics. I would have departed with the notion that the land question was insoluble and that most cadres were either too self-centered or too inept to carry the revolution through. And I would have been greatly mistaken.

Today's parallel is close. In 1971 we found the Chinese Communist Party and the Chinese people struggling to free themselves from a "left" dogmatic line which tended to distort every facet of life, raise impossible goals, and reject countless good cadres as inept and venal. Everywhere large numbers of "set aside" civilians still remained in May 7 Cadre schools or on detached service in the countryside while army personnel, some of it poorly qualified, held down a disproportionate number of positions on the revolutionary committees and in the administrative apparatus of the provinces, the regions, the counties, and the municipalities. Judged by the "left" standards propagated by Lin Piao, there was no sound way to evaluate the "set aside" cadre. It is only now, since the defense minister has fallen, that a wholesale review of unsettled cases has been undertaken, leading to a large-scale movement for rehabilitation.

Key spots such as Tsinghua University, where questions of rehabilitation were solved relatively early, seem to be the exception rather than the rule. Tsinghua's advanced position was due to the fact that it had been chosen as a "breakthrough point" by Mao Tse-tung, and that it had been personally led by the best, most politically developed officers of the 8341 Army.* Under this kind of leadership Tsinghua became one of the models, one of the beacon lights, for the whole country showing the way toward "uniting all forces that can be united," for the great task of "struggle-criticism-transformation" which alone could replace the bourgeois superstructure of the past with the socialist superstructure of the future.

---

*To what extent the 8341 Army may have been under Lin Piao's influence is another question with disturbing implications. It is a question impossible to answer at this time.